HEALTHY
HEART
COOKBOOK

HEALTHY HEART
COOKBOOK

By Edith Tibbetts
&
Karin Cadwell, Ph.D., R.N.

Sterling Publishing Co., Inc.
New York

Library of Congress Cataloging-in-Publication Data Available

10 9 8 7 6 5 4 3 2 1

Published by Sterling Publishing Co., Inc.
387 Park Avenue South, New York, NY 10016

Previously published as *The Complete Low-Sodium/Low-Salt Cookbook*
© 1984, 2005 by Sterling Publishing Co., Inc.
Distributed in Canada by Sterling Publishing
$^c/o$ Canadian Manda Group, 165 Dufferin Street
Toronto, Ontario, Canada M6K 3H6

Distributed in Great Britain by Chrysalis Books Group PLC
The Chrysalis Building, Bramley Road, London W10 6SP, England
Distributed in Australia by Capricorn Link (Australia) Pty. Ltd.
P.O. Box 704, Windsor, NSW 2756, Australia

Sterling ISBN 1-4027-1681-8

CONTENTS

Acknowledgments

The authors want to thank the people who helped with the manuscript:

Louann Walther, who cheerfully and patiently typed endless revisions, whom we couldn't get along without;

Betty Dennis, the world's fastest typist, who typed the entire manuscript for American cooks and then revised the entire manuscript with metric measurements;

Donna Byerly, who checked and double-checked the recipes in addition to typing;

Jean Meers, who led the taste testing;

Joanne McIlhenny, who computed the sodium and calorie content of the recipes;

Theresa Gutsch, R.D., and Sylvia Mortenson, R.D., who reviewed the manuscript from the dietitian's point of view; and

All the people who participated in our low-sodium classes and tested the recipes in their own kitchens.

CONVERSION GUIDE

Ounces	Cups	Tablespoons	Teaspoons	Milliliters
			1/4 teaspoon	1 mL
			1/2 teaspoon	2 mL
			1 teaspoon	5 mL
			2 teaspoons	10 mL
1/2 ounce		1 tablespoon	3 teaspoons	15 mL
1 ounce		2 tablespoons	6 teaspoons	30 mL
2 ounces	1/4 cup	4 tablespoons	12 teaspoons	60 mL
4 ounces	1/2 cup	8 tablespoons	24 teaspoons	125 mL
8 ounces	1 cup	16 tablespoons	48 teaspoons	250 mL

Keep in mind that these conversions are not exact, but generally may be used for food measurement.

FOREWORD

I wonder if you can think of any carnivorous animal that eats salt or adds salt to its food as we humans do. From the medical standpoint, the use of additional salt may be detrimental to your health. There is no medical argument about the influence of salt on blood pressure, its role in the status of the pregnant woman's health, and the effect that excessive salt ingestion may have on kidney function.

Excess salt and the use of salt in cooking and as a food additive are most probably cultural phenomena. As a result of these cultural phenomena, we program our taste buds at a very young age to enjoy adding salt to all the foods we eat. Because of this habit, I believe it is rather difficult to make people understand the necessity for a low-salt or low-sodium diet.

Authors Edith Tibbetts and Karin Cadwell should be congratulated on having undertaken such a monumental task in developing the contents of *Healthy Heart Cookbook* to help all of us adapt to using less salt in preparing our foods. The background of the authors certainly qualifies them for this undertaking.

The most exciting part of the book may well be that it reads like a story. Even though the subject is primarily food preparation, I found the book to be easily readable and placed in perspective. Not only does the book explain menus and cooking methods, but it allows us to know the sodium content per serving as well as the calories per serving. So, if you are obese and hypertensive, I think this cookbook will be of great value to you.

The chapters beyond the introduction are valuable in suggesting a variety of dishes. But you must spend time reading and understanding the content of the introduction. The introduction will give you the medical background and reasons why you find it difficult to stop eating and using salt, why you should consider cutting down on salt and sodium intake, and lastly, the medical conditions that require you to avoid avoiding salt and salted foods as much as possible.

Philosophically, can we make a judgment as to whether or not the human really requires any added salt in cooking or in food preparation? In ancient times, salt was used to preserve food, because we had no refrigeration. One wonders whether or not that is a valid reason today for preserving food in salt. There's probably a minimal number of indications for the addition of salt, that is, sodium, to any recipe.

I can name many medical conditions in which the use of salt or salted products is absolutely contraindicated. These reasons are well known to all of you, but for emphasis, let me name just a few of them, such as hypertension, pregnancy, kidney disease, and premenstrual syndrome.

I believe you will enjoy reading this book and that you will certainly have fun preparing these low-sodium diet recipes. I am quite pleased that the authors wrote this book.

ALVIN F. GOLDFARB, M.D.,
PROFESSOR, JEFFERSON MEDICAL COLLEGE OF
THOMAS JEFFERSON UNIVERSITY,
PHILADELPHIA, PENNSYLVANIA

PREFACE

We wrote this book for people like you—people who love good regular cooking but who want to cut down on salt. Whether you must be on a restricted sodium diet or whether you choose to live with less sodium because of its association with high blood pressure, this book will help you. It is different from all other low-salt cookbooks. How is it different?

The *Healthy Heart Cookbook* provides an understanding of sodium restriction and gives practical help in the types of situations you encounter daily—restaurant eating, traveling, visiting, shopping, cooking, planning meals, and selecting low-sodium ingredients, both naturally and commercially prepared kinds.

This book tells you how to cook the foods you and your family really like. Recipes include pizza, pancakes, tacos, egg rolls, hamburgers, onion dip, lasagne, curried tuna canapés, barbecued chicken and spareribs—dishes usually high in sodium—tested for you and written with clear directions. The recipes also include the full nutritional information for each serving.

Our work in conducting classes for people on low-sodium diets produced the ideas to begin and complete this book. In talking to hundreds of men and women with high blood pressure, or their spouses, we found that they needed a lot more than the traditional advice, "Just cut down on your salt." Above all, they needed to know how to make low-sodium food taste good. Working with many people and two dietitians, who checked the nutritional content, we chose the most delicious recipes—using ingredients available in your grocery store.

INTRODUCTION

The *Healthy Heart Cookbook* is more than just a cookbook—it is a complete guide to eating for a healthy heart. This book explains how and why to make healthy eating choices; the scientific and medical reasons behind the benefits of this diet; and how to avoid unhealthy eating habits you may engage in without even knowing it. Understanding the big picture will teach you that healthy eating answers aren't going to be found in foods like low-carb doughnuts or fat-free cookies. It's important to be aware of all the ingredients in your foods and how eating those things will affect your body. Rather than substituting one bad ingredient for another, we advocate avoiding canned, frozen, and prepackaged foods. These items almost always contain exceedingly high amounts of sodium and are not usually as healthy and delicious as dishes prepared with fresh ingredients. This cookbook will show you how to make the change.

Heart healthy eating isn't just for those who already have heart problems: by making the right diet choices, you can fight major risk factors that cause and contribute to heart disease. This is a way of eating for life, not a fad diet. The best way to eat for a healthy heart is to choose a diet low in sodium, saturated fat, trans fat, and cholesterol that includes a wide variety of fruits, vegetables, and grains. Heart-healthy eating is a crucial step toward a healthy heart lifestyle, and here you'll find delicious recipes for home-cooked meals, snacks, and desserts guided by these principles.

The *Healthy Heart Cookbook* will also be your guide for everyday challenges such as what to eat at restaurants, while traveling, visiting friends or relatives, or shopping. It will help you make good choices as you plan your meals and buy ingredients for tasty recipes you and your family will enjoy.

The *Healthy Heart Cookbook* includes recipes for homemade seasonings, condiments, and relishes so that your food will always be perfectly flavored. The nutritional information for these recipes has been tested by two dietitians, and the cookbook includes charts showing the sodium contents of common foods so that you will never have to make potentially risky or inaccurate guesses.

Fun and flavorful recipes like Vegetable Tempura, Gazpacho, Pineapple Coleslaw, Scandinavian Mashed Potatoes, and Pasta Primavera prove that heart-healthy meals can be exciting. The *Healthy Heart Cookbook* is also packed with classic dishes like the Steak Sandwich, Chicken Fricassee,

Southern Fried Chicken, Italian Meatballs, Pork Chops, Moussaka, Baked Beans, Blueberry Muffins, and Pumpkin Pie, which have all the flavors you love without unnecessary bad-for-you ingredients.

For a healthy heart, your diet is a big factor, but it is also important to exercise and maintain a healthy weight. Major risk factors for heart attack include high blood pressure, high blood cholesterol, and being over-weight.

According to the American Heart Association, about 1 in 4 American adults have high blood pressure, and about 22% of American adults have "prehypertension." The prevalence of high blood pressure increases drasti-cally as we age—for American men 75 and older, it is about 69%, and for American women of the same age, it is about 84%. Nor is high blood pres-sure the only area of concern: about 1 in 5 American adults have some form of cardiovascular disease, 51% have high blood cholesterol, and 65% are overweight or obese. These statistics are alarming—what conclusions should we draw? These figures are telling us that many people have heart disease, and many more are at risk: therefore, we all need to pay attention to leading a heart-healthy lifestyle. Some forms of heart disease or risk fac-tors may be hereditary—so why don't you get your whole family started on a heart-healthy lifestyle? For your family's meals, choose low-sodium, low-cholesterol foods that are fresh, wholesome, and nutritious, and find a fun way to exercise together.

Healthy Heart Awareness

If there is one guiding principle toward a healthy heart lifestyle, it is awareness. Awareness means knowing and understanding which choices we make are good for our hearts, and which ones are potentially detrimental. You may want to keep a journal to record your food and exercise choices to develop healthy heart awareness. If you don't know your blood pressure, blood cholesterol, and weight, then you may not be aware of a problem. Work with your doctor to discover this important information and to understand it.

Understanding your blood pressure

Your blood pressure reading has two numbers: the systolic pressure (the pressure when the heart is beating) and the diastolic pressure (the pressure when the heart rests between beats). It is represented as the systolic pressure over the diastolic pressure, and is measured in milligrams of mercury (mm Hg). High blood pressure, or hypertension, is usually defined as a systolic pressure of more than 140 mm Hg or a diastolic pressure of more than 90 mm Hg. High blood pressure is a risk factor for heart disease, heart attack, or stroke and makes your heart and arteries work very hard.

Normal blood pressure is defined as a systolic pressure of less than 120 mm Hg and a diastolic pressure of less than 80 mm Hg. Blood pressures that are normal (or somewhat below normal) are usually the healthiest. One example of a normal blood pressure might be read as 110 over 70, or 110/70, with the first number representing the systolic pressure and the second number representing the diastolic pressure. Blood pressures that are above normal, but not quite hypertension (systolic pressure of 120–139 mm Hg or diastolic pressure of 80–89 mm Hg) signal prehypertension, and should be watched carefully.

Lifestyle changes can lower blood pressure—if you smoke, it is strongly advised that you quit, especially if you have above normal blood pressure, to reduce your risk of heart attack or stroke. If your blood pressure is above normal, your doctor might also recommend that you not drink alcoholic beverages, or limit your drinking to a moderate amount (no more than one alcoholic drink per day for women or two per day for men). There are also medications that can treat high blood pressure.

Understanding your blood cholesterol

There are three aspects of your cholesterol that you should be aware of: total cholesterol, LDL (bad) cholesterol, and HDL (good) cholesterol. Cholesterol is measured in mg/dL: milligrams of cholesterol per deciliter of blood. Total cholesterol levels below 200 mg/dL are desirable; between 200 and 239 mg/dL are borderline high risk, and 240 mg/dL and over are high risk.

With LDL (bad) cholesterol, low levels are ideal. Less than 100 mg/dL is optimal, 100–129 mg/dL is near optimal, 130–159 mg/dL is borderline high, 160–189 mg/dL is high, and 190 mg/dL and above is very high.

HDL (good) cholesterol is a little different: low levels of this kind of cholesterol put you at risk for heart disease. For women, HDL cholesterol on average ranges from 50 to 60 mg/dL, while men's average is 40 to 50 mg/dL. Less than 40 mg/dL of HDL cholesterol is considered low.

Eating less saturated fat, trans-fatty acids, and cholesterol as well as incorporating physical activity into your routine can help manage your blood cholesterol. Maintaining a healthy weight is also beneficial. High blood cholesterol is a risk factor for heart disease, heart attack, and strokes. Lifestyle changes such as these are the recommended treatment for high blood cholesterol, but cholesterol-lowering medications may be prescribed for those with very high blood cholesterol, or those for whom exercise and dietary changes are not helping enough.

The Healthy Heart Diet

The best diet for a healthy heart is low in sodium, saturated fat, trans fat, and cholesterol, and includes a wide variety of fruits, vegetables, and grains. In *Healthy Heart Cookbook*, you'll find recipes that follow these guidelines and taste delicious. Many prepared, processed, and packaged foods deliver little nutrition but are high in calories and unhealthy ingredients like sodium and saturated fat. Home-cooked meals are a better choice for a heart-healthy diet because you can control exactly how the food is prepared, and which ingredients to use, and make it a healthy choice for you.

A diet that is high in sodium has been associated with higher blood pressure. Sodium is involved in the body's process of controlling blood pressure and fluids, and this is why so many doctors recommend a low-sodium diet for patients with high blood pressure. Much of the sodium in our diets comes from salt, but there are other high-sodium sources to watch out for, such as baking soda and MSG, so avoiding sodium goes way beyond not salting your food at the table. In general, canned, packaged, and processed foods are much higher in sodium than fresh and plain frozen foods. These packaged convenience foods are usually so high in sodium that they ought to be eliminated from a heart-healthy diet.

Many sauces, condiments, and seasonings are high in sodium and should not be used, or should be used only in measured amounts. Other foods that are quite high in sodium are fast food, cured meats, potato chips, canned vegetables, stuffing, and cheese. Check the nutritional label for the amount of sodium in foods you buy—you may be surprised to see how much sodium is added to canned beans, ketchup, dried soups, and other everyday foods. Homemade seasonings and condiments are a good alternative to these high-sodium foods that can affect your blood pressure.

Eat less of the foods that are high in saturated fats, such as whole milk, cheese, butter, fatty meats, lard, and coconut and palm oil, because they can raise your blood cholesterol. For the same reason, it is best to avoid foods that are high in cholesterol such as liver, egg yolks, and dairy fats. Any food that has a high amount of trans-fatty acids can also raise blood cholesterol. Tran-fatty acids, or trans fats, can be found in partially hydrogenated vegetable oils which are often ingredients in margarines, shortenings, and some fried or baked goods. You can check the nutrition labels of foods to find out how much of these blood-cholesterol-raising ingredients are present. Because dairy products can be such a good source of calcium, rather than take them out of your diet entirely, you might opt for some fat-free or low-fat dairy products like skim milk, which contain less saturated fats.

Although you want to keep your total fat intake low, when you do eat fat in your diet, try to replace foods containing saturated fats with foods that have unsaturated fats, which do not raise your blood cholesterol. Try replacing lard or shortening in cooking with unsaturated vegetable oils, like olive and soybean oil. Avocados, salmon, most nuts, and vegetable oils contain unsaturated fats, and you can eat small amounts of them. Salmon, tuna, and mackerel have omega-3 fatty acids that even have some qualities that may protect against heart disease.

The USDA's *Nutrition and Your Health: Dietary Guidlines for Americans* suggests eating at least five servings of fruits and vegetables each day: at least 2 servings of fruit and at least 3 servings of vegetables. Most fruits and vegetables are low in calories, sodium, and unhealthy fats and have many vitamins and nutrients. By eating a wide variety of fruits and vegetables, you will be getting a healthy spectrum of vitamins and nutrients like potassium, folate, and vitamins A and C. Because juices contain very little fiber compared with most whole fruits or vegetables, it is better to choose the whole fruits and vegetables. Fiber is an important part of any healthy diet.

Whole grains are another good source of fiber, and are low in fat. Brown rice, oatmeal, whole wheat, and even popcorn are tasty whole grains that you should add to your diet. Try replacing white rice with brown rice, white bread with whole wheat bread, plain pasta with whole wheat pasta, potato chips with plain popcorn, a croissant with oatmeal, and so on. All of those whole grain foods have more fiber than their white-flour counterparts.

Foods and beverages with added sugars, like nondiet sodas, candies, cookies, and sweets add extra calories to your diet, provide little nutritional benefit, and often don't leave you feeling satisfied. You should limit how often you eat them and try to choose healthier alternatives when you are craving a snack. Sometimes we reach for a candy bar or soda pop just because it is convenient—make it easier to resist that temptation by buying or preparing heart healthy snacks and keeping them on hand. Unsalted nuts, fruits and vegetables for dipping, and the tasty and satisfying snacks we have included in *Healthy Heart Cookbook* could be just what you're looking for. When you are thirsty, instead of having a soda pop, make yourself some unsweetened iced tea or sip a bottle of sparkling water.

Advice About Exercise

Beginning a new exercise routine can be challenging, but if you start slowly and work towards a healthy, active lifestyle, it can be easier than you think. Set aside time each day to be active, and stick to it. When you schedule exercise into your day, you are telling yourself that it is just as important as the other appointments and commitments you wouldn't miss. Maybe you could wake up earlier and go to a fitness center, or perhaps you can use part of your lunch time to take a long walk around the neighborhood. Another good way to do it is to integrate exercise into your routine: opt to walk rather than drive when you can; use the stairs rather than the escalator. Some of us are so busy it seems impossible to make time to exercise, but you can make something you already do more active. Look at your daily routine carefully. If you like to read books or magazines, you could ride an exercise bike or walk on a treadmill while doing so. If you take public transportation, getting off the bus or subway a stop earlier means getting a little more active without sacrificing much time. Vacuuming burns calories, and so do other forms of housework. Raking the yard or gardening are great forms of exercise. Making these kinds of choices can lower your risk for heart disease. If, however, you have chronic health problems, are over 40 (for men) or 50 (for women), or have a high risk for heart disease, you should follow your doctor's recommendations before starting an exercise program.

When you are beginning an exercise routine, it will probably seem difficult at first. That's why it's important to take it slowly and let your strength and endurance build up. As you become more active, it will start to feel easier. Make sure to wear comfortable athletic clothing and shoes that fit your feet and are right for the activity. Stretch first and warm up for a few minutes, and don't forget to cool down afterwards.

There are many exciting exercise options for everyone—have you tried yoga, riding your bike to work, or dancing? If there are some forms of exercise you don't care for, or your doctor doesn't recommend, try something new. You could try doing a different form of exercise every day—ballet on Mondays, pilates on Tuesdays, water aerobics on Wednesdays, walking on Thursdays, African dance on Fridays, yoga on Saturdays, a bike ride on Sundays—whatever you like! Having an enjoyable and varied exercise routine means you always have something to look forward to. It can be especially fun and motivating to exercise with a friend or family member. Your dog would probably love a good walk or jog, and his or her health will benefit too.

We've already mentioned that the American Heart Association reports that about 65% of American adults are overweight or obese, and that this is a risk factor for heart disease. But did you know that it is estimated that 8,830,000 children and teenagers ages 6–19 are overweight or obese? Even among very young children, weight can be an issue: more than 10 percent of preschool children ages 2–5 are overweight. One of the best things you can do for the children in your life is to help them be healthy and learn good eating and exercise habits that are likely to stick with them. Going for a family walk or bike ride is a great way to spend quality time together. Don't underestimate the influence you have on your family—you can be a healthy heart role model!

When you and your family are getting active and choosing healthy, heart-friendly foods in the right portions, you are already working toward your ideal weights. Many people try to slim down for swimsuit season or to fit into those jeans from high school, but the single most important reason to lose weight is for your health. Of all the forms of exercise, aerobic exercise is one of the best for fighting heart disease. Aerobic exercise doesn't just mean "aerobics" classes—walking, jogging, running, bike riding, and using stair-climbing machines are all aerobic activities.

Making It Happen:
Fitting Heart-Healthy Eating
into Your Life

Have you noticed how often new diet books appear in stores? Are you getting used to doctors and celebrities explaining their diets on television? New diets appear all the time, and each one has a new promise. Most of these diets are weight-loss diets that people have trouble sticking with—they lose a few pounds and stop dieting, or gain weight and go on another diet. Heart-healthy eating is different—it is a way of eating for life, and it is part of a whole healthy heart lifestyle. It isn't just about losing weight—it is about knowing and understanding what makes certain food choices either healthy or bad for you.

One important component of the healthy heart diet is that it is low in sodium. This follows many doctors' recommendations and research about how sodium affects blood pressure, and we've explained how important this is. People who need to cut down on sodium aren't usually cured of the condition that made beginning a low-sodium diet important; so they need to stick with it. But people sometimes have problems staying on their low-sodium diets because they can't find ways to make it convenient. If you get into the habit of making your low sodium diet an easy way of eating, you are more likely to stay on it. This is especially true if you have become accustomed to using convenient (but high-sodium) prepared foods. We acknowledge that heart-healthy eating will never be as easy as grabbing a premade meal from the grocery store shelves, but when you plan your cooking, it can be simpler than it seems. (And you'll be rewarded for your efforts with fresh, nutritious, and tasty meals.)

If you've salted your food all your life, and if you've come to eat a lot of prepackaged, processed foods, it may take you a little while to get used to low-sodium eating. This chapter is a collection of hints to make the transition easier. These are hints that have worked for other people.

1. Don't Try to Guess How Much Sodium Is in Food

Which food has more sodium, 1 Heinz pickle or 4 slices of Oscar Mayer bacon? Did you guess that the pickle has more than three times as much sodium as the bacon? The pickle has 1,428 mg versus 452 mg for the bacon.

Which has more sodium, a serving of Wish-Bone Italian dressing, or 1 ounce (30 g) of Planters cocktail peanuts? The salad dressing has 293 mg and the peanuts have only 138 mg, even though these are salted peanuts.

If you guessed wrong, don't worry, you are not alone. Many people have trouble remembering even approximately how much sodium is in different foods. In one study, doctors who recommended sodium restriction to their patients were asked to identify high-sodium foods. In fact, the doctors were asked to answer the same questions that were asked above, plus more examples. The doctors guessed correctly only 46 percent of the time. They answered more than half of the specific questions wrong! Obviously, even doctors who are convinced of the benefits of low-sodium eating can have trouble remembering the numbers.

You don't need to memorize the sodium values of foods. But if you know where to find that information, staying with low-sodium eating will be easier. There are several ways of identifying high-sodium foods.

- The circle charts (pages 36 and 37) will tell you which foods are high and which are low in sodium.

- Books with sodium values of common foods and brand names are for sale at bookstores or are available at your library. The internet can also be a terrific source of information about the sodium contents of foods.

- New products that appear daily on grocery stores shelves will not, of course, appear in printed books for some time (but you may be able to find them on the manufacturer's website, or low-sodium information websites). Information on the sodium content should appear on the label. If not, jot down the manufacturer's name and address and the name of the product while you're at the market. Then you can write for sodium information before you spend any money.

2. Don't Trick Yourself into Thinking You Are on a Low-Sodium Diet When You're Not

The traditional advice for a person who needs only to cut down on sodium a little has been to tell him or her to just stop adding salt at the table, or sometimes also in cooking. When you look at the actual sodium content of many popular foods, it's easy to see that you're probably not on a low-sodium diet if the only change you made is to stop salting your food.

This is an easy mistake to make, but when you learn about the sodium contents of foods, you can avoid making it. Here is an actual example of one dinner eaten by a man with high blood pressure—a man who sincerely wants to cut down on salt. He stopped adding salt to his food at the table, his wife adds none in cooking, and they do not use any high-sodium cooking aids such as MSG, tenderizer, and soy sauce. But without realizing it, this man was still on a high-sodium diet. His meal and the sodium content are shown in the following table. Another table, "A Few Easy Changes" (page 23), illustrates how he reduced his sodium intake.

Although this example shows that it is possible to reduce sodium intake while still eating very similar meals, further modifications may be wiser still. For example, he may need to eat less red meat.

Make Your Own Chart

People who need to change their diets are often asked to write down everything they ate in one day. This exercise can help you to tell how much sodium you've been taking in. Before you begin, keep in mind that snacks and nibbling need to be included along with regular meals. One problem with many meal plans is that they assume that people eat most of their foods at "meals," with an occasional snack. Surveys show that this is not true for many people. They eat between meals or they eat casually instead of having formal meals, yet tend to overlook foods eaten informally when they're reporting what they ate.

Dr. Paul A. Fine reported to the American Medical Association that the average family in the United States does not eat three square meals a day, even though people in the family may believe that this is the case. Rather, the average family actually engages in 20 "food contacts," although people are reluctant to admit this, even to themselves.

You need to look at the way you actually eat. When you eat matters less than what you eat. Even if you are eating at an "informal contact," the food item needs to be low in sodium. Take a few minutes now and make a simple chart like the previous example (page 22). Jot down what you ate yesterday. Be honest with yourself and include everything you put in your mouth—a few potato chips you casually munched on or a few cookies you had while watching TV.

Now, look up each food that you wrote down. Write down the number of mg of sodium next to each food. For example, if you had two pieces of white bread toast, you can look up bread and see that there are 228 mg in two slices.

After you jot down the sodium content of each of yesterday's foods, add them up to tell how much sodium was in the food. Be sure the size of the

Time	Food	Food Used in Preparation or Added at Table	Notes	Amount of Sodium (in mg)
5:00 PM–7:00 PM	steak	Kraft barbecue sauce (1 oz. or 30 g)	dinner at home at 6:30 pm a generous piece of steak maybe about 9 ounces (255 g); there are 55 mg of sodium in a 3 ounce (90 g) serving.	steak–165 sauce–466
	scalloped potatoes made from a packaged mix without cheese (1/3 of the total)	as directed on box—with milk, margarine	1/3 of the box of potatoes is not a particularly large serving	potatoes–290
	peas frozen with butter sauce (1/2 of package)			peas–622
	salad: lettuce, 1/2 of a tomato, packaged croutons, blue cheese salad dressing from a bottle (3 tablespoons or 45 mL)		one ounce (30 g) of seasoned Pepperidge Farm croutons has 519 mg of sodium!-	lettuce = 2 tomato = 3 croutons = 519
	2 Pillsbury crescent rolls	margarine for the rolls (2 tablespoons or 30 mL)		margarine = 280 2 rolls = 1,330
	coffee	milk (1 tablespoon or 15 mL)		coffee = 2 milk = 8
	homemade apple pie (1/6 of a pie)	piecrust was prepared from a packaged mix; apples were canned apple pie filling	using convenience products such as a piecrust mix adds large amounts	for 1/8 of a 2-crust pie made from mix crust=389
				TOTAL = 4,628 in this meal

A Few Easy Changes By making a few changes, it is possible to drastically reduce the amount of sodium.

Time	Food	Food Used in Preparation or Added at Table	Notes	Amount of Sodium (in mg)
5:00 PM–7:00 PM	steak (3 oz. or 90 g)	barbecue sauce (1 ounce or 30 mL; homemade, low-sodium)	dinner at home at 6:30 PM	steak = 55 sauce = 5
	baked potato			potato = 5
	(frozen) green beans (frozen) ear of corn		serving 3 vegetables helps to fill up- the dinner plate	beans = 2 corn = 4
	salad: lettuce, 1/2 of a tomato, low-sodium salad dressing (3 tablespoons or 45 mL)			lettuce = 2 tomato = 3 dressing = trace
	low-sodium bread or rolls	2 tablespoons (30 mL) unsalted	by eliminating the croutons and substituting low-sodium salad dressing, the salad has become a low-sodium item	bread = 10 margarine = 2
	coffee	milk (1 T. or 15mL)		coffee = 2 milk = 8
	homemade apple pie (1/8 of a pie)	piecrust was made from scratch; fresh apples	substituting fruit for the fruit pie would be wiser still	crust = trace apples = 2
				TOTAL = 100 in this meal

23

portions corresponds to how much you actually ate. Example: a three-ounce (90-g) serving of beef has 55 mg of sodium. This is a fairly small serving, about the size of a small hamburger patty at a fast-food restaurant. If you had a "good size" serving of beef, you may have had three or four times this amount, or 220 mg of sodium. Be sure to count things that were added, such as salt, MSG, tenderizer, shaking and baking mixes, and all seasonings.

If your total was less than 1,000 mg of sodium—congratulations!—it was truly low in sodium.

If your total was between 1,000 and 3,000 mg, it was moderately low in sodium.

If the total was more than 5,000 mg, it was high in sodium. But remember that this was for yesterday. Today you can do better.

3. Stock Your Kitchen Wisely

If your kitchen shelves are now stocked with canned vegetables and canned soups, packaged mixes, pickles, and tenderizer, you may have a problem. Ask yourself or your spouse: "What are we going to do with all those high-sodium foods?" Use them up to save money? High-sodium foods used for noble motives (like saving money) are just as bad for you as any other high-sodium food. You could give them to a soup kitchen or just throw them away.

When you first start to plan low-sodium cooking on a regular basis, it's easy to imagine what you won't be using: salt, MSG, and baking soda. But you also need to buy some items that you may never have bought. Low-sodium products are an obvious first thought. But we advise you to buy only one of each new item and taste it to see if you find the food palatable. It makes sense to stock up on items that you know your family likes, such as uncooked spaghetti, fruits, and so forth. If your spice cupboard is rather bare, buy some fresh ones. We recommend basil, cinnamon, dill, pepper, dry mustard, paprika, garlic powder, and onion powder (see Seasonings, page 39).

Wine is a favorite ingredient for people who take pride in making low-sodium dishes taste as good as any without restrictions. All the alcohol cooks away, but a nice flavor is left. But do not use cooking wines that have added salt. (This is an old-time practice to discourage the cook from drinking it.) If you want to try just one bottle, we recommend that you buy a bottle of dry vermouth. Because the flavor is fairly strong, it adds a lot of flavor. With plain food, such as chicken soup, leaving out the salt makes a very bland dish until you add vermouth and let it cook. Adding wine or vermouth does not make the food taste like wine, and the alcoholic content diminishes as it cooks off. Wine or vermouth can help unsalted food have a more interesting, robust taste. If you prefer not to use wine, substitute fresh or frozen lemon juice. Substitute half as much lemon juice as the amount of wine called for in the recipe.

4. Stay with Low-Sodium Eating and You'll Adjust Faster

When a food has salt on or in it, you notice the taste as soon as it is in your mouth. Unsalted food does not give you that quick zap of instant flavor recognition; it delivers its flavors a little more slowly. When you put a piece of salted steak into your mouth, you taste the salt instantly and then you notice the taste of the meat. With unsalted meat, there is no instantaneous zap—only the slower appreciation of the flavor of the meat itself. If you keep this in mind, you won't be looking for an instant zap of flavor from unsalted foods.

When you first start eating unsalted and low-sodium foods, many foods seem rather tasteless. But the good news is that this reaction does not last. After about 2 to 3 weeks of being on a true low-sodium diet, most people find that their taste sense starts to adjust. They no longer expect the instantaneous flavor of salt; they detect and enjoy the subtle flavors that are found in various foods. Fresh unsalted vegetables, for example, taste better because you become more aware of the vegetables' natural flavors. But remember, it takes a little while on a low-sodium diet before this change takes place.

The other thing that happens is a reaction to sodium itself. You begin to detect sodium or a "salty" taste in products that used to taste normal. For example, dry cereals or packaged frosting mixes begin to taste objectionably salty. This change is actually a good thing. Instead of craving salty foods, you will begin to enjoy low-sodium foods much more than you did at first. Many people who give up all high-sodium foods notice this change. But it does not happen to people who give up only table salt. You can use this taste readjustment to your advantage. If you stay on a low-sodium diet day after day, you will automatically begin to enjoy the many flavors of different foods. But this also means that it is particularly foolish to cheat on a low-sodium diet. If you go back to eating foods with a lot of sodium, your perception of saltiness may change, and low-sodium foods will seem too bland again, as they did in the first days of low-sodium eating.

Let's be realistic—if you have enjoyed salting your food all your life, you're going to miss the salt, especially at first. But if you switch back and forth between low- and high-sodium eating, you are making the change harder on yourself, because you won't get the physical readjustment in taste. So our hint is to stay with low-sodium eating on a regular basis.

5. Add Lots of Other Seasonings and Make the Meal Look Appealing

If you learn to make food taste delicious, you and other people in your family are not so likely to get discouraged and reach for the salt shaker. In cooking, fresh vegetables, herbs, and spices add flavor, as do table wine and lemon juice. Instead of putting the salt shaker on the table, put out lots of other seasonings. Treat yourself to a nice pepper mill. Try lemon juice, vinegar, onion powder, or any herb or spice that you like. Put out the Unsalt Shaker (recipes, pages 39–41).

You'll notice that our recipes often call for garlic, green peppers, mushrooms, herbs, spices, tomato paste, wine, or onions. These ingredients all add delicious flavor to the recipes, and help create a taste that is naturally good without salt. The better your food tastes, and the more delightful the flavor is, the less you'll miss the unhealthy sodium. Aromatic, flavorful ingredients make a heart-healthy diet enticing!

Foods that traditionally have little flavor except salt (such as commercially prepared chicken soup or chicken pie) are the ones that are most difficult to make into delicious low-salt versions. It may be wise to wait a few weeks or until your taste has really readjusted to low-salt eating before you expect unsalted chicken pie to seem tasty. Chicken pot pie is one dish that relies too heavily on the flavor of salt for there to be a really good low-sodium alternative. But making a tasty low-salt Chicken Cacciatore (page 160) is fairly easy, because the usual flavors—tomato and onion—are there to add taste.

In this book, portions for a person who needs to cut down on salt (or fat or calories) are figured to be a certain size. For meat, the portion size is 4 ounces (120 g) of raw meat. This will cook down to approximately 3 ounces (90 g) when cooked—you may be surprised at how small this looks. The best way to know meat weight is to buy a kitchen scale. Since a 3-ounce (90-g) cooked serving of meat or fish looks small, it helps to fill the dinner plate with other foods. A generous serving of rice, noodles, pasta, potatoes, or vegetables can help. Or serve one green and one yellow vegetable.

Attractive garnishes help, too—Corn Relish, Five-Minute Chutney (pages 50 and 51). Low-sodium mustard (pages 44–45) will have your dishes looking and tasting wonderful. You can put low-sodium Ketchup (page 43) in a squeeze bottle if you want it to look like familiar old ketchup.

6. Make Extra to Freeze

Is that a piece of advice you've heard again and again? That's because freezing low-sodium foods helps to make them convenient. Having delicious low-sodium foods on hand will make it easier to stay on your diet. Some foods freeze well and are delicious when defrosted and reheated. Other foods dry out and are not as tasty as when cooked fresh and just served. You will find out what works for you as you go along.

As a general rule, it's a good idea to freeze the amount that you will want to serve. For example, you might make two meat loaves: one for a family meal and the other to freeze for sandwiches. It makes sense to slice the second meat loaf and wrap each slice before freezing. That way you have a convenient low-sodium sandwich filling. Try slicing bread before freezing, too. You can freeze the loaf of bread wrapped in one piece and take out slices as needed. Plan ahead for freezing: Use freezer-quality plastic bags, freezer paper, or aluminum foil for wrapping; glass canning jars with screw tops are ideal for freezing soups and sauces; plastic freezer containers are easy to buy and use. Keep your freezing equipment on hand so you can make another convenient meal.

Remember, liquids expand as they freeze, don't overfill your containers. Leave some room when freezing soups and sauces in glass or plastic containers. When freezing food in plastic bags, you need to leave room for expansion; don't put the tie down too close to the food. Cover foods tightly; freezers, especially the frost-free type, rob foods of moisture. Be careful about how you pack your food in the freezer—then, when it's defrosted, your food will still be delicious.

Keep ingredients such as chicken stock handy in the freezer. Homemade low-sodium chicken stock is such a delicious addition to a recipe, it's worth the extra effort to make it ahead to have on hand.

Freeze leftover tomato sauce in ice cube trays. When they're fully frozen, you can take them out of the trays and put them in a freezer bag. Then when you're ready to use them, you'll be able to grab just the amount you need. You can use the cubes to flavor sauces and to toss over noodles or pasta.

Defrost frozen foods in a hurry by running hot water around the outside of the container. Run the water until the block of food is loose and you can place it into the top of a double boiler. Then heat the food over medium heat until it's defrosted and hot. Although the double-boiler method is easy, it's not nearly as fast as using a microwave oven. A microwave oven is a great kitchen tool for making low-sodium eating more convenient. The combination of freezing serving-sized portions and then defrosting and heating them in a microwave shortens meal preparation time.

7. Buy and Use the Right Equipment

Do you have a really sharp kitchen knife and a good vegetable peeler? These are inexpensive items that can be conveniently purchased in supermarkets, hardware stores, and discount stores.

Low-sodium cooking is more convenient if your kitchen is stocked with the tools you need such as a frying pan with a flat bottom, small and large saucepans with lids, a soup pot, a wire whisk, a mixing bowl or two, a sharp kitchen knife, a vegetable peeler, a big stirring spoon (either wood or metal), and a vegetable steamer.

8. Be Careful When You Substitute

Experienced cooks often change recipes and substitute one ingredient for another. But it's not as easy to substitute when you are on a sodium-restricted diet because sodium is hidden in so many foods that do not taste salty.

Let's take the example of tomatoes. The cook finds a recipe calling for fresh tomatoes that will be cooked, but cooking tomatoes are out of season and the cook needs to find a low-sodium substitute. The fresh tomatoes, cooked without salt, would have 28 mg of sodium. What about substituting a can of whole or stewed tomatoes? A medium-size can of stewed tomatoes has about 1,303 mg of sodium. A can of whole tomatoes has 900 mg of sodium. Tomato purée has 1,701 mg of sodium. A can of tomato sauce has 2,130 mg of sodium. None of these are acceptable substitutes. A small can of no-salt-added tomato paste has only 69 mg of sodium. Unsalted canned tomatoes make a good substitute.

If you have a favorite recipe that you are thinking about making for low-sodium eating, remember not to guess how high a particular food is in sodium. Check the sodium values of the ingredients, and then decide whether the recipe can still work with substitutions and omissions. Ingredients such as salt and MSG (monosodium glutamate) can be left out of a recipe. Since their contribution is flavor, the food may seem somewhat less flavorful, but the recipe will still work. Some dishes have only salt for flavor and are bland when salt is omitted; stuffing for turkey is one example. There is no recipe for bread stuffing in this book because the real flavor in stuffing is salt; even with sage or savory, in our experience, unsalted stuffing tastes rather like wet bread.

Baking soda and baking powder are both high in sodium. If you are on a restricted diet it would be very unwise to allot your few milligrams of sodium to baking soda, which has 821 mg in a teaspoon (5 mL). Unfortunately, baking soda (sodium bicarbonate) has no commonly available low-sodium replacement. You may have read that potassium bicarbonate can be bought at pharmacies and used as a substitute, but the pharmacies we checked no longer stock it.

Baking powder has fewer mg of sodium—339 per teaspoon (5 mL). Low-sodium baking powders have less than 1 mg in each teaspoon (5 mL). The instructions on the low-sodium baking powders advise the cook to use 1^1/$_2$ times the amount the recipe calls for when replacing regular baking powder. We had the best results when we shook the jar every time before measuring. We found that low-sodium baking powder was most successful in pancakes, waffles, and muffins but did not work in cakes or quick breads such as banana bread. You may want to consider using regular baking powder in recipes that don't work with low-sodium baking powder.

If the doctor has told you to limit the number of eggs you eat in a week, you may want to try one of the egg substitutes, such as Fleischmann's Egg Beaters. They work well in cooking, and work for tasks such as binding a meat loaf. The sodium content is slightly higher than that of an egg; a quarter cup (60 mL) of Egg Beaters (equivalent to one large egg) contains 90mg of sodium.

You will probably find that some recipes cannot be adapted to low-sodium cooking. Recipes that depend on an ingredient that has no low-sodium counterpart most likely won't work out. Recipes that rely on a convenience food are also especially difficult to convert to low-sodium foods.

9. Be Careful When You're Eating Away from Home

These days, Americans eat many of their meals away from home. The more restrictive your diet is, the harder it is to choose items from standard menus. Many restaurants today make extensive use of prepared frozen foods, which are sometimes just reheated in a microwave oven. Such foods are high in sodium. This is especially true of restaurant chains; the practice is not at all limited to fast-food restaurants.

There are restaurants that make all their own food from scratch so inquire politely to determine how food is prepared at restaurants where you might eat. Many family-operated restaurants pride themselves on making their own food; try to find one in your area.

When you eat out, be prepared to order plain foods such as a baked potato and a broiled piece of meat without sauces—foods that do not need to be cooked in advance with sauces. Be prepared to politely ask your waitress or waiter which food items are not the preassembled ones that need only reheating. Ask which entrees are cooked from raw foods. Be prepared to ask that no salt or salty ingredients be added to your food. If you don't speak up, you may be surprised to find soy sauce on your prime rib, as we did. Learn to be cautious about some of the things you are told. In an attempt to please a potential customer, or because he or she is not familiar with which ingredients might be high in sodium, your waiter or waitress may even offer you false reassurance about the supposedly low-sodium content of the food.

Most fast-food restaurants will prepare their food items for you as you request. You can order unsalted french fries. You can order a plain hamburger, and ask that they hold the pickles, cheese, ketchup, mayonnaise, salt, and any special sauce. Ask for extra onion, lettuce, and tomato, if you wish. If you are on a mild level of sodium restriction, you can eat the roll and figure that it adds approximately 300 milligrams of sodium. The plain hamburger patty probably has about 55 mg.

There are quite a few low-sodium choices in beverages—coffee, tea, soft drinks. Or you can order milk as part of your calcium intake.

Some fast-food chains have salad bars where you can make low-sodium choices. Usually this means no premixed dressing (you can bring your own), no beans, bacon bits, croutons, or cheeses. The salad bar probably has containers of oil and vinegar that you can use.

When you go to regular restaurants, open the menu with realistic expectations. There will probably be fewer low-sodium choices than you thought.

Breakfast—a few tips:

Fruits, fruit juices, coffee, and tea are all low in sodium.

Cold cereals which are low in sodium include shredded wheat and puffed rice. (Since they are not popular, many restaurants do not carry them.) The other cold cereals are high in sodium; you may want to carry a plastic bag of low-sodium cereal just in case. Then you can ask the waitress if she has any of the cold cereals that are on your diet. If there are none available, explain that you have your own. Order a bowl and milk. You can order fruit too, if you like. You can offer to pay for the cereal that would have come with the bowl. Hot cereals in restaurants are generally instant (probably very high in sodium) or cooked in salt. They are not a good choice for low-sodium eaters.

One large egg has approximately 59 mg of sodium. You might consider having a hard- or soft-cooked egg if your doctor has not advised you to limit the number of eggs you eat.

Breakfast potatoes have probably been boiled in salted water and salted again during frying. They are not a good choice.

Lunch—if you don't carry your own:

Nearly all common luncheon choices except hamburgers (without commercial rolls) are very high in sodium: cold cuts (bologna, pastrami, ham, salami), commercial bread and rolls, potato chips, dill pickles, coleslaw, tuna, chicken salad, cheese, and soup. Salad can be low in sodium. Mix an oil and vinegar dressing yourself. Leave off the high-sodium salad ingredients.

Dinner—needs planning:

For dinner, it's a good idea to choose a restaurant that specializes in plain foods rather than casseroles and foods with gravies and sauces. Chinese and some other Asian restaurants may use soy sauce and MSG, which make their foods very high in sodium.

Fruit cocktail, fruit, and fruit juices are all low in sodium.

Salad can be low in sodium if you leave out the high-sodium fixings.

Baked potatoes are low in sodium. Request that your baked potato be brought to you unopened. (You may want to bring your own unsalted margarine if your diet is very restricted.) Rice and pasta are often cooked in salted water. You can ask if an order of pasta can be cooked for you in unsalted water.

Ask if the restaurant has any fresh fish that could be broiled for you without sauces.

Roast beef, prime rib, and turkey are often served covered with high sodium sauces or gravies, but you can ask if they have plain meat (with no sauce or gravy). An inside slice of a roast should be fairly low in sodium.

Coffee, tea, soda, wine, beer, and liquor are all low in sodium.

You may enjoy your food a lot more if you try what we have done. Pack a bag with unsalted margarine, your favorite unsalted salad dressing, some good unsalted bread, bread stick, a roll, or a matzo. You can quietly take such items out of your bag to go with the meal.

If you are having dessert, fruit gelatins, sherbet, and ice cream are the only choices that are not too high in sodium. If you skipped the fresh fruit as an appetizer, consider having it as a refreshing end to your meal.

More Tips When Eating Out

In interviewing people for this book, we learned that many people eat only breakfast at home. People who eat most of their other meals in restaurants tend to be busy married couples whose children are grown, or single people who hate to cook for one person, and are usually the ones with high income levels—less affluent people simply cannot afford to eat out twice a day. In addition to their comfortable income levels, many of these people have high blood pressure or other medical problems that have led their doctors to recommend a low-sodium diet. How can they cut down on sodium and still eat out? In addition to the suggestions for breakfast, lunch and dinner if you eat out occasionally, here are more suggestions:

- Consider bringing a lunch from home since low-sodium lunches are very difficult to find in restaurants.

- Avoid Chinese restaurants, delicatessens, and restaurants that heat up prepackaged foods.

- Find one or more good restaurants that care enough about you and other discriminating customers to go along with your special requests (for example, allowing you to bring your own salad dressing).

- Get in the habit of never even looking at the choices in the foods that are always high in sodium: soups, breads, dishes with fancy sauces, especially barbecue sauces.

Eating on Airplanes

You can ask your travel agent to request low-sodium menus, or request them yourself if you purchase tickets online. Be sure to order them at least 24 hours in advance, and be aware that problems can arise. One major problem is that low-sodium choices are available only for full meals, such as dinner. Sometimes, the airline considers what it serves to be a snack and there are no special choices available for snack lunches.

When the airline is serving a full meal, special low-sodium dishes are available. But occasionally the special meals fail to arrive or get confused. If you do get a "low-sodium" meal, it may not really be low-sodium. We have been served sausages, salted salad dressing, salami, salt, and salted butter as part of "low-sodium" meals.

When you are traveling, you may want to bring along a kit of low-sodium foods—just in case available foods are inappropriate when you are hungry.

Visiting

When invited to eat at someone's home, it's a good idea to think about ways to handle your diet. If it is a large party where no one notices what you eat or whether you eat at all, you can eat before you go to the party (there probably won't be any low-sodium choices unless you bring your own).

At an intimate dinner where food is the high point of the evening—the main focus of the social occasion—you will want to tell your hostess in advance about your diet. Together, you can work out arrangements. Perhaps a low-sodium choice can be included in her plans. Dinner with close friends or family who understand your diet may plan low-sodium foods for everyone when you are invited over.

10. Try to Get a Friend or Family Member to Go Along with Low-Sodium Eating

Having the moral support of a friend or family member can help when you feel discouraged. But don't make the mistake of turning the responsibility over to someone else. Other people can be a help, but you are the one who decides what food to put in your mouth. For example, since you know that pickles are high in sodium, you can avoid putting them on the plate. People who get involved in planning their own diet are more likely to stay with it. If you aren't the cook at your house, you can still read labels and make positive suggestions.

Shopping, meal planning, and cooking will be more convenient if you don't make separate high- and low-sodium meals. The major reason for not preparing two separate meals, however, is the realization that this procedure usually results in one tasty high-sodium meal and one tasteless low-sodium meal.

Other family members can add a little salt at the table. But they would be well advised to salt lightly. The offspring of people with high blood pressure are fairly likely to develop this condition when they are older, especially if they eat high-sodium foods. You can do family members a tremendous favor if you teach them to enjoy foods that are delicious without being high in sodium.

11. Don't Fall into the Trap of Making Excuses for Eating High-Sodium Foods

If you hear yourself making these excuses, stop:

"It's only a little piece of ham, so it's okay."

"The recipe won't be traditional without __."

"It doesn't taste salty."

The best bet is to stick with your diet consistently, even when it gets challenging.

12. Use This Book to Help You Get Used to Low-Sodium Cooking

By using recipes that are designed to keep sodium intake low, you get used to this type of cooking and will be ready to evaluate other recipes. Each time you look at a new or old recipe, think about each ingredient for a minute and ask yourself if it is appropriate for low-sodium eating. If it's not, you can leave it out (salt, tenderizer) or you can substitute something that is low in sodium (low-sodium tuna for regular tuna, frozen corn for canned corn).

The recipes in this book can help you adjust to low-sodium cooking. Most are planned to serve four people. But on the other hand, these four servings are an approximation. The recipes would not serve four teenage boys or others with large appetites. Alice B. Toklas was once asked how many people a recipe would serve. She answered, "How should I know how many it serves? It depends on their appetites—what else they have for dinner—whether they like it or not."

A few recipes state that they will serve more or fewer guests. With a recipe for baked bread for example, it's not feasible to make bread that just serves four.

Following the recipes, we have given the nutritional information for each serving. Take a look at this information before cooking the recipe—the nutritional information should meet your guidelines for healthy heart eating.

In some recipes in this book, no sodium or calorie content is given. Recipes such as tacos have so many different possibilities of combinations that selecting one version would be arbitrary. A taco with bean filling or meat? With or without cheese? What kind of cheese? In other cases it is impossible to know what the yield is. Let's say that a carrot is cut up and used to flavor a chicken stock, but is removed from the stock. How would you know how much of the sodium or calories were removed and how much stayed in the stock?

Also, since a healthy heart diet is low in sodium and cholesterol, the recipes in this book were planned to be without ingredients like heavy cream, sour cream, eggs, egg yolks, and butter. The *Healthy Heart Cookbook* does have a few recipes for low-sodium but high-cholesterol ingredients (shrimp, whole-milk cheeses) that should be eaten sparingly. If your doctor has told you to eat red meats (beef, lamb, pork) only a few times a week, concentrate on the recipes for chicken, fish, vegetables, pasta, and beans. According to USDA guidelines, adults need daily: two servings of foods rich in calcium such as milk, yogurt or some cheese; two or more servings of protein foods, such as chicken, fish, meat, peanuts, or dry cooked beans; four or more servings of fruits and vegetables, four or more servings of breads, cereals, pasta, etc. Only a small amount of fat is needed. The recipes in this book have been planned to use only a small amount of fat.

If you stay with low-sodium cooking, you will be able to derive the satisfaction from having served your family food that is good for them and will help them stay healthy. When you go to the trouble of making delicious low-sodium foods, you deserve a lot of credit. We hope that you enjoy the tasty recipes we've included in *Healthy Heart Cookbook*, and that they help you enjoy your heart-healthy lifestyle!

Sodium in Foods

○ **Low** (inner circle): USE FREELY
◐ **Medium** (middle circle: USE IN MEASURED AMOUNTS
● **High** (outer circle): DO NOT USE

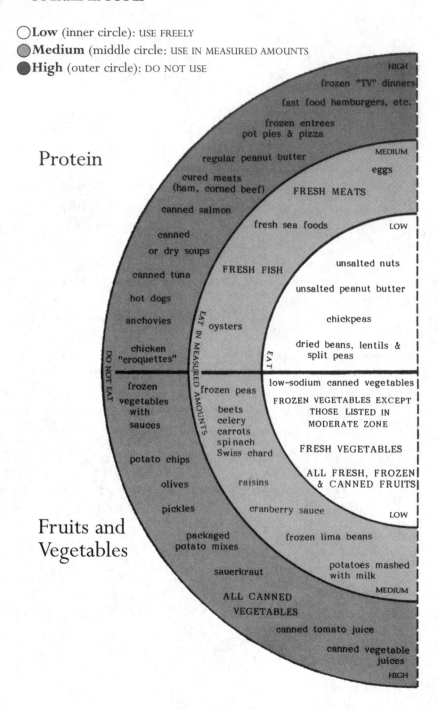

Protein

HIGH
frozen "TV" dinners
fast food hamburgers, etc.
frozen entrees
pot pies & pizza
MEDIUM
regular peanut butter
eggs
cured meats
(ham, corned beef)
FRESH MEATS
canned salmon
fresh sea foods
LOW
canned
or dry soups
FRESH FISH
unsalted nuts
canned tuna
unsalted peanut butter
hot dogs
chickpeas
anchovies   oysters
dried beans, lentils &
split peas
chicken
"croquettes"

DO NOT EAT

EAT IN MEASURED AMOUNTS

EAT

frozen   frozen peas   low-sodium canned vegetables
vegetables   FROZEN VEGETABLES EXCEPT
with   beets   THOSE LISTED IN
sauces   celery   MODERATE ZONE
                carrots
                spinach   FRESH VEGETABLES
                Swiss chard
potato chips   ALL FRESH, FROZEN
                                 & CANNED FRUITS
olives   raisins
pickles   cranberry sauce
                                 LOW
Fruits and   packaged   frozen lima beans
Vegetables   potato mixes
                                 potatoes mashed
                sauerkraut   with milk
                                 MEDIUM
                ALL CANNED
                VEGETABLES
                    canned tomato juice
                        canned vegetable
                            juices
                                 HIGH

macaroni & cheese

prepared dinner rolls
(packaged or frozen)

instant corn meal

packaged mixes
of rice or noodles

store-bought breads

"stuffing" in bags
or mixes

homeade biscuits

Cereals and Grain
Products

English muffins

pancake mix

pasta   rice   most muffins

instantized flour

wheat germ

instant oatmeal

matzo

cake &
pie crust mixes

breakfast cereal

low-sodium cereals

biscuit mixes

oatmeal (regular)

low-sodium bread

salted popcorn

Shredded Wheat

grits   flours   noodles

crackers

Cream of Wheat (regular)

pretzels

milk

low-sodium cheese

ALL CHEESES

yogurt

cottage cheese

cream

ice cream

Dairy

sour cream

prepared instant
pudding mixes

commercial buttermilk

Reprinted by permission of Health Education Associates Inc.

Sodium in Foods

○ **Low** (inner circle): USE FREELY
◑ **Medium** (middle circle: USE IN MEASURED AMOUNTS
● **High** (outer circle): DO NOT USE

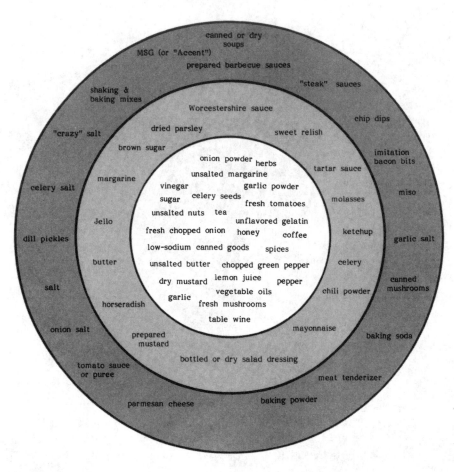

Reprinted by permission of Health Education Associates Inc.

SEASONINGS, CONDIMENTS, *and* RELISHES

◆◆◆◆◆

Low sodium food can be bland—a real problem. If you or your family feel that way, don't just sit there—do something. Make and use flavorful, low-sodium condiments.

Some popular condiments are naturally low in sodium: jams and jellies—3 mg in 1 tablespoon (15 mL); mint jelly—3 mg in 1 tablespoon (15 mL); cranberry orange relish—12 mg in 1/2 cup (125 mL); applesauce—3 mg in 1/2 cup (125 mL).

When beginning low-sodium cooking, you will be grateful for products such as commercial low-sodium ketchup even when they lack the flavor you would prefer. The new unsalted ketchups made by the large food companies, luckily, taste much better than some of the older ones. If you can't find any that you like, try one or both of these homemade ketchups.

This chapter includes zesty seasonings to liven up your dishes, popular condiments, and also marinades to flavor food—and each recipe needs only five or ten minutes to whip up. You'll find sauces in other chapters as well; check the index.

SEASONINGS
◆◆

◆ The Unsalt Shaker ◆

If you find it hard not to pick up the salt shaker and "shake" when you sit down to eat, you can make up an unsalt shaker. Try using different blends on various foods. A few shakes of any combination adds just a trace of sodium. Enjoy shaking the Unsalt Shaker! Empty the salt out of a shaker; wash and dry it. Mix one of the following spice blends or create your own. Spoon the mixture into the clean shaker. Add a few grains of uncooked rice to prevent it from caking.

Exotic Blend

1	tablespoon (15 mL) dry mustard
1 1/2	teaspoons (7 mL) white pepper
1	teaspoon (5 mL) curry powder
3	tablespoons (45 mL) onion powder
1/2	teaspoon (2 mL) garlic powder

Gentle Italian

2	tablespoons (30 mL) onion powder
1	teaspoon (5 mL) powdered oregano (leaf oregano may clog up the shaker)
1	teaspoon (5 mL) celery seed

Classic Blend

1/2	teaspoon (2 mL) white pepper
1/2	teaspoon (2 mL) celery seed
5	teaspoons (25 mL) onion powder
2	teaspoons (10 mL) garlic powder
2 1/2	teaspoons (12 mL) dry mustard

World Favorite

5	teaspoons (25 mL) onion powder
1	tablespoon (15 mL) garlic powder
1	tablespoon (15 mL) paprika
1	tablespoon (15 mL) dry mustard
1	teaspoon (5 mL) thyme
1/2	teaspoon (2 mL) white pepper
1/2	teaspoon (2 mL) celery seeds

Herb Blend

(use a shaker with large holes)

1	teaspoon (5 mL) thyme
1	teaspoon (5 mL) marjoram
1	teaspoon (5 mL) sage
1	teaspoon (5 mL) powdered basil
1	teaspoon (5 mL) lemon peel

◆ Salt-Free Chili Powder ◆

Ideal for seasoning chili beans, beef tacos, burritos—any "spicy" food.

   2   **tablespoons (30 mL) Durkee's paprika**
   2   **teaspoons (10 mL) Durkee's imported oregano**
1 1/4   **teaspoons (6 mL) Durkee's ground cumin**
1 1/4   **teaspoons (6 mL) Durkee's garlic powder**
 3/4   **teaspoon (3 mL) Durkee's ground red pepper**
 3/4   **teaspoon (3 mL) Durkee's onion powder**

Mix all ingredients thoroughly. Store in airtight container. Use as desired.

Note: Commercial chili powder varies in sodium content from brand to brand. Don't assume that the brand on your shelf is low in sodium until you find out for yourself (by calling or writing to the manufacturer). Since most brands do have salt, you may need to figure that each teaspoon (5 mL) of a brand with salt adds approximately 31 mg.

Reprinted by permission of Durkee Famous Foods, Westlake, Ohio

Calories per tablespoon: 20, Fat: 1 g (0 g saturated), Protein: 1 g, Cholesterol: 0 mg, Carbohydrates: 4 g, Sodium: 3 mg

Hot Peppers or Chiles and ◆ Hot Sauce ◆

Using hot peppers or chiles can be a natural part of low-sodium cooking. Chiles are naturally low in sodium with only a few milligrams per pepper. And they counteract the bane of low-sodium cooking— "It's tasteless."

Use fresh chiles with skins removed: To remove skins, broil a few inches from the heat, turning frequently for about 5 minutes or until the skins blister on all sides. Pop the blistered chilies into a closed plastic bag for 15 minutes. Then the skins will easily tear off. Or, if in a hurry, hold with a tong the heated chili under running water; peel and remove seeds. Use fresh, or freeze for another day.

Avoid hot peppers commercially packed in oil, since they have some added salt. Brands range from 10 to 138 mg per tablespoon. To learn the exact amount of added salt, write to the manufacturer whose brand you like.

Tabasco sauce and Louisiana red hot sauce are liquid hot pepper seasonings. Using a sauce from a bottle is much more convenient, but these products do contain salt—in small amounts. McIlhenny-brand Tabasco sauce, distributed in most countries, is lower in sodium and may be a wiser choice for people on low-sodium diets.

◆ Roll and Bake Coating Mix ◆

Make up a batch to keep on hand to bread your chicken, fish, or pork chops!

1	8-ounce box (227 g) low-sodium cornflakes
2/3	cup (180 mL) flour
2	teaspoons (10 mL) paprika
2	teaspoons (10 mL) onion powder
1 1/2	teaspoons (7 mL) garlic powder
3/4	teaspoon (4 mL) fresh ground pepper
1 1/2	tablespoons (22 mL) safflower oil
1 1/2	tablespoons (22 mL) sugar

Crush the cornflakes very fine using a blender or food processor; or crush flakes in a plastic bag with a rolling pin. Mix cornflake crumbs in a bowl with remaining ingredients (clean fingers work as well as anything). Store in a covered container in a cool, dry place; it keeps for weeks.

Calories per tablespoon: 11, Fat: 0 g (0 g saturated), Protein: 0 g, Cholesterol: 0 mg, Carbohydrates: 2 g, Sodium: 0 mg

CONDIMENTS

◆ Ketchup ◆

1	medium onion, coarsely chopped
1/2	cup (125 mL) water
12	ounces (340 mL) no-salt-added tomato paste
1/4	cup (60 mL) sugar
3/4	cup (180 mL) vinegar
1/4	teaspoon (1 mL) cinnamon
1/2	teaspoon (2 mL) dry mustard

Whip onion and water in blender at high speed until onion is liquefied. In a small saucepan, combine the onion-water mixture with remaining ingredients; stir with a wire whisk. Cook over low heat for about 10 minutes. Cool. Store in the refrigerator in a covered container (preferably a plastic squeeze bottle).

Calories per tablespoon: 13, Fat: 0 g (0 g saturated), Protein: 0 g, Cholesterol: 0 mg, Carbohydrates: 3 g, Sodium: 7 mg

◆ Peach Ketchup ◆

MAKES 2¹/₂ CUPS

A sweeter version.

    12 ounces (340 mL) no-salt-added tomato paste
    1/2 cup (125 mL) water
    1   teaspoon (5 mL) onion powder
    2   tablespoons (30 mL) corn syrup
    2   tablespoons (30 mL) sugar
    3/4 cup (190 mL) vinegar
    1   teaspoon (5 mL) dry mustard
    1/4 teaspoon (1 mL) cinnamon
    1   small jar baby food peaches
    1/4 teaspoon (1 mL) liquid hickory smoke (optional)

Combine all ingredients in a saucepan. Over medium heat, stir with a wire whisk for two minutes or until the sugar has dissolved and the mixture is smooth. Store, covered, in refrigerator.

Calories per tablespoon: 16, Fat: 0 g (0 g saturated), Protein: 0 g, Cholesterol: 0 mg, Carbohydrates: 4 g, Sodium: 9 mg

◆ Mayonnaise ◆

MAKES 1–1¹/₂ CUPS

This delicious mayonnaise is so easy to whip up in a blender or food processor—much better than commercial low-sodium mayonnaise. Remember, homemade mayonnaise does not keep as well as the commercial ones. Make each batch when needed. (Egg substitute does not work in blender mayonnaise, but one tablespoon of this mayonnaise contains only the cholesterol in ¹/₂₄ of an egg.)

1   *egg*
2   *tablespoons (30 mL) fresh lemon juice*
1/2 *teaspoon (2 mL) dry mustard*
1   *cup (250 mL) safflower oil*

Combine egg, lemon juice, mustard, and 1/4 of the oil in blender or food processor. Mix on low speed and quickly add remaining oil in a steady stream; beat for 20 seconds. Spoon into a jar and store, covered, in the refrigerator.

Calories per tablespoon: 84, Fat: 9 g (1 g saturated), Protein: 0 g, Cholesterol: 9 mg, Carbohydrates: 0 g, Sodium: 3 mg

◆ Hot Mustard ◆

MAKES 1/2 CUP

1/4 *cup (60 mL) flour*
1/4 *cup (60 mL) dry mustard*
1   *teaspoon (5 mL) sugar*
1/2 *teaspoon (2 mL) unsalted margarine*
1/3 *cup (80 mL) water, boiling*
1/4 *cup (60 mL) vinegar, boiling*

Mix first 4 ingredients in a small bowl. Add the boiling water and stir to make a stiff dough. Gradually add boiling vinegar and mix to a desired consistency.

Calories per tablespoon: 46, Fat: 2 g (0 g saturated), Protein: 2 g, Cholesterol: 0 mg, Carbohydrates: 6 g, Sodium: 0 mg

◆ Mild Mustard ◆

MAKES 1/2 CUP

3   *tablespoons (45 mL) flour*
2   *tablespoons (30 mL) dry mustard*
2   *teaspoons (10 mL) sugar*
1/4 *teaspoon (1 mL) turmeric*
1/2 *teaspoon (2 mL) unsalted margarine*
1/4 *cup (60 mL) water, boiling*
1   *tablespoon (15 mL) white wine (optional)*
2   *tablespoons (30 mL) cider vinegar, boiling*

Mix the first 5 ingredients together in a small bowl. Add the boiling water and mix. Then add the wine, if using, and the boiling vinegar.

Calories per tablespoon: 39, Fat: 2 g (0 g saturated), Protein: 1 g, Cholesterol: 0 mg, Carbohydrates: 5 g, Sodium: 1 mg

◆ Horseradish ◆

MAKES 1 CUP

Buy a horseradish root the right size to make one cup (250 mL) of chunks. (Horseradish root has an unusual, gnarled appearance.) If the fresh horseradish you bought yields more than one cup, use it all and add more vinegar—as long as there is about 3/4 as much vinegar as horseradish. Since fresh horseradish root is not always available, you may want to make extra horseradish and freeze it in small batches. One tablespoon (15 mL) of commercially prepared horseradish has about 200 mg of sodium.

  1 *piece (8 ounces / 226 g) horseradish root*
3/4 *cup (180 mL) white vinegar*

Wash and peel horseradish root using a vegetable peeler; cut into large chunks. Place about 1 cup (250 mL) in a blender or food processor. Add the vinegar. Blend until mixture is fairly smooth. Drain off any excess vinegar by placing the horseradish in a colander or mesh strainer and discard the liquid. Store horseradish, covered, in the refrigerator.

Calories per tablespoon: 10, Fat: 0 g (0 g saturated), Protein: 1 g, Cholesterol: 0 mg, Carbohydrates: 2 g, Sodium: 35 mg

◆ Horseradish Gravy ◆

MAKES 1 CUP

Serve with broiled fish or meat. Add more horseradish for a "hot" taste.

  2 *tablespoons (30 mL) unsalted margarine*
  2 *tablespoons (30 mL) flour*
3/4 *cup (180 mL) skim milk*
  3 *tablespoons (45 mL) Horseradish (above)*
  1 *teaspoon (5 mL) vinegar*
  1 *teaspoon (5 mL) sugar*

Melt margarine in a small saucepan. Add flour, stir, and cook for a minute or so. Add the milk, stirring with a wire whisk over medium heat until the mixture thickens; remove from heat. Stir in the horseradish, vinegar, and sugar.

Calories per tablespoon: 23, Fat: 2 g (0 g saturated), Protein: 1 g, Cholesterol: 0 mg, Carbohydrates: 2 g, Sodium: 13 mg

◆ Barbecue Sauce ◆

MAKES 1¹/2 CUPS

As good a barbecue sauce as any in a restaurant, and better than bottled barbecue sauces. If you're cutting down on meat, but love the flavor of barbecue, try this sauce over cooked navy or great northern beans.

- 1   *tablespoon (15 mL) unsalted margarine*
- 1/4 *cup (60 mL) low-sodium ketchup*
- 1/2 *cup (125 mL) cider vinegar*
- 3   *tablespoons (45 mL) molasses*
- 2   *tablespoons (30 mL) sugar*
- 1/4 *teaspoon (1 mL) paprika*
-     *dash Tabasco sauce*
- 1   *small jar baby food peaches*
- 1/2 *teaspoon (2 mL) dry mustard*
- 1/2 *teaspoon (2 mL) ginger*
- 1/4 *teaspoon (1 mL) liquid hickory smoke (optional)*

Combine all the ingredients in a saucepan and cook gently for 15 minutes.

Calories per tablespoon: 22, Fat: 1 g (0 g saturated), Protein: 0 g, Cholesterol: 0 mg, Carbohydrates: 5 g, Sodium: 3 mg

◆ Chili Sauce ◆

MAKES 1 CUP

If you find a brand of chili powder with no salt listed on the ingredient list, you will avoid 31 mg of sodium. To make your own, try Salt-Free Chili Powder (page 41).

1 cup (250 mL) Ketchup (page 42)
2 dashes Tabasco sauce (more if you like it "hotter")
1 teaspoon (5 mL) onion powder
1 tablespoon (15 mL) sugar
2 tablespoons (30 mL) vinegar
1/2 teaspoon (3 mL) no-salt-added chili powder

Combine all ingredients. Store in refrigerator.

Calories per tablespoon: 17, Fat: 0 g (0 g saturated), Protein 0 g, Cholesterol: 0 mg, Carbohydrates: 4 g, Sodium: 8 mg

◆ Hamburger Sauce ◆

MAKES 1 CUP

If you love fast-food style hamburgers, make up this sauce for your own homemade hamburgers (pages 91 and 92).

3/4 cup (180 mL) Mayonnaise (page 43)
2 tablespoons (30 mL) Ketchup (page 42)
2 tablespoons (30 mL) Sweet Relish (page 50)
2 teaspoons (10 mL) sugar
2 teaspoons (10 mL) vinegar
1/4 teaspoon (1 mL) dry mustard

Stir together all ingredients. Store, covered, in refrigerator.

Calories per tablespoon: 72, Fat: 7 g (1 g saturated), Protein: 0 g, Cholesterol: 7 mg, Carbohydrates: 2 g, Sodium: 4 mg

◆ Hot Cocktail Sauce ◆

MAKES 6 TABLESPOONS

1/4 cup (60 mL) Ketchup (page 42)
1 tablespoon (15 mL) Horseradish, less for a milder flavor, (page 45)
2 dashes Tabasco sauce

Combine ketchup, horseradish, and Tabasco sauce in a small bowl.

Calories per tablespoon: 13, Fat: 0 g (0 g saturated), Protein: 0 g, Cholesterol: 0 mg, Carbohydrates: 3 g, Sodium: 14 mg

◆ Sweet-and-Sour Pineapple Sauce ◆

MAKES 2¹/₄ CUPS

This sauce can be cooked with chicken or pork or served with vegetable, fish, and grain dishes.

1/2 cup (125 mL) water
1 cup (250 mL) drained crushed pineapple
1/2 cup (125 mL) juice drained from pineapple can
1 tablespoon (15 mL) molasses
3 tablespoons (45 mL) sugar
1/2 teaspoon (2 mL) ginger
1/2 cup (125 mL) vinegar
3 tablespoons (45 mL) cornstarch

Stir all ingredients in a saucepan over medium heat until mixture boils. Reduce heat and cook gently for about 10 minutes.

Calories per tablespoon: 13, Fat: 0 g (0 g saturated), Protein: 0 g, Cholesterol: 0 mg, Carbohydrates: 3 g, Sodium: 0 mg

◆ Tartar Sauce ◆

MAKES ¹/₄ CUP (60 ML)

3 tablespoons (45 mL) Mayonnaise (page 43)
1 tablespoon (15 mL) Sweet Relish, drained (page 50)

Combine mayonnaise and relish in a small bowl. Serve immediately or refrigerate, covered, until mealtime.

Calories per tablespoon: 68 Fat: 7 g (1 g saturated), Protein: 0 g, Cholesterol: 7 mg, Carbohydrates: 1 g, Sodium: 2 mg

◆ Soy Sauce Substitute ◆

MAKES ²/₃ CUP

Use as a soy sauce substitute. No, it doesn't taste just like soy sauce, because soy sauce tastes very salty. In fact, there are 1,319 mg of sodium in one tablespoon (15 mL) of soy sauce—a clue that it is mainly salt.*

1/2 cup (125 mL) cola drink
  2 teaspoons (10 mL) cornstarch
  2 teaspoons (10 mL) molasses
  2 tablespoons (30 mL) lemon juice
1/8 teaspoon (1/2 mL) ginger
1/4 teaspoon (1 mL) Angostura bitters
  1 tablespoon (15 mL) sherry (not cooking sherry)

In a small saucepan, stir all of the ingredients over low heat. Cook for a minute or less. Using a funnel, pour into a container such as a bottle with a shaker top. If you save, wash, and reuse a soy sauce bottle with a shaker top, the sauce will seem more "authentic." Store in the refrigerator.

* New commercial soy sauces continually appear on grocery shelves. These are lower in sodium, but they are not low-sodium; it will be necessary to read the labels.

Calories per tablespoon: 12, Fat: 0 g (0 g saturated), Protein: 0 g, Cholesterol: 0 mg, Carbohydrates: 3 g, Sodium: 1 mg

◆ Chinese Peach Sauce ◆

MAKES 3/4 CUP

1/2 cup (125 mL) peach preserves
  2 tablespoons (30 mL) vinegar (cider vinegar is best)
1/8 teaspoon (.5 mL) ground ginger
1/8 teaspoon (.5 mL) garlic powder

Combine all the ingredients* in a small saucepan over low heat and cook for one minute. Store extra sauce in a covered container in the refrigerator. Serve hot or cold.

* Double the amount for the 96 Egg Roll Hors d'Oeuvres (page 81).

Calories per tablespoon: 38, Fat: 0 g (0 g saturated), Protein: 0 g, Cholesterol: 0 mg, Carbohydrates: 9 g, Sodium: 4 mg

◆◆

◆ Sweet Relish ◆

MAKES ABOUT 1 3/4 CUPS

    4   sweet green peppers
    1   medium onion
  1/3   cup (90 mL) sugar
  1/2   teaspoon (2 mL) celery seed
    1   teaspoon (5 mL) mustard seed
        dash cinnamon
        dash allspice
  3/4   cup (185 mL) vinegar

Chop peppers and onion using a food grinder or food processor or chop with sharp knife on cutting board. Transfer pepper-onion mixture to saucepan; stir in 1/2 cup (125 mL) of the vinegar. Cook over medium heat for 10 minutes, stirring often. Drain vegetables and discard liquid. Return the vegetables to the pan. Add the spices and the remaining 1/4 cup (60 mL) vinegar. Cook gently about 5 minutes. Cool. Store in a covered container or glass jar in the refrigerator.

Calories per tablespoon: 17, Fat: 0 g (0 g saturated), Protein: 0 g, Cholesterol: 0 mg, Carbohydrates: 4 g, Sodium: 1 mg

◆ Corn Relish ◆

MAKES 2 1/2 CUPS

Easy and delicious. Serve corn relish with baked beans to help complete the protein. Or serve as a garnish to any "plain" meal.

  2/3   cup (180 mL) cider vinegar
    2   tablespoons (30 mL) cornstarch
    1   teaspoon (5 mL) pickling spice
  1/4   teaspoon (1 mL) cinnamon
  1/3   cup (90 mL) sugar
   10   ounces (300 g) frozen corn
  1/2   red or green pepper, finely diced

Combine the vinegar, cornstarch, pickling spice, cinnamon and sugar in a saucepan. Simmer for 15 minutes, stirring occasionally. Meanwhile, cook frozen corn as directed on label (but leave out the salt); drain. Mix with chopped pepper in a bowl. Pour the sauce over the corn and peppers (or you can strain and discard spices). Refrigerate overnight to blend flavors.

**Calories per 1/2 cup: 59, Fat: 0 g (0 g saturated), Protein: 1 g,
Cholesterol: 0 mg, Carbohydrates: 15 g, Sodium: 2 mg**

◆ Five-Minute Chutney ◆

MAKES 1 CUP

A tasty accompaniment for curry and easy to make. Try chutney on no-salt cheese, meat, chicken, or tuna sandwiches instead of butter or mayonnaise.

  1 *7³/4-ounce jar (200 g) junior baby food apricots*
1/4 *cup (60 mL) apricot preserves*
1/4 *cup (60 mL) cider vinegar*
  1 *tablespoon (15 mL) brown sugar*
1/4 *teaspoon (1 mL) onion powder*
  2 *pinches cayenne red pepper*
  1 *pinch allspice*
  1 *teaspoon (5 mL) ginger (use less if you want a milder taste)*
  1 *tablespoon cornstarch (15 mL)*

Combine all of the ingredients except the cornstarch in a saucepan. Heat gently and stir until the brown sugar dissolves. Spoon the cornstarch into a bowl. Using a whisk or spoon, gradually stir in about 1/2 cup (125 mL) of the fruit mixture. Add the cornstarch-fruit mixture to the saucepan; heat gently and stir until thickened.

**Calories per tablespoon: 24, Fat: 0 g (0 g saturated), Protein: 0 g,
Cholesterol: 0 mg, Carbohydrates: 6 g, Sodium: 2 mg**

DRESSINGS, MARINADES, *and* SAUCES

✦✦◆✦✦

DRESSINGS

◆◆

✦ Good and Good for You Dressing ✦

MAKES 2 1/2 CUPS

1   *cup (250 mL) water*
1/4 *cup (60 mL)sugar*
1/4 *cup (60 mL) lemon juice*
1/4 *cup (60 mL) vinegar*
1   *tablespoon (15 mL) safflower oil*
1/2 *cup (125 mL) low-sodium ketchup*
1   *clove garlic*
2   *teaspoons (10 mL) celery seeds*
1   *small onion, grated*
    ground black pepper

Put all ingredients together in a jar. Shake well. Chill before using. Store in refrigerator. Shake well before serving.

Calories per tablespoon: 22, Fat: 1 g (0 g saturated), Protein: 0 g, Cholesterol: 0 mg, Carbohydrates: 4 g, Sodium: 2 mg

❖ Oil-and-Vinegar Dressing ❖

MAKES 1 CUP

2/3   cup (180 mL) safflower oil
1/3   cup (80 mL) tarragon vinegar, or other vinegar
      or lemon juice
      dash pepper
  1   clove garlic, peeled
1/2   teaspoon (2 mL) dry mustard
      dash Tabasco sauce
1/2   teaspoon (2 mL) paprika
1 1/2 tablespoons (22 mL) sugar
1/2   teaspoon (2 mL) basil, dill, or other herb that you like

Shake all the ingredients in a covered container. Store in the refrigerator.

**Calories per tablespoon: 86, Fat: 9 g (1 g saturated), Protein: 0 g,
Cholesterol: 0 mg, Carbohydrates: 2 g, Sodium: 0 mg**

❖ Tangy Red Dressing ❖

MAKES 2 1/4 CUPS

Delicious and attractive, this dressing is great even on plain lettuce.

1/2   cup (125 mL) low-sodium ketchup
1/4   cup (60 mL) safflower oil
1/4   cup (60 mL) water
1/2   cup (125 mL) sugar
1/3   cup (80 mL) lemon juice
1/4   teaspoon (1 mL) onion powder
      ground black pepper
1/2   cup (125 mL) vinegar
  1   clove garlic, peeled

Shake all ingredients in a covered jar. Store in the refrigerator. Shake before
each use.

**Calories per tablespoon: 43, Fat: 2 g (0 g saturated), Protein: 0 g,
Cholesterol: 0 mg, Carbohydrates: 6 g, Sodium: 1 mg**

◆ Low-Calorie Italian Dressing ◆

MAKES 1 CUP

It is best to make several hours before serving so that the flavors blend.

- 1/2 cup (125 mL) vinegar
- 2 tablespoons (30 mL) safflowr oil
- 1 tablespoon (15 mL) cornstarch
- 1/2 cup + 1 tablespoon (125 mL +15 mL) water
- 1/4 teaspoon (1 mL) paprika
- 1/4 teaspoon (1 mL) dry mustard
- 1/2 teaspoon (2mL) celery seed
- 1/4 teaspoon (1 mL) oregano
- 1 medium clove garlic, pressed
- 1/4 teaspoon (1 mL) basil
- 1 tablespoon (15 mL) sugar

Stir vinegar, oil, and 1/2 cup (125 mL) water in a small saucepan until it boils. Mix cornstarch and 1 tablespoon (15 mL) water in a small dish. Add the cornstarch mixture to the saucepan and continue cooking over low heateaspoon When mixture boils again, remove from heat; add other ingredients. Pour the dressing into a container, cover tightly, and refrigerate.

Calories per tablespoon: 22, Fat: 2 g, (0 g saturated), Protein: 0 g, Cholesterol: 0 mg, Carbohydrates: 2 g, Sodium: 0 mg

◆ Light 'n Easy Cucumber Dressing ◆

MAKES 2 CUPS

- 1/4 cup (60 mL) low-fat yogurt
- 1 medium cucumber, peeled and cubed
- 1/2 green pepper, seeded and sliced
- 1 clove garlic
- 2 dashes white pepper
- 2 dashes onion powder
- 1/4 cup (60 mL) Mayonnaise (page 43)

Combine everything except mayonnaise in the blender. Blend and pour into a storage container. Stir in mayonnaise. Cover tightly and refrigerate.

Calories per tablespoon: 13, Fat: 1 g (0 g saturated), Protein: 0 g, Cholesterol: 1 mg, Carbohydrates: 1 g, Sodium: 2 mg

◆ Creamy Italian Dressing ◆

Wonderful and easy.

      1   cup (250 mL) Mayonnaise (page 43)
    1/2   teaspoon (2 mL) garlic powder
    1/2   teaspoon (2 mL) onion powder
    1/2   teaspoon (2 mL) crushed dried red pepper
    1/4   cup (60 mL) cider vinegar
      1   teaspoon (5 mL) sugar
      3   tablespoons (45 mL) Sweet Relish (page 50)
          ground black pepper

Mix all of the ingredients together. Store in a tightly covered container in the refrigerator. Mix again before serving.

Calories per tablespoon: 72, Fat: 8 g (1 g saturated), Protein: 0 g, Cholesterol: 7 mg, Carbohydrates: 1 g, Sodium: 2 mg

◆ Russian Dressing ◆

If you add some chopped low-sodium pickles, you'll have a thousand island dressing. You could also add diced green pepper or cucumber.

      4   tablespoons (60 mL) Mayonnaise (page 43)
      2   tablespoons (30 mL) Ketchup (page 42)

Mix the mayonnaise and ketchup just before serving. Store in the refrigerator.

Calories per tablespoon: 60, Fat: 6 g (0 g saturated), Protein: 0 g, Cholesterol: 6 mg, Carbohydrates: 1 g, Sodium: 4 mg

◆ Fruit Dressings ◆

Honey Dressing

This dressing is especially nice with fruit salads.

- 1/4 cup (60 mL) honey
- 1/4 cup (60 mL) vinegar
- 2 tablespoons (30 mL) safflower oil
- 2 tablespoons (30 mL) water

Combine all ingredients in a covered container and shake to combine. For best flavor, keep chilled until you're ready to use it. Store in the refrigerator.

Calories per tablespoon: 42, Fat: 2 g (0 g saturated), Protein: 0 g, Cholesterol: 0 mg, Carbohydrates: 6 g, Sodium: 0 mg

Spicy Dressing

Good on fruit salads any time of year.

- 1/2 cup (125 mL) Mayonnaise (page 43)
- 2 tablespoons (30 mL) lemon juice
- 2 tablespoons (30 mL) skim milk
- 1/2 teaspoon (2 mL) celery seed
- 1/8 teaspoon (1/2 mL) cinnamon
  dash ginger
- 1 tablespoon (15 mL) sugar

Combine all the ingredients in a small bowl. Store in a covered container in the refrigerator. Shake before using.

Calories per tablespoon: 62, Fat: 6 g (0 g saturated), Protein: 0 g, Cholesterol: 6 mg, Carbohydrates: 2 g, Sodium: 3 mg

MARINADES

——◆◆——

Marinades add flavor to foods and also help to tenderize tougher meat cuts. To marinate: Place the food in a nonmetal container; cover with the marinade for at least one hour, or preferably longer (all day or overnight), in refrigerator.

Plan ahead. When you are thinking about serving a meat, place it in a marinade instead of just leaving it in the wrapping paper. It is difficult to calculate how much of the marinade or sauce is absorbed by each piece of meat, so we can't be sure how much sodium and how many calories are added to any meat.

All the recipes for marinades in this book are very low in sodium. If you are marinating a very tough cut of meat, you may want to add a little unsalted tenderizer to the marinade. Meat tenderizer is so high in sodium—5,490 mg in one tablespoon (15 mL)—that it should not be used by anyone who needs to cut down on salt.

◆ Lemony Marinade ◆

MAKES 3/4 CUP

Brush marinade on raw chicken parts before broiling for a great chicken dish.

6 *tablespoons (90 mL) lemon juice*
4 *tablespoons (60 mL) unsalted margarine*
4 *tablespoons (60 mL) low-sodium ketchup*

In a saucepan, stir all ingredients and simmer over low heat for 10 minutes.

Calories per tablespoon: 41, Fat: 4 g (1 g saturated), Protein: 0 g, Cholesterol: 0 mg, Carbohydrates: 2 g, Sodium: 2 mg

◆ Sweet-and-Sour Marinade ◆

MAKES 1 CUP

The pineapple sweetens chicken or pork, especially.

1/4 cup (60 mL) cider vinegar
1/2 cup (125 mL) crushed pineapple (unsweetened)
2 tablespoons (30 mL) honey
1 tablespoon (15 mL) low-sodium ketchup

Stir together all the ingredients to make the marinade.

**Calories per tablespoon: 12, Fat: 0 g (0 g saturated), Protein: 0 g,
Cholesterol: 0 mg, Carbohydrates 3 g, Sodium: 0 mg**

◆ White Wine Marinade ◆

MAKES 1 1/2 CUPS

Good for chicken, pork, or lamb.

1   cup (250 mL) white wine such as Chablis
1/4   cup (60 mL) lemon juice
2   tablespoons (30 mL) honey
1/4   teaspoon (1 mL) garlic powder
1/4   teaspoon (1 mL) dry mustard
2   tablespoons (30 mL) safflower oil

In a small saucepan stir all of the ingredients. Heat gently until dissolved.

**Calories per tablespoon: 23, Fat: 1 g (0 g saturated), Protein: 0 g,
Cholesterol: 0 mg, Carbohydrates: 2 g, Sodium: 1 mg**

◆ Tomato Wine Marinade ◆

Adds a powerful flavor to beef.

1   cup (250 mL) red wine, such as Burgundy
2   cloves garlic, finely minced
6   ounces (180 mL) no-salt-added tomato paste
¹/₂ teaspoon (2 mL) basil

Whisk together all of the ingredients.

Calories per tablespoon: 13, Fat: 0 g (0 g saturated), Protein: 0 g, Cholesterol: 0 mg, Carbohydrates: 2 g, Sodium: 7 mg

◆ Orange Juice Marinade ◆

Good on chicken.

¹/₃ cup (80 mL) orange juice
1   tablespoon (15 mL) safflower oil
¹/₄ cup (60 mL) vinegar
1   clove garlic, finely chopped
1   small onion, finely chopped
¹/₂ teaspoon (2 mL) dry mustard
1   teaspoon (5 mL) cinnamon

Combine all ingredients in a bowl to make the marinade.

Calories per tablespoon: 19, Fat: 1 g (0 g saturated), Protein: 0 g, Cholesterol: 0 mg, Carbohydrates: 2 g, Sodium: 1 mg

◆ Burgundy Marinade ◆

This robust marinade is terrific for tenderizing tough cuts of beef, such as round.

   2   *tablespoons (30 mL) olive oil*
   1   *medium onion, sliced very thin*
   1   *garlic clove, crushed*
  1/4 *cup (60 mL) red wine vinegar*
  1/2 *cup (125 mL) Burgundy or other dry red wine*
  1/4 *cup (60 mL) water*
   1   *teaspoon (5 mL) thyme*
       ground black pepper
   1   *bay leaf*

Heat the oil in a small saucepan and stir in the onion; cook over moderate heat until onion is soft and yellow. Add the garlic and cook for a minute or two. Add the wine vinegar, stir for 3 minutes more, then add remaining ingredients and cook 5 minutes. Cool.

Calories per tablespoon: 16, Fat: 1 g (0 g saturated), Protein: 0 g, Cholesterol: 0 mg, Carbohydrates: 1 g, Sodium: 1 mg

◆ Herb Marinade ◆

Good for tenderizing and adding flavor to tougher cuts of lamb or beef.

   3   *tablespoons (45 mL) lemon juice*
   2   *tablespoons (30 mL) oil*
   1   *clove garlic, minced*
  1/4 *teaspoon (1 mL) thyme*
  1/4 *teaspoon (1 mL) oregano*
  1/2 *teaspoon (2 mL) rosemary*
   1   *medium onion, thinly sliced*
       ground black pepper

In a nonmetal container with a cover, shake all ingredients.

Calories per tablespoon: 38, Fat: 3 g (0 g saturated), Protein: 0 g, Cholesterol: 0 mg, Carbohydrates: 2 g, Sodium: 1 mg

SAUCES

—◆◆—

◆ Fresh Tomato Sauce ◆

This *pomodori crudi* is a wonderful way to serve summer tomatoes. Serve over pasta, such as small shaped macaroni, ziti, rotelle, or little shells. For a hotter version, try Fresh Tomato Sauce with Chili (page 198).

  2   *pounds (900 g) very ripe fresh tomatoes*
  2   *cloves garlic, minced*
1/4 *teaspoon (1 mL) oregano*
  1   *tablespoon (15 mL) fresh parsley, chopped*
1/3 *cup (80 mL) olive oil*
1/4 *pound (110 g) no-salt-added Swiss cheese*

Place tomatoes in a pot of boiling water for a minute or so until their skins break open. Scoop the tomatoes out of the boiling water. Peel off the tomato skin, and scoop out the seeds. Save as much juice as you can. Cut the tomatoes into chunks. Mix the tomatoes with their juice, the garlic, oregano, parsley, oil, and cheese in a bowl. Let stand at room temperature for at least an hour, to let flavors blend. Toss tomato sauce with pasta. Serve while hot.

Calories: 322, Fat: 28 g (8 g saturated), Protein: 9 g,
Cholesterol: 28 mg, Carbohydrates: 12 g, Sodium: 27 mg

◆ Meat Sauce ◆

If you want to make a meat sauce, sauté 1/2 pound (225 g) of very lean ground beef in a separate pan. After it is cooked, drain off the fat and add meat to Tomato Sauce (page 62). Simmer to combine the flavors.

◆ Tomato Sauce ◆

This easy sauce can be used on pizza,* on spaghetti, or in other recipes. There is no fat added to this recipe. You can add Italian meatballs. Cook the meatballs separately using the recipe on page 179. Drain off the fat and add the meatballs to the tomato sauce. Simmer to combine the flavors.

- 12 ounces (340 g) no-salt-added tomato paste
- 1 teaspoon (5 mL) basil
- 1 teaspoon (5 mL) oregano
- 1/8 teaspoon (1/2 mL) pepper
- 1 teaspoon (5 mL) onion powder
- 1/2 teaspoon (2 mL) garlic powder
- 2 tablespoons (30 mL) sugar
- 2 cups (500 mL) water
- 2 tablespoons (30 mL) vinegar

Put all ingredients in a large saucepan. Stir with a whisk to combine. Simmer for at least 20 minutes.

* Make half this recipe for Pizza (page 144) and simmer while preparing the dough, or freeze in small amounts for quick use.

Calories per 1/2 cup: 66, Fat: 0 g (0 g saturated), Protein: 2 g, Cholesterol: 0 mg, Carbohydrates: 16 g, Sodium: 50 mg

Tomato Sauce with ◆ Peppers and Mushrooms ◆

Add 1 cup (250 mL) of sliced mushrooms and 1/2 of a green pepper, finely chopped. Simmer until the vegetables are as tender as you like.

Calories per 1/2 cup: 72, Fat: 0 g (0 g saturated), Protein: 3 g, Cholesterol: 0 mg, Carbohydrates: 17 g, Sodium: 51 mg

BREAKFAST

◆◆◆◆◆

Breakfast is the easiest meal of the day for many low-sodium dieters. Low-sodium eating at home certainly is easier than eating in a restaurant. Favorite breakfast choices—coffee or tea, orange juice, some cold cereals, eggs, potatoes—are naturally low in sodium. Popular breakfast foods, such as pancakes, that are usually high in sodium, can be made at home with a much lower sodium content (page 67). You'll find muffins, nut breads, and yeast breads in the Breads chapter (page 209).

FRUIT AND FRUIT JUICE

If you like to start breakfast with juice or fruit, you can choose any pure juice. Avoid tomato juice and V-8 vegetable juice, which have more than 800 mg of sodium in one cup (250 mL)—obviously much too high for anyone on any kind of a sodium restricted diet. Low-sodium tomato and blended vegetable juices are available; try a small can to see if you like the taste before you stock up.

Juice drinks are slightly higher in sodium than pure juices. But there is an even more compelling reason not to buy them—they contain mostly water with a small amount of juice (about 5–10 percent) plus coloring agents and sugar. Considering that the price is almost as high as the price of pure juices, you are not getting much for your money.

Whole fresh fruits are not only naturally low in sodium—they also provide more filling food than juices with the same calories and vitamins. Adding a piece of fruit to breakfast is a real morale booster. Seasonal fruits are not too expensive—grapefruit in the winter and melon in the summer, for example. Hot broiled grapefruit is almost as easy as chilled grapefruit and makes a special treat on a cold morning.

◆ Broiled Grapefruit ◆

After cutting the grapefruit in half, sprinkle on a little sugar or honey. Broil for about 5 to 10 minutes, or until it is hot and bubbly.

Calories: 37, Fat: 0.1 g (0 g Saturated), Protein: 1 g, Cholesterol: 0 mg, Carbohydrates: 9 g, Sodium: 0 mg

COLD CEREALS

Cold cereals are standard breakfast dishes in many homes. Although the grains from which all cereals are made contain just a trace of sodium, many manufacturers add large amounts. Unfortunately, cereals that are advertised claiming "good nutrition" tend to be among the highest in sodium. In one ounce (30 g) they are high in sodium mg: All-Bran, 287; cornflakes, 291; Special K, 218; Total, 375; Wheaties, 393.

Luckily, most low-sodium cold cereals list the sodium contents on the label. These are available: Sovex fruit and nut granola, Sovex unprocessed wheat bran, Quaker unprocessed bran, Puffa Puffa Rice, puffed rice (not the fancy kind), puffed wheat, plain shredded wheat (Spoon Size Shredded Wheat is the same), Frosted Mini-Wheats, and toasted wheat germ.

Familia Swiss Birchermuesli, a combination of grains and fruits, is available in many markets. There are several different versions, so select the one with no added salt. Look for the red box.

Also, you may want to try to see if you like low-sodium cereals, such as cornflakes. Use them as a substitute for bread crumbs in recipes. (See Roll and Bake Coating Mix, page 42.)

If you have been a cereal eater, you should be able to find one low in sodium that you like. A half cup (125 mL) of milk adds about 63 mg of sodium plus valuable calcium. And the complete protein in the milk complements the incomplete protein in the cereal.

HOT CEREALS

◆◆

If you like hot cereal, you are lucky—all of the popular ones are naturally low in sodium (1 to 3 milligrams in a serving): oatmeal, Cream of Rice, Cream of Wheat, farina, Maltex, Malt-O-Meal, and Wheatena.

Although the long-cooking cereals are all low in sodium, instant and quick-cooking types vary considerably: regular and "quick" oats, 1 mg per serving; Quaker "instant" oats, 400 mg; Nabisco "instant" Cream of Wheat, 10 mg. Manufacturers often change the formulas for their products. Read the labels every time you shop.

Cereals cook just as well when you leave out the salt. For more flavor, try adding cinnamon, nutmeg, and a little sugar or honey. Be careful with brown sugar: there are 4 mg sodium in a level tablespoon (15 mL). Or slice a banana or peach on your cereal.

◆ Granola ◆

MAKES 9 SERVINGS

Granola has become a popular breakfast cereal. But commercial granolas are loaded with sodium and calories. If you're interested, just check the boxes. This granola recipe, on the other hand, is surprisingly low in calories.

   3 cups (750 mL) oatmeal (regular)
 1/2 cup (125 mL) wheat germ
 2/3 cup (180 mL) sliced unsalted almonds or other
       unsalted nuts
   1 tablespoon (15 mL) safflower oil
 1/4 cup (60 mL) honey
   2 tablespoons (30 mL) molasses
 1/4 cup (60 mL) apple juice

Mix oatmeal, wheat germ, and almonds in a flat lasagne or jelly roll pan. In a saucepan, combine and heat the oil, honey, molasses, and apple juice. Drizzle over the oatmeal mixture; use a spatula to push the mixture around in the pan. Bake in a 325°F (165°C) oven for about 30 minutes. Then, mix again and bake 10 minutes. (The longer you cook it, the crunchier it gets.)

**Calories: 344, Fat: 11 g (1 g saturated), Protein: 13 g,
Cholesterol: 0 mg, Carbohydrates: 51 g, Sodium: 7 mg**

SPECIAL BREAKFAST OR BRUNCH

For a low-sodium breakfast or brunch with an informal flair, arrange the waffle iron, waffle batter, and toppings on the buffet. These toppings also create a special waffle dessert:

Strawberry: Defrost frozen strawberries and fill an attractive serving dish with them for guests to spoon over waffles.

Applesauce: Heat applesauce in a saucepan, adding a dash of cinnamon or nutmeg.

Pineapple: Crushed pineapple is tasty.

◆ Pancake and Waffle Batter ◆

MAKES 16 PANCAKES

For a change in the morning, you might want to make pancakes,* waffles, or French toast.

Making pancakes from the following recipe takes about one minute longer than commercial pancake mix, which is very high in sodium.

Low-sodium baking powder works well in this recipe. For toppings, maple and pancake syrups are fairly low in sodium but high in calories. So if you're watching calories, try applesauce.

> 3/4 cup (180 mL) skim milk
> 1 1/2 tablespoons (22 mL) safflower oil
> 1 egg or egg substitute
> 1 tablespoon (15 mL) low-sodium baking powder (shake and stir before measuring)
> 3 tablespoons (45 mL) sugar
> 1 cup (250 mL) flour

In a large bowl, combine the milk, oil, and egg or egg substitute. Stir in the baking powder, sugar, and flour. Mix just enough to moisten flour; do not overmix. (The batter will still have small lumps.) Griddle according to directions that follow.

Mix a scant cup (240 mL) of fresh or frozen whole blueberries into your pancake batter or add chopped apples to your waffle batter for flavor. The fruits add a very small amount of sodium.

Calories per pancake: 58, Fat: 2 g (0.2 g saturated), Protein: 2 g, Cholesterol: 14 mg, Carbohydrates: 9 g, Sodium: 11 mg

◆ Pancakes ◆

Preheat a lightly oiled griddle or frying pan while mixing the batter. Griddle must be hot—drops of water will sizzle and "dance" when dropped on it. Pour about 1/4 cup (60 mL) or less for each pancake onto the griddle or frying pan. With a spatula turn pancakes when bubbly and edges are cooked. Serve hot. To freeze, cool and wrap in freezer wrap. To reheat, use toaster, oven, or microwave oven.

◆ Waffles ◆

Preheat waffle iron when mixing your batter. Test the waffle iron by sprinkling a drop of water on it. If the water "dances," the iron is hot enough. To prevent sticking, brush waffle iron with oil, or spray with a vegetable coating spray. Pour in about 1/3 of a cup (80 mL) for each waffle. When there is less steam escaping from the corners of the waffle iron, the waffles are done. If you like crispy waffles, continuing cooking until almost no steam escapes. Serve hot. To freeze and reheat, see Pancakes above.

◆ Toast ◆

Toast is a favorite breakfast food, and low-sodium breads are increasingly available in the freezer department of grocery stores. Especially, homemade low-sodium breads make wonderful toast. Try making some when you feel ambitious (see Breads, page 209). If your sodium intake is highly restricted, be careful about making toast from regular commercial bread; there are about 228 mg in 2 slices.

◆ French Toast ◆

MAKES 2 SERVINGS

Serve French toast with maple or pancake syrup or try lower calorie applesauce for a delicious change. Leftover slices of any kind of bread can be used.

    1 teaspoon (5 mL) unsalted margarine
  1/4 cup (60 mL) skim milk
    1 egg or egg substitute
    4 slices low-sodium bread

Preheat a frying pan or griddle over medium heat. Melt the margarine in the pan. Using a fork, in a bowl combine the milk and egg or egg substitute. Dip both sides of the bread into this mixture. Fry on both sides until browned.

**Calories: 198, Fat: 6 g (2 g saturated), Protein: 8 g,
Cholesterol: 107 mg, Carbohydrates: 27 g, Sodium: 62 mg**

◆ English Muffins ◆

MAKES 12 MUFFINS

Commercial English muffins are packed with added sodium—from 225 to 600 mg per muffin. Brands vary a great deal; check before you buy. You may have to write to the manufacturer to get this information.

Homemade English muffins are delicious, although, admittedly, they do take time for the dough to rise. But the muffins are not hard to make. If you make up a batch when you are going to be home anyhow, it won't seem like much trouble at all.

These muffins are cooked on a griddle the old-fashioned way! And they freeze well.

*1/4 cup (60 mL) warm water (water used with packaged
     yeast should feel warm, but not hot, to the touch)
  1 tablespoon (15 mL) sugar
  1 package dry yeast
1/2 cup (125 mL) skim milk
  2 tablespoons (30 mL) safflower oil
  2 tablespoons (30 mL) unsalted margarine
1/4 cup (60 mL) cool water
  3 cups (750 mL) flour, more if necessary
  2 tablespoons (30 mL) corn meal*

Pour the warm water into a mixing bowl, stir in the sugar, and sprinkle the yeast on top. Wait a minute, then stir and set aside until yeast bubbles up, about 10 minutes. Meanwhile, heat milk in small pan, add oil and margarine. Stir and heat until margarine melts, add the cool water and remove from heat. Pour in large bowl; cool to lukewarm. Add yeast mixture and all but half cup (125 mL) of the flour. Mix by hand or wooden spoon until flour is absorbed. Sprinkle half of the remaining flour on a working surface. Knead, adding more flour if the dough is sticky, until smooth and elastic.

Place dough in mixing bowl, and cover with clean cloth. Put bowl in a warm place away from drafts; let rise until doubled, about 1 hour.

Punch dough down; divide into 12 parts and shape with hands into muffins about 3 1/2" (9 cm) in diameter. Dust a cookie sheet lightly with cornmeal. Place muffins on the cookie sheet and lightly dust the tops with cornmeal. Cover with a clean cloth and let rise for about 1 hour. Heat an ungreased griddle or cast-iron frying pan until moderately hot. Cook muffins for 9 minutes on each side until golden brown. Regulate the heat so that the muffins cook through but don't burn. Cool muffins before splitting. Store in refrigerator or freezer.

Calories per muffin: 165, Fat: 5 g (1 g saturated), Protein: 4 g, Cholesterol: 0.2 mg, Carbohydrates: 27 g, Sodium: 7 mg

◆ Quick Biscuits ◆

MAKES 6 LARGE BISCUITS

Self-rising flour, often used for biscuits, is outrageously high in sodium. All-purpose flour works well with low-sodium baking powder in this recipe. You can use unsalted margarine or honey or jelly on your biscuits—very low in sodium, but high in calories. For more quick breads see Breads (page 209).

  1 *cup (250 mL) flour*
2 1/2 *teaspoons (12 mL) low-sodium baking powder (shake or stir before using)*
  1 *teaspoon (5 mL) sugar*
  2 *tablespoons (30 mL) unsalted margarine*
 1/3 *cup (80 mL) skim milk*

Sift the flour, baking powder, and sugar together twice into a mixing bowl. Using fork or pastry blender, cut the margarine into the flour mixture until it has the consistency of coarse cornmeal. Add milk and stir just enough to moisten. Shape the dough into a ball. Sprinkle flour on a work surface. Using a rolling pin, roll the dough until 1/2-inch (1=cm) thick. Cut with a 2-inch (5-cm) biscuit cutter to make approximately 6 biscuits. If you do not have a biscuit cutter, use any round top. Spray a cookie sheet with a vegetable coating spray. Place biscuits on the cookie sheet. Bake in a 450°F (230°C) oven about 10 minutes.

Calories per biscuit: 119, Fat: 4 g (1 g saturated), Protein: 3 g, Cholesterol: 0.3 mg, Carbohydrates: 18 g, Sodium: 11 mg

◆ Home Fries ◆

You can also add a small amount of chopped onion.

2 tablespoons (30 mL) safflower oil
1 tablespoon (15 mL) paprika
4 medium potatoes, cooked, peeled, and diced

Heat oil in frying pan. Sprinkle paprika over the potato pieces. Drop potatoes into the frying pan and fry over medium heat for a few minutes, stirring frequently.

Calories: 121, Fat: 5 g (0.3 g saturated), Protein: 2 g, Cholesterol: 0 mg, Carbohydrates: 19 g, Sodium: 5 mg

EGGS AND EGG SUBSTITUTES

—◆◆—

Your doctor can tell you how many eggs per week you should eat. For a person cutting down on cholesterol, the egg yolk is the one to avoid, and the white is OK; for a person who needs to cut down on sodium, the yolk is OK, while the white is fairly high. The yolk has about 9 mg of sodium and the white about 50.

When you can enjoy an egg, the traditional cooking styles are fine and by using a nonstick frying pan, you will avoid using fats. Chopped chives or minced onion perk up scrambled eggs or omelettes. Egg substitutes, such as Fleischmann's Egg Beaters, available in the frozen food section of grocery stores, are somewhat higher in sodium; the equivalent to one egg, 1/4 cup (60 mL) of Egg Beaters, has 90 mg of sodium. But egg substitutes contain no cholesterol. If you are cutting down on cholesterol, you may want to try egg substitutes to make scrambled "eggs," French toast, or pancakes. Unsalted scrambled egg substitute will need your most creative seasoning to make anything close to a delicious breakfast. Check the label for the sodium content of new brands.

BREAKFAST MEATS

All traditional breakfast meats are too high in sodium. If you need convincing, look at the sodium content: bacon—274 mg in 2 slices; ham—1,114 mg in 3 ounces (90 g); sausage—812 mg in 3 ounces (90 g).

When you serve an egg without the meat and the plate does look very empty, try breakfast potatoes as a substitution. Hash browns or cottage fries have made "diner" breakfasts very popular. Plan ahead. When you're boiling or baking potatoes for dinner, cook a few extras for the next day's breakfast and store them in the refrigerator. As you prepare breakfast, you can cook potatoes quickly. Just add cold diced potatoes to the skillet, sprinkle with paprika, then add the egg (or egg substitute).

SNACKS *and* APPETIZERS

◆◆◆◆◆

Snacking may be frowned on, but eating small amounts of food throughout the day is healthier than eating three very large meals a day. The problem is that "snack foods" are often very salty or less nutritious than they could be. So if the snack is a good one, there is no reason to give up snacking. Just remember to count the total number of calories and the total number of milligrams of sodium per day. Even foods you eat standing up count!

Sometimes you may want a snack that is convenient and no trouble to fix. When you've invited guests to your home who need to cut down on sodium, you may not mind going to a little more trouble. Guests will be grateful if you serve delicious low-sodium snacks and will probably ask you for the recipe.

Unsalted nuts (peanuts, almonds, walnuts, etc.) are widely available, and potato chip companies are chipping away at the unsalted snack-food business—somewhat bland but not bad tasting at all.

Raw fruits and vegetables are always excellent choices for snacking. Try cutting them into little cubes, and serve them on toothpicks (you may dip fruit into lemon juice to prevent darkening). Keep fruits in your home "snack" places. And homemade popcorn satisfies the urge to munch with very few calories, no fat, and no sodium. The type of corn popper that uses hot air (without oil) is a good gift for someone who loves to munch while losing weight. Season with the Unsalt Shaker (page 39).

CRUDITÉS

---◆◆---

Crudités is a French word meaning "raw." Served as hors d'oeuvres, crudités are very popular at fancy restaurants and parties. Serve crudités with a dipping sauce from this chapter, or any of the salad dressing recipes (pages 52–56). If salad dressing is made up in advance, preparing crudités will be quick. Cut up seasonal vegetables that your family likes. Nibbling raw vegetables satisfies the snacking urge with very few calories.

These popular raw vegetable choices are all low in calories and sodium: chunks of zucchini, cherry tomatoes, sections of broccoli, carrot sticks, cucumber slices, small mushrooms, scallions (green onions), and cubes of green pepper.

◆ Yogurt Dip for Crudités ◆

MAKES 3/4 CUP (3 SERVINGS)

1   8-ounce (240 g) container of yogurt
2   tablespoons (30 mL) Mild Mustard (page 45)

Combine with a wire whisk.

Calories: 87, Fat: 3 g (1 g saturated), Protein: 5 g, Cholesterol: 3 mg, Carbohydrates: 11 g, Sodium: 41 mg

◆ Fruits for Dipping ◆

Cut up pieces of fruit and toss them with a little lemon, pineapple, or grapefruit juice to keep the fruit from turning brown. Try fruits like apples, pears, plums, nectarines. Dip with Spicy Dressing and Honey Dressing (page 56).

◆ Onion Dip ◆

MAKES 1 1/2 CUPS (9 SERVINGS)

This onion dip does not taste like the popular dip made from sour cream and dry onion soup mix. We hope you won't be disappointed and will appreciate this one on its own merits (much lower sodium). It's best made ahead so that the flavors blend.

1 tablespoon (15 mL) olive oil
1 large onion, finely diced or grated
2 tablespoons (30 mL) cornstarch
1/2 cup (125 mL) skim milk
1/4 teaspoon (1 mL) onion powder
1/2 teaspoon (2 mL) liquid hickory smoke
1/2 teaspoon (2 mL) dry mustard
     dash Tabasco sauce (more if you like it hotter)
1 8-ounce (240 g) container of yogurt

Warm the oil in a skillet and cook onion over medium heat for approximately 10 minutes until lightly browned. Add the cornstarch and stir with a wire whisk for a couple of minutes. Add the milk and seasonings and stir with a wire whisk, simmering until the mixture is smooth and thick. Pour into a small bowl and cool slightly. Fold the yogurt into the onion mixture.

Calories: 47, Fat: 2 g (1 g saturated), Protein: 2 g, Cholesterol: 2 mg, Carbohydrates: 5 g, Sodium: 29 mg

OTHER IDEAS FOR DIPS

Many salad dressings can be used as dipping sauces. We recommend that you try: Good and Good for You Dressing (page 52); Creamy Italian Dressing (page 55); Light 'n Easy Cucumber Dressing (page 54); Russian Dressing (page 55). Recipes from the condiment section also make good dipping sauces: Hot Cocktail Sauce (page 47); Barbecue Sauce (page 46).

◆ Pinto Bean Dip ◆

MAKES 1 1/2 CUPS (18 SERVINGS)

This recipe is a natural for everyone on low-sodium, low-cholesterol diets. If you can't find a low-sodium, low-cholesterol cheese, simply omit the cheese. The recipe will still be flavorful. You can substitute other kinds of beans.

1 tablespoon (15 mL) olive oil
1 medium onion, diced
1 clove garlic, minced
     dash liquid hickory smoke

1 teaspoon (5 mL) no-salt chili powder
   dash Tabasco sauce
2 cups (500 mL) pinto beans, cooked without salt
2 ounces (60 g) no-salt-added cheese
2 tablespoons (30 mL) vinegar (cider is best)
1 tablespoon (15 mL) sugar

Heat the oil in a skillet over medium heat and sauté onion and garlic for a few minutes until soft. Add the hickory smoke, chili powder, and Tabasco sauce. Grate the cheese and stir into the beans with the vinegar and sugar. Whip all together in a food processor or blender until the dip is smooth. Add more Tabasco if you like a "hotter" flavor. Store, covered, in the refrigerator.

Calories: 101, Fat: 4 g (2 g saturated), Protein: 5 g, Cholesterol: 6 mg, Carbohydrates: 13 g, Sodium: 30 mg

◆ Red Bean Dip ◆

MAKES 3 CUPS (18 SERVINGS)

Taco shells with no added sodium, broken into small pieces, make ideal dippers. Cold crisp vegetables are even better—try cherry tomatoes, cucumber sticks, pieces of green pepper, and other crudités.

1/4 cup (60 mL) low-sodium ketchup
  2 tablespoons (30 mL) cider vinegar
     dash Tabasco sauce (more if you like it hotter)
1/4 teaspoon (1 mL) liquid hickory smoke
  1 teaspoon (5 mL) garlic powder
  3 cups (750 mL) kidney beans, cooked without salt

Measure all ingredients into a blender or food processor and blend until smooth. Scrape into small jars or bowls and chill. At serving time, garnish with parsley, cucumber slices, scallions, cherry tomatoes, or whatever vegetables are in season.

Calories: 42, Fat: 0.2 g (0 g saturated), Protein: 3 g, Cholesterol: 0 mg, Carbohydrates: 72 g, Sodium: 2 mg

◆ Guacamole Dip ◆

Never bought an avocado? Try this dip as your first avocado dish. Serve fresh, since avocado does not keep well. An avocado is ripe when the flesh yields to gentle pressure.

- 1 *large avocado, soft and ripe*
- 1 *tablespoon (15 mL) onion, minced*
- 1 *large ripe tomato*
- 1 *tablespoon (15 mL) lemon juice*
- 1/4 *teaspoon (1 mL) ground black pepper*
  dash Tabasco sauce (optional)

Cut the avocado in half, lengthwise. Discard the large pit and scoop the avocado into a bowl (save the skins to refill, if you like). Peel and dice the tomato and add to the avocado with the seasonings; mash, using a fork, potato masher, or the plastic blade of a food processor. Serve immediately or chill before serving.

Calories: 48, Fat: 4 g (1 g saturated), Protein: 1 g, Cholesterol: 0 mg, Carbohydrates: 3 g, Sodium: 5 mg

◆ Cheese Spread ◆

A soft and appetizing cheese for spreading on vegetables, low-sodium crackers, or bread. Double this recipe and roll the cheese into a log or ball. Roll in chopped walnuts or pecans for a festive occasion.

- 2 *tablespoons (30 mL) unsalted margarine*
- 3 *tablespoons (45 mL) cornstarch*
- 1/2 *cup (125 mL) skim milk*
- 1/4 *teaspoon (1 mL) garlic powder*
- 1/4 *pound (120 g) unsalted cheese, grated*
- 1½ *teaspoons (7 mL) dry mustard (less if you want a milder flavor)*
- 1 *teaspoon (5 mL) paprika*

Melt the margarine in a saucepan. Stir in the cornstarch. Gradually add the milk and cook until smooth. Add the garlic powder, stir, and cook for 2 minutes. Remove from heat. When the margarine mixture is cool, add cheese, mustard, and paprika. Stir and cook briefly over low heat until mixture is smooth. Store in the refrigerator.

Calories: 137, Fat: 10 g (5 g saturated), Protein: 6 g,
Cholesterol: 19 mg, Carbohydrates: 6 g, Sodium: 15 mg

◆ Curried Tuna Canapés ◆

MAKES 50 CANAPÉS

Curry provides an interesting flavor. Leftover cooked chicken can be used in place of the tuna.

7 ounces (198 g) low-sodium tuna
1/3 cup (80 mL) low-sodium mayonnaise
1/4 teaspoon (1 mL) onion powder
1/2 teaspoon (2 mL) curry powder
Five-Minute Chutney (page 51, optional)
50 small matzo crackers (or unsalted Melba toast)

Drain the tuna, discard liquid, and mash tuna in a bowl. Add the mayonnaise, onion powder, and curry powder. Stir until well mixed and tuna is flaky. Spoon curried tuna on each cracker. Spread a layer of Five-Minute Chutney on the crackers, if using. Broil for a minute or two before serving.

Calories per canapé: 47, Fat: 2 g (0 g saturated), Protein: 2 g,
Cholesterol: 8 mg, Carbohydrates: 6 g, Sodium: 4 mg

◆ Baked Cheese Snacks ◆

MAKES 50 CHEESE SNACKS

4 tablespoons (60 mL) unsalted margarine
1 cup unsalted (250 mL) cheese, such as Swiss
1/2 cup (125 mL) sifted flour
dash cayenne pepper
1/2 teaspoon (2 mL) dry mustard
poppy or sesame seeds

In a mixer or food processor, cream the margarine until light and fluffy. Finely grate the cheese and add it with flour, cayenne pepper, and mustard to the margarine. Beat well. Using your fingers, shape the mixture into a roll 1 inch (2.5 cm) in diameter. Wrap the roll in plastic wrap or wax paper. Refrigerate until firm. (You can do this ahead of time and cook later.) Slice the roll into 1/4-inch (.5 cm) "buttons." Arrange on a cookie sheet, allowing room for them to spread out. Sprinkle the tops with sesame seeds or poppy seeds. Bake in 350°F (175°C) oven for 10 minutes. Serve hot or cold. Store in a tightly covered container.

Calories per cheese snack: 21, Fat: 2 g (1 g saturated), Protein: 1 g, Cholesterol: 2 mg, Carbohydrates: 1 g, Sodium: 6 mg

◆ Shredded Wheat Snacks ◆

MAKES 3 CUPS

A fantastic idea for low-sodium snacking—easy to mix and eat. It's faster to make than popcorn.

1/3   cup (80 mL) unsalted margarine
1/2   teaspoon (2 mL) curry powder
1/2   teaspoon (2 mL) onion powder
1/8   teaspoon (1/2 mL) ginger
3   cups (750 mL) Spoon Size Shredded Wheat

Melt margarine in a large frying pan and stir in the curry powder, onion powder, and ginger. Toss the shredded wheat in the seasoned margarine and stir while heating for 5 more minutes.

Calories per 1/2 cup: 174, Fat: 10 g (2 g saturated), Protein: 3 g, Cholesterol: 0 mg, Carbohydrates: 21 g, Sodium: 2 mg

◆ Marinated Mushrooms ◆

MAKES ABOUT 100 MUSHROOMS

These are worth the effort and keep well in the refrigerator. By comparison, a pound of canned mushrooms contains about 2,000 mg of sodium.

1   pound (450 g) fresh small mushrooms
1/4   cup (60 mL) dry vermouth
1/2   cup (125 mL) water
2   tablespoons (30 mL) olive oil
1   tablespoon (15 mL) vinegar
2   tablespoons (30 mL) fresh parsley, finely chopped
3   cloves garlic, minced

Wash the mushrooms, trim the stems, and drop them into a saucepan. Add the vermouth and water and simmer for 5 minutes. Ladle the mushrooms and the liquid into a bowl. Stir in the oil, vinegar, parsley, and garlic and refrigerate.

Calories per mushroom: 4, Fat: 0 g (0 g saturated), Protein: 0 g, Cholesterol: 0 mg, Carbohydrates: 0 g, Sodium: 0 mg

◆ Mushroom Roll-Ups ◆

MAKES 14 ROLL-UPS

Great to make ahead of time and heat up before serving.

  3 *tablespoons (45 mL) unsalted margarine, at room temperature*
1/2 *pound (225 g) mushrooms, chopped*
  2 *tablespoons (30 mL) onion, finely chopped*
14 *slices low-sodium bread*

Melt 1 tablespoon (15 mL) of the margarine in a frying pan. Add the mushrooms and onion and cook gently for about 5 minutes; cool. Trim the crusts from the bread and flatten each slice with a rolling pin. Spread remaining margarine on the bread. Divide the filling on the bread. Roll up each slice like a jelly roll and place on a cookie sheet, seam side down. Without cutting all the way through, with a sharp knife make 4 small slashes across each roll. (Wrap and freeze until needed, if you like.) Just before serving, bake in a 350° F (175° C) oven until brown, about 10 minutes.

Calories per roll up: 93, Fat: 3 g (1 g saturated), Protein: 3 g, Cholesterol: 0.3 mg, Carbohydrates: 13 g, Sodium: 8 mg

◆ Sautéed Chicken Tidbits ◆

We suggest serving these party tidbits with little bowls of your favorite condiments.*

1/3   *cup (80 mL) flour*
       dash white or black pepper
11/4   *pound (600 g) boneless chicken breast cutlets*
  1   *tablespoon (15 mL) unsalted margarine*
  1   *tablespoon (15 mL) olive oil*

Mix the flour and pepper together in a bowl. Cut the cutlets into bite-size pieces. Coat the chicken by shaking the chicken and flour in a closed paper bag. Heat margarine with the oil in a large frying pan. Add the pieces of chicken and cook over medium high heat until they are just cooked through and golden brown. Turn the pieces while cooking so that they brown evenly. Cutlets cook fairly quickly, so be careful not to overcook. Serve with toothpicks to dunk the chicken.

* *Try Sweet-and-Sour Pineapple Sauce (page 48); Five-Minute Chutney (page 51); Barbecue Sauce (page 46); or Mustard (mild or hot) thinned with a little water and vinegar (pages 44–45). For memories of fast-food chicken pieces (Chicken Nuggets), try honey, too.*

Calories: 125, Fat: 4 g (1 g saturated), Protein: 17 g, Cholesterol: 41mg, Carbohydrates: 4 g, Sodium: 46mg

◆ Baked Potato Skins ◆

These are the latest in fancy restaurant hors d'oeuvres. Sodium content and calories are quite low.

  4   *baking potatoes, baked in their skins*
  2   *tablespoons (30 mL) unsalted margarine*
1/2   *teaspoon (2 mL) onion powder*
1/2   *teaspoon (2 mL) garlic powder*
1/2   *teaspoon (2 mL) paprika*

Cut baked potatoes in half lengthwise and scoop out the insides, leaving a layer of potato near the skin. (You might like to make Home Fries, (page 70), with the part you scoop out.) Melt margarine in a saucepan and mix in the onion powder, garlic powder, and paprika. Arrange the potato skins, open side up, on a cookie sheet. Brush potatoes with the flavored mixture. Bake in a 400°F (205°C) oven, 15–20 minutes or until lightly browned. You can add a filling or cheese and return the potatoes to the oven for a few minutes.* Or, put out dishes of sauces and let your friends choose their own toppings.

* *There are many good fillings: Sweet Relish (page 50); Hot Cocktail Sauce (page 47); Ketchup (page 42); Mustard (pages 44–45); Barbecue Sauce (page 46); Sweet-and-Sour Pineapple Sauce (page 48).*

Calories: 63, Fat: 3 g (1 g saturated), Protein: 1 g, Cholesterol: 0 mg, Carbohydrates: 9 g, Sodium: 3 mg

◆ Party Pizzas ◆

MAKES 16 2¹/₂-INCH PIZZAS

Terrific for low-sodium snacks!

Make Pizza Dough (page 144) and Tomato Sauce (page 61). Prepare cookie sheets by dusting with a fine layer of cornmeal. After the dough has been mixed, break off small amounts of dough, each about the size of a walnut. With your hands, shape each piece of dough into a ball and then flatten it into a circle about 2¹/₂ inches (6 cm) across. Place circles on a cookie sheet. Spoon on a little pizza sauce and top with grated low-sodium cheese (unsalted Swiss cheese is good). If you want extras on your pizzas, try thin slices of sautéed mushrooms, green pepper, or onion. Or try ground beef cooked with fennel (page 146)—a topping that tastes like sausage. Bake in 450° F (230° C) oven for about 10 minutes.

◆ Egg Roll Hors d'Oeuvres ◆

MAKES 96 HORS D'OEUVRES

For cute and delicious party appetizers, adapt Egg Rolls (page 206). Just cut each egg roll wrapper into quarters. Place one teaspoon (5 mL) of filling in each wrapper; roll and fry as in the basic recipe. You need 24 egg roll wrappers to make 96. Make them in advance and keep in a warm oven or on a special warming tray.

◆ Vegetable Tempura or Onion Rings ◆

A special snack for special get-togethers, such as watching the big game. Use available vegetables: zucchini, cauliflower florets, broccoli florets, sliced broccoli stems, and green beans. Onion rings are always the favorites.

    2 large onions, sliced or grated
    4 cups (1 L) fresh vegetables in bite-size pieces
    4 tablespoons (60 mL) flour
    1 tablespoon (15 mL) cornstarch
  1/2 teaspoon (2 mL) low-sodium baking powder
  1/4 cup (60 mL) water
    1 tablespoon (15 mL) egg substitute
       oil for frying

Combine 3 tablespoons flour, cornstarch, baking powder, water, and egg substitute in a bowl. Beat with a wire whisk until the batter is smooth and foamy. Steam vegetables for approximately 5 minutes or less time if you like the vegetables crispy. Put the remaining tablespoon of flour into a paper bag and add the onions or vegetable pieces. Shake well to coat lightly. Drop the onions or vegetables into the batter. Turn each piece over and over in the batter to coat well.

Pour the oil into a frying pan and heat to 375°F (190°C). (An electric frying pan is best.) Slip each vegetable segment into oil. Using a long-handled spoon to turn, cook for approximately 5 minutes until golden brown. Drain on paper towels. Serve at once

Calories: 92, Fat: 7 g (1 g saturated), Protein: 1 g, Cholesterol: 0 mg, Carbohydrates: 6 g, Sodium: 5 mg

◆ Party Spareribs ◆

A finger-licking snack for special get-togethers!

   3 *pounds (1.4 kg) spareribs*
   1 *tablespoon (15 mL) unsalted margarine*
 1/4 *cup (60 mL) low-sodium ketchup*
 1/2 *cup (125 mL) cider vinegar*
   3 *tablespoons (45 mL) molasses*
   2 *tablespoons (30 mL) sugar*
 1/4 *teaspoon (1 mL) paprika*
      dash Tabasco sauce
   1 *small jar baby food peaches*
 1/2 *teaspoon (2 mL) dry mustard*
 1/2 *teaspoon (2 mL) ginger*
 1/4 *teaspoon (1 mL) liquid hickory smoke (optional)*

Cut the spareribs between the bones. To remove excess fat, parboil for about 5 minutes. Drain ribs in a colander. Refill the pot with cold water, plunge ribs in cold water to firm; drain. While the ribs are cooking, make the sauce by mixing remaining ingredients in a saucepan. Cook gently for 15 minutes. (If it's more convenient to finish the recipe later, put the ribs in a bowl, cover with the sauce, and refrigerate.) When ready to cook, arrange the ribs on the rack of a broiler pan. Brush with sauce. Bake in a 450° F (230° C) oven for 15 minutes. Turn on oven broiler. Brush ribs with more sauce and broil for a minute or two. Turn, brush with sauce, and broil on other side. Serve with plenty of napkins!

**Calories: 558, Fat 42 g (16 g saturated), Protein: 29 g,
Cholesterol: 133 mg, Carbohydrates: 15 g, Sodium: 135 mg**

SANDWICHES

◆◆◆◆◆

Recipes and advice about sandwiches and other foods that you can take with you are found in this chapter. You can also keep these sandwich ideas in mind for meals at home. When busy or tired, many people prefer a light soup and sandwich meal.

Popular high-sodium sandwich fillings—cold cuts, hot dogs, turkey roll or breast, chicken loaf—are taboo for low-sodium eating. The only "deli" meat low in sodium is plain roast beef.

Companies that make cold cuts, in some instances, have started making unsalted cold cuts—turkey breast, etc. You may have to write to the manufacturer to find out how much sodium cold cuts actually contain.

There are quite a few other low-sodium sandwich fillings. No one needs a recipe for peanut butter and jelly. Fortunately, all jams and jellies are naturally low in sodium. Unsalted peanut butter is available in nearly all large grocery stores; health food stores sell it also. Try peanut butter on apple, pear, or banana slices, for a change.

Other low-sodium sandwich ideas include low-sodium tuna salad, egg salad (if your cholesterol allowance includes eggs), low-sodium cheese with mustard or horseradish, and thin slices of leftover chicken, turkey or beef, with cranberry sauce for extra flavor.

Try restaurant favorites at home—Meatball Sandwiches (page 90) or Tacos (page 200) are easy and delicious.

ADDING HOT ITEMS TO
A COLD LUNCH

—◆◆—

A widemouthed Thermos insulated container is terrific for packing hot soup or a serving of a casserole for lunch to carry out from home. To make sure that the food is still hot several hours after it's packed, pour boiling water into the Thermos, put on the cover, and let it sit. At the same time, put the soup or other food into a saucepan and heat until it's very hot. Then dump out the boiling water and add the hot food and cover the Thermos. This method works well for all of the hot soups (pages 96 to 104). You might find it most convenient to make up batches of soup and freeze the extra soup in the amount that will be used in the Thermos.

Some casseroles pack very well and make good lunches. As with soups, let the Thermos sit covered with boiling water in it while you heat the food. These foods pack well: Curry (page 196); Macaroni and Beef Casserole (page 142); Old-Fashioned Beef Stew (page 174); Beef Goulash (page 173).

For more classic recipes, designed for low-sodium diets, try the following sandwiches.

◆ Steak Sandwich ◆

MAKES 4 SERVINGS

1   tablespoon (15 mL) safflower oil (optional)
1   medium onion, thinly sliced (optional)*
1   pound (450 g) no-salt-added meat for steak sandwiches
    (usually available in freezer cases—check label)
4   Soft Rolls (page 220) shaped long
2   ounces (60 g) low-sodium cheese (optional)*

Heat oil in a skillet or griddle over medium high heat and sauté onions, if using. Add the meat and heat briefly on each side. For a "Philadelphia" cheese steak, spread a thin slice of cheese on the partially cooked meat and let it melt. Fold the steak over to cover the cheese.

* You may like to skip the onion or cheese and add some Tomato Sauce (page 61).

Calories (without options): 490, Fat: 20 g (6 g saturated), Protein: 44 g, Cholesterol: 123 mg, Carbohydrates: 31 g, Sodium: 59 mg

Submarine, Hero, Hoagie,
◆ Grinder, Po'boy... ◆

Make long rolls and pack a submarine sandwich (also called a grinder, a hoagie, a po'boy, etc.).* The secret to the special taste: Prepare the sliced onion ahead of time so that the seasonings are absorbed.

1 *tablespoon (15 mL) olive oil*
2 *tablespoons (30 mL) cider vinegar*
1 *teaspoon (5 mL) oregano*
1 *small onion, sliced thinly*
1 *Soft Roll (page 220)*
2 *ounces (60 g) unsalted cheese, such as Swiss*
  tomato, thinly sliced
  lettuce, finely shredded

Whisk the olive oil, vinegar, and oregano in a bowl. Add the onion slices, mix, and cover the bowl. Marinate for at least 3 hours. Slice and open the roll. (Some people like to pull the roll open and remove part of the inside to make room for the filling.) Add the cheese, tomato slices, and lettuce; drain the onion and add to the filling. Drizzle with the flavored marinade. To pack for lunch, wrap with plastic wrap. If you prefer your sandwich hot, wrap it in aluminum foil and heat in a 325°F (165°C) oven for approximately 10 minutes, or wrap it with plastic wrap and heat briefly in a microwave oven.

* *If you like hot peppers, buy fresh ones, cut them in half, and discard the seeds before adding to the sandwich. Hot peppers that come in jars are more convenient but have added salt. Also, try fillings of low-sodium tuna or hot Italian Meatballs (page 179).*

Calories: 556, Fat: 33 g (12 g saturated), Protein: 23 g, Cholesterol: 63 mg, Carbohydrates: 45 g, Sodium: 157 mg

HOT OPEN-FACED SANDWICHES

◆◆

Hot open-faced sandwiches are popular for quick meals. For instance, you can mix low-sodium tuna with low-sodium mayonnaise. Spread on a piece of bread and broil a few inches from the heat for approximately 5 minutes.

COLD PITA SANDWICHES

◆◆

You can vary your pita sandwiches. Use Pita Pocket Bread (page 225) and fill the pocket with the tasty combinations that follow.

Stuff a little lettuce into the bottom of the pocket. Add Chicken Salad, (page 93), tuna salad (made with low-sodium tuna), no-salt cheese, thinly sliced roast beef, or leftover ground beef. Top with a slice of fresh tomato, chopped onion, bean or alfalfa sprouts, slivered celery, carrots, or other vegetables, if you like. Just wrap the sandwich and you're ready to go.

◆ Zesty Cheese Filling ◆

MAKES 1 SERVING

Use this filling in a pita or roll. For zestier fillings, try Meat Filling for Tacos or Burritos (page 201) or Chicken Filling for Tacos (page 202).

> 2 ounces (60 g) low-sodium cheese
> 2 tablespoons (30 mL) olive oil
> 1 tablespoon (15 mL) cider vinegar
> 1/4 teaspoon (1 mL) oregano
> ground black pepper
> 1/4 teaspoon (1 mL) garlic powder (optional)
> 1 Pita Pocket Bread (page 225) or 1 Soft Roll (page 220)

Cube the cheese. Combine all the other ingredients in a small bowl. Add the cheese cubes; marinate 30 minutes. Slice pita or roll and fill with marinated cheese.

Calories: 643, Fat: 49 g (16 g saturated), Protein: 19 g, Cholesterol: 67 mg, Carbohydrates: 33 g, Sodium: 18 mg

Hot Pita Sandwiches

Hot pita sandwiches make a delicious change for lunch at home or a quick dinner. Stuff your pocket sandwich with either of the fillings that follow.

Steak Filling

  1 *tablespoon (15 mL) safflower oil*
1/2 *medium green pepper, cut into small chunks*
1/4 *cup (60 mL) mushrooms, sliced*
  1 *medium onion, cut into small chunks*
  2 *ounces (60 g) frozen sandwich steaks, 100 percent beef, no salt added*
  1 *medium pita bread, sliced in half*

Heat the oil in a skillet. Add the green pepper, mushrooms, and onion; stir and cook gently until the vegetables are soft and the onion is golden. Add the sandwich steaks; cook on one side about 45 seconds, then turn and cook on the other side until brown. Scoop the steaks and vegetables into the pita bread. Serve hot.

**Calories: 454, Fat: 21 g (3 g saturated), Protein: 26 g,
Cholesterol: 51 mg, Carbohydrates: 40 g, Sodium: 32 mg**

Vegetarian Filling

  1 *tablespoon (15 mL) safflower oil*
1/2 *medium onion, cut into small chunks*
1/2 *medium green pepper, cut into small chunks*
1/4 *cup (60 mL) mushrooms, sliced*
  1 *ounce (30 g) no-salt cheese, thinly sliced*
  1 *Pita Pocket Bread (page 225)*

Heat the oil in a skillet and add the vegetables. Stir-fry until the vegetables are soft. Lay the cheese slices on top of the vegetables. Cook for one minute until the cheese begins to melt. Slice the pita and scoop the melting cheese and vegetables into the bread. Serve hot.

**Calories: 396, Fat: 24 g (7 g saturated), Protein: 12 g,
Cholesterol: 28 mg, Carbohydrates: 35 g, Sodium: 11 mg**

◆ Grilled Cheese Sandwich ◆

MAKES 1 SANDWICH

This popular sandwich will be delicious if you are able to find a source of good low-sodium cheese. If your favorite low-sodium cheese does not yet come presliced, slice it at home.

   2   slices low-sodium bread
   1   ounce (30 g) no-salt cheese such as Swiss
   1   teaspoon (5 mL) unsalted margarine
       thin slices of onion, tomato, and tuna (optional)

Preheat a griddle or frying pan over medium heat. Slice the cheese very thin and place it with onion, tomato, and any extras you want on the bread. Close it up like a sandwich. Spread the margarine on both sides of the bread. Grill on both sides until bread is toasted and cheese melts.

**Calories: 280, Fat: 15 g (7 g saturated), Protein: 11 g,
Cholesterol: 29 mg, Carbohydrates: 26 g, Sodium: 20 mg**

◆ Rachel Sandwich ◆

MAKES 1 SANDWICH

If you are on a low-sodium diet you can't eat a Reuben—grilled corned beef, Swiss cheese, and sauerkraut on rye—with 2,317 mg of sodium! Have you ever heard of a Rachel? Rachels are almost as popular as Reubens in some delicatessens. Serve with hot or mild mustard (pages 44–45).

   2   ounces (60 g) lean trimmed roast beef, thinly sliced
   1   ounce (30 g) no-salt cheese
   2   tablespoons (30 mL) Russian Dressing (page 55)
   2   slices low-sodium bread, preferably Rye (page 224)
   1   teaspoon (5 mL) unsalted margarine, softened

Preheat your skillet or griddle over medium high heat. Meanwhile, spread the meat, cheese, and dressing on one slice of bread. Cover with the other piece of bread. Spread a thin layer of margarine on the outside of both slices of bread. Cook until nicely browned on both sides.

**Calories: 491, Fat: 32 g (10 g saturated), Protein: 23 g,
Cholesterol: 78 mg, Carbohydrates: 28 g, Sodium: 71 mg**

Variations on a Rachel Sandwich

For other tasty ideas, try: thinly sliced, leftover roast chicken or turkey for the beef; substitute homemade Coleslaw (page 111) for the Russian Dressing; add thinly sliced onion or tomato.

You can make any of these variations as cold sandwiches. Use a small amount of salad dressing on the inside of the sandwich instead of margarine.

◆ Cheese Dreams ◆

MAKES 4 SANDWICHES

1   tablespoon (15 mL) safflower oil
1/8 teaspoon (.5 mL) liquid hickory smoke
1   large tomato
6   ounces (180 g) low-sodium cheese
4   slices low-sodium bread

Combine the oil and hickory smoke in a small shallow bowl. Slice the tomato into thin slices and dip into the flavored oil. Slice the cheese thinly and cover the bread. Spread tomato slices on top. Place on a broiler pan and broil a few inches from the heat for approximately 5 minutes.

Calories per sandwich: 273, Fat: 18 g (9 g saturated), Protein: 13 g, Cholesterol: 43 mg, Carbohydrates: 15 g, Sodium: 19 mg

◆ Meatball Sandwich ◆

MAKES 1 SANDWICH

Cook extra meatballs when you're making them for dinner. Use the leftovers for sandwiches. Freeze in small packs with the sauce so that you have enough for one sandwich.

1/4 pound (120 g) Italian Meatballs (page 179)
1/3 cup (90 mL) Tomato Sauce (page 61)
1   Soft Roll (page 220)

If the meatballs are large, slice them in half. Heat the meatballs and sauce in a saucepan. If eating at home, arrange meatballs in the roll and serve. If packing a lunch, be sure that the meatballs and sauce are very hot. Wrap the roll and pack it separately.

Calories: 660, Fat: 25 g (9 g saturated), Protein: 33 g, Cholesterol: 153 mg, Carbohydrates: 74 g, Sodium: 162 mg

HAMBURGERS

Hamburgers can be grilled, broiled, fried, or charcoal-broiled. You probably have ideas about what tastes good on a hamburger. If you add a thin slice of low-sodium cheese, you'll have a low-sodium cheeseburger.

Popular hamburger toppings include: Ketchup (page 42), Barbecue Sauce or Chili Sauce (pages 46 and 47); a slice of tomato; lettuce; thin onion slices; sliced or diced onion, sautéed in a small amount of unsalted margarine; sautéed green pepper slices; sautéed mushroom slices; and Russian Dressing (page 55).

◆ Fast-Food-Style Hamburgers ◆

MAKES 4 WHOPPERS-OR BIG MAC-STYLE HAMBURGERS

Arguments over which is better—McDonald's "Big Mac" or Burger King's "Whopper"—may continue to rage among people who admit to being fast-food fanatics. Someone in your family may be fond of fast-food style hamburgers—they have sold billions, after all. If so, you can make low-sodium versions at home, which are pretty good substitutes for the Big Mac (which has 1,060 sodium mg) or the Whopper (which has 990 mg sodium).

1   *pound (450 g) very lean ground beef*
2   *ounces (60 g) low-sodium cheese, sliced very thin*
    (optional)
4   *Soft Rolls (page 220)*

Divide the meat into 4 or 8* patties. Broil or grill over medium-high heat until done as desired (rare, medium, or well-done). After you turn the patties over to the second side, add a very small piece of low-sodium cheese, if desired.

To assemble a "Big Mac" hamburger, cut each roll across two times to make three pieces. Put one patty on each of the two bottom pieces. Top with desired garnishes.

To assemble a "Whopper" hamburger, cut across each roll in half; fill with hamburger and garnishes.

* *You may want to make one large patty out of the 1/4 pound of meat per person. Or if you want to make Big Mac–style hamburgers, divide each 1/4 pound in half and cook two very thin patties per person.*

Calories: 500, Fat: 28 g (11 g saturated), Protein: 30 g,
Cholesterol: 114 mg, Carbohydrates: 31 g, Sodium: 86 mg

◆ Garnishes, Whopper Style ◆

1/4 cup (60 mL) shredded lettuce
1 medium onion, thinly sliced
1 tomato, thinly sliced
4 tablespoons (60 mL) low-sodium mayonnaise
1 low-sodium pickle, thinly sliced

Low-sodium pickles are available at some health food stores. If you can't find them, just omit this ingredient. Do not substitute a regular pickle.

Calories : 118, Fat: 11 g (2 g saturated), Protein: 1 g, Cholesterol: 8 mg, Carbohydrates: 5 g, Sodium: 8 mg

◆ Garnishes, Big Mac Style ◆

MAKES GARNISHES FOR 4 HAMBURGERS

1/4 cup (60 mL) shredded lettuce
4 tablespoons (60 mL) Hamburger Sauce (page 47)
1 small onion, diced
1 low-sodium pickle, thinly sliced

Calories : 85, Fat: 7 g (1 g saturated), Protein: 1 g, Cholesterol: 7 mg, Carbohydrates: 5 g, Sodium: 6 mg

◆ Chili Burger ◆

MAKES 1 CHILI BURGER

1/4 pound (120 g) very lean ground beef
1/4 cup (60 mL) Chili con Carne (page 203)
1 Soft Roll (page 220)

Form the beef into a patty and pan-fry in a skillet, or broil on a broiler pan. While the hamburger is cooking, heat the Chili con Carne in a saucepan. Set the burger on half of the roll and add the chili. Serve hot.

Calories: 531, Fat: 27 g (10 g saturated), Protein: 32 g, Cholesterol: 103 mg, Carbohydrates: 38 g, Sodium: 103 mg

◆ Club Sandwich ◆

 3 *slices low-sodium bread*
1/8 *teaspoon (.5 mL) liquid hickory smoke*
 1 *tablespoon (15 mL) low-sodium mayonnaise*
1 1/2 *ounces (45 g) cooked chicken or turkey, thinly sliced*
 1 *small tomato, sliced*
 1 *leaf of lettuce*

Toast the bread. Mix liquid smoke and mayonnaise in a small bowl and spread thinly on one side of 3 pieces of toast. Place the chicken on the mayonnaise side of one piece of toast. Cover with a second piece of toast. Put the tomato slices and lettuce on the second piece of toast. Cover with the last piece of toast. Cut sandwich on the diagonal and then across again to make 4 triangles. Spear with a toothpick, if desired, to hold it together.

**Calories: 390, Fat: 15 g (3 g saturated), Protein: 20 g,
Cholesterol: 42 mg, Carbohydrates: 43 g, Sodium: 63 mg**

◆ Chicken Salad ◆

If chicken salad with unsalted mayonnaise seems bland, spice it with a low-sodium salad dressing such as Creamy Italian, Light 'n Easy Cucumber, or Good and Good for You (pages 52–55). Add celery seeds, paprika, or curry powder to the mayonnaise before mixing it with chicken.

12 *ounces (360 g) cooked, diced chicken*
 3 *tablespoons (45 mL) low-sodium mayonnaise*
    celery, chopped
    onion, chopped (optional)

Mix chicken in a bowl with mayonnaise until the chicken is coated. Add chopped onion and a small amount of chopped celery, if desired. Stir to combine.

**Calories: 168, Fat: 9 g (2 g saturated), Protein: 20 g,
Cholesterol: 55 mg, Carbohydrates: 0 g, Sodium: 58 mg.**

◆ Sloppy Joes ◆

A favorite food with young people. This low-sodium version is tasty enough to please even people who are not used to low-sodium food. It can also be frozen in small portions, for later defrosting, to make a quick meal or sandwich. If you made Sloppy Joes with a commercial seasoning mix, there would be more than 3,500 mg of sodium per commercial sandwich.

1	*pound (450 g) very lean ground beef*
6	*ounces (170 g) no-salt-added tomato paste*
1¹/4	*cup (300 mL) water*
2	*teaspoons (10 mL) cornstarch*
1/2	*teaspoon (2 mL) onion powder*
1/4	*teaspoon (1 mL) garlic powder*
1/2	*teaspoon (2 mL) celery seed*
1/2	*teaspoon (2 mL) Salt-Free Chili Powder (page 41)*
1/2	*teaspoon (2 mL) dry mustard*
1¹/2	*tablespoons (22 mL) sugar*
	dash Tabasco sauce (more if you like it hot)
1/4	*cup (60 mL) wine vinegar*
1	*small onion, finely chopped*
1/2	*green pepper, finely chopped*

Brown the ground beef in a frying pan, mashing the meat with a fork as it cooks. Combine remaining ingredients in a saucepan. Stir and cook over low heat. Skim off any fat and add the browned meat to the sauce; stir. Serve on toasted low-sodium bread (7 mg sodium each); or if you have some homemade rolls in the freezer, this is a logical choice.

Calories (without roll): 345, Fat: 20 g (8 g saturated), Protein: 23 g, Cholesterol: 78 mg, Carbohydrates: 19 g, Sodium: 118 mg

SOUPS

❖◆❖◆❖

People who eat soup take in fewer calories than those who do not eat soup. It may be that people feel more satisfied. Soup takes longer to eat. Soup is also a good choice for someone who is having problems chewing or who is not feeling up to eating a full meal. Whether you're feeling sick or well, soup is always comforting.

Regular canned soups are very convenient, but with a sodium content of 1,810 to 2,475 mg per can, forget them! Canned low-sodium soups are just as convenient and available, although more expensive per serving. To be honest with you, none of the people who taste-tested foods for us found the commercial low-sodium soups delicious or even acceptable. Both of the canned low-sodium chicken soups tested by *Consumer Reports* were rated "poor in sensory quality."

Homemade low-sodium soups, if well-seasoned, are better than commercial ones. Some people who do not have the time or inclination to make soup may want to try flavoring the canned soups.

Plan ahead and keep chicken stock in the freezer. For 15 minutes of work you will create delicious soup to satisfy you for hours. If you are not home during the day, make soup on a weekend or in the evening. And if you have a microwave oven, you can defrost and heat homemade soup as quickly and easily as you would heat a can of soup. In other words, low-sodium cooking can be convenient.

We have a tip for you if your family has been used to canned soup: Cut the vegetables into very small pieces so that the soup will have more of a familiar look. Especially, be careful about which vegetables you add to soup, since the sodium does go into the liquid. That's why carrots and celery are called for in small amounts.

Do you like croutons in your soup? Unfortunately, commercial croutons are extremely high in sodium, and homemade croutons made with low-sodium bread and unsalted margarine bear little resemblance to the store-bought ones. You might be surprised at what a nice crunchiness plain popcorn adds when sprinkled on top of soup. Try it with Split Pea Soup (page 101) and Senate Bean Soup (page 102).

◆ Chicken Stock ◆

Soups and other recipes often call for homemade chicken stock. Homemade unsalted chicken stock is very helpful for low-sodium cooking because the other choices (milk or regular bouillon) are high in sodium. There are low-sodium, dry packaged instant broths available. We tried them and, frankly, did not like the potassium chloride aftertaste. Try this recipe and you may never need to try commercial ones again.

- 1 **tablespoon (15 mL) olive oil**
- 1 **package soup vegetables***
- 1/4 **cup (60 mL) parsley**
- 2 **pounds (900 g) chicken breasts, bone in, skin removed**
- 1 **bay leaf**
- 2 **quarts (2 L) water (If it takes more water than this to cover the ingredients, your cooking pot is too wide.)**
- 1/3 **cup (80 mL) vermouth**
  - **dash cayenne pepper**
  - **dash black or white pepper**

Heat the oil in a soup pot and pan-fry the peeled and diced vegetables over medium heat; a good way to do this is to get one vegetable ready at a time and add to the warm oil. Keep cooking and preparing until all the vegetables have been added. Add remaining ingredients. Turn the heat to high and bring to a boil, turn down heat and simmer for about 2 1/2 hours. Strain over a bowl. Use the chicken for Curry (page 196), Chicken Salad (page 93), etc., and freeze the stock in one-meal quantities.

* *If your store does not sell soup vegetables, you can just buy separate vegetables (a package of soup vegetables usually contains two carrots, two stalks of celery, a medium onion, a yellow turnip, and a parsnip). Don't overlook vegetables such as turnips or parsnips; they add a lot of flavor to the liquid.*

Calories per cup: 38, Fat: 1 g (0 g saturated), Protein: 5 g, Cholesterol: 0 mg, Carbohydrates: 1 g, Sodium: 43 mg

Mushroom Barley Soup

This hearty soup freezes well.

1 *tablespoon (15 mL) unsalted margarine*
1 *tablespoon (15 mL) safflower oil*
1 *small onion, chopped fine*
4 *cups (1 L) Chicken Stock (opposite)*
1/2 *pound (225 g) fresh mushrooms, diced*
1/4 *teaspoon (1 mL) onion powder*
1 *bay leaf*
2 *tablespoons (30 mL) chopped parsley*
1/4 *teaspoon (1 mL) white pepper*
3 *tablespoons (45 mL) barley*
2 *tablespoons (30 mL) cornstarch*
1 *cup (250 mL) skim milk*
1/4 *cup (60 mL) sherry (not cooking sherry)*

Melt margarine in a soup pot; add the oil and onion and sauté for about 5 minutes. Add the chicken stock, mushrooms, onion powder, bay leaf, parsley, white pepper, and barley; cook over low heat for 45 minutes, stirring occasionally. In a small bowl, mix the cornstarch and the milk, stirring with a wire whisk until smooth. Add to the soup pot. Reduce heat and cook gently for 2 to 3 minutes until thickened, stirring constantly; remove bay leaf. Before serving, stir in the sherry.

Calories per cup: 161, Fat: 7 g (1 g saturated), Protein: 8 g, Cholesterol: 1 mg, Carbohydrates: 16 g, Sodium: 65 mg

Chicken Noodle Soup

A popular canned chicken noodle soup has 960 mg of sodium per 1 cup (250 mL) serving (only 1/3 of the can of soup since a can is theoretically figured to have 2.69 servings). Campbell's chicken noodle soup contains 2,580 mg of sodium.

6 *cups (1.5 L) Chicken Stock (opposite)*
1 *cup (250 mL) thin noodles, cooked and drained*

Cook chicken stock and use tongs to remove chicken; leave the vegetables in the soup, but discard bay leaf. When chicken is cool enough to handle, discard bones and cut chicken into bite-size pieces. Add chicken and noodles. Serve hot.

Calories per cup: 75, Fat: 2 g (1 g saturated), Protein: 6 g, Cholesterol: 9 mg, Carbohydrates: 8 g, Sodium: 50 mg

◆ Onion Soup ◆

MAKES 6 CUPS

A simple and tasty recipe.* You may want to freeze part of the recipe in portions. A cup of soup made from a mix would contain almost 1,000 mg of sodium.

    4   tablespoons (60 mL) unsalted margarine
    2   tablespoons (30 mL) safflower oil
    4   large onions, thinly sliced
    3   tablespoons (45 mL) flour
    6   cups (1.5 L) Chicken Stock (page 96)
        ground black pepper
  1/4   cup (60 mL) white wine

Use a large cooking pot. Heat the margarine and oil and sauté the onions over low heat for about 20 minutes, until the onions are golden and soft. Stir occasionally and do not let the onions brown. Sprinkle the flour over the onion. Stir occasionally to avoid burning and cook for 2 minutes. Stir in the chicken stock, wine, and black pepper. Simmer over low heat for 20 to 30 minutes. Serve hot.

* *To serve French style, ladle a serving of soup into an ovenproof bowl. Toast bread (low-sodium for strict dieters or French bread) and rub each piece of toast with a cut garlic clove. Sprinkle grated low-sodium cheese on top of the toast. Broil until the cheese has melted and is golden. Serve hot.*

Calories per cup: 196, Fat: 14 g (2 g saturated), Protein: 6 g, Cholesterol: 0 mg, Carbohydrates: 10 g, Sodium: 50 mg

◆ Beef Stock ◆

Use vegetables you have on hand, but small amounts of the vegetables that are fairly high in sodium (spinach, beets, celery, carrots).

2 *pounds (900 g) marrow bones or other soup bones*
1 *teaspoon (5 mL) olive oil*
2 *cups (500 mL) vegetables to add flavor, such as 1 carrot, 1 yellow turnip, 1 onion, 1 stalk celery, small handful parsley*
8 *cups (2 L) water*
 ground black pepper
 dash Tabasco sauce
1 *bay leaf*
1/2 *teaspoon (2 mL) dry mustard*
1 *teaspoon (5 mL) basil*
1/2 *cup (125 mL) red wine, such as Burgundy*
2 *tablespoons (30 mL) no-salt-added tomato paste*
1 *cup (250 mL) small noodles or macaroni (optional)*

Brown the marrow bones in warm oil in a large soup pot. Coarsely chop the vegetables and add, stirring occasionally with a wooden spoon. Add the water and remaining ingredients. Simmer for at least 2 hours. Cool and refrigerate overnight. The next day, remove and discard the layer of fat and bones. If you prefer clear stock, strain to remove the vegetables and bones. Or leave the vegetables in the soup. You can also cook separately a cup of small noodles or half cup of ABC macaroni to thicken the vegetable soup. Store in small portions in the freezer. (An ice cube tray works for very small amounts. Freeze and pop out; store in a freezer bag. Use stock cubes to flavor unsalted rice and gravy.)

Calories per cup: 66, Fat: 2 g (1 g saturated), Protein: 3 g, Cholesterol: 5 mg, Carbohydrates: 6 g, Sodium: 32 mg

◆ Vegetable Beef Soup ◆

   1 teaspoon (5 mL) safflower oil
 3/4 pound (338 g) very lean beef, cubed
   1 package soup vegetables, diced (see note* under
     Chicken Stock, (page 96)
   2 quarts (2 L) water
   1 bay leaf
     ground black pepper
 1/2 teaspoon (2 mL) basil
   3 tablespoons (45 mL) no-salt-added tomato paste
 1/2 cup (125 mL) vermouth
   1 cup (250 mL) small thin noodles or
 1/2 cup (125 mL) macaroni

Heat the safflower oil in a large soup pot and brown the beef. Add the diced vegetables to the pot, stir, and add remaining ingredients. Simmer for 2 to 2 1/2 hours. Skim off foam every hour; stir occasionally. To remove fat, cool and refrigerate overnight. Skim off fat layer and reheat. Or, if in a hurry, place paper towel on top to remove fat. Cook noodles or macaroni separately and add to the soup.

Calories per cup: 210, Fat: 9 g (3 g saturated), Protein: 12 g, Cholesterol: 34 mg, Carbohydrates: 17 g, Sodium: 61 mg

◆ Ground Beef and Vegetable Soup ◆

1 1/2 pounds (675 g) very lean ground beef
   8 cups (2 L) water
   6 ounces (170 mL) no-salt-added tomato paste
   2 tablespoons (30 mL) vinegar
   2 teaspoons (10 mL) basil
   1 teaspoon (5 mL) dry mustard
   2 teaspoons (10 mL) dill
   1 teaspoon (5 mL) garlic powder
 1/8 to 1/4 teaspoon (1/2–1 mL) black pepper, or to taste
 1/2 cup (125 mL) vermouth
   1 bay leaf

1/4 cup (60 mL) chopped parsley
2 carrots, finely diced
2 cups (500 mL) finely chopped cabbage
1 yellow turnip, finely diced
1 parsnip, finely diced
10 ounces (300 g) frozen corn
9 ounces (270 g) frozen green beans

Brown the meat in a soup pot. Drain off the fat, wipe the pan, and drain meat on a paper towel. Return the meat to the pot. Add all remaining ingredients and simmer over low heat for approximately 2 hours.

Calories per cup: 213, Fat: 11 g (4 g saturated), Protein: 14 g, Cholesterol: 43 mg, Carbohydrates: 14 g, Sodium: 73 mg

◆ Split Pea Soup ◆

MAKES 7 CUPS

Try this soup with liquid hickory smoke for the smoky flavor of the missing ham bone without added sodium.

1 pound (450 g) green or yellow split peas
1 stalk celery, diced
2 small carrots, diced
2 medium onions, diced
8 cups (2 L) water
1 bay leaf
1/2 teaspoon (2 mL) thyme
1/2 teaspoon (2 mL) white or black pepper
1 teaspoon (5 mL) hickory liquid smoke (optional)
2 tablespoons (30 mL) sherry (not cooking sherry) (optional)
1 cup (250 mL) skim milk

Wash and pick out any discolored peas and combine with the vegetables in a soup pot. Add the water and the seasonings. Simmer until the peas are soft, about 2 hours. Remove the bay leaf. In a food mill or blender, purée the soup 2 cups (500 mL) at a time. If you like your soup lumpy, do not blend it all. Stir in the sherry, if using, the milk, and any additional water needed for a thinner consistency. Serve hot.

Calories per cup: 260, Fat: 1 g (0 g saturated), Protein: 18 g, Cholesterol: 1 mg, Carbohydrates: 46 g, Sodium: 40 mg

◆ Quick Lentil Barley Soup ◆

Good on a cold day for a brown bag lunch. Try freezing this soup in one-cup portions for easy reheating.

1	*small onion, chopped*
1/4	*cup (60 mL) safflower oil*
9	*cups (2.2 L) water*
12	*ounces (340 g) no-salt-added tomato paste*
1/2	*teaspoon (2 mL) celery seed*
1/2	*cup (125 mL) dry lentils*
1/3	*cup (80 mL) whole barley*
1/4	*teaspoon (1 mL) black pepper*
1/8	*teaspoon (1/2 mL) rosemary*
3/4	*teaspoon (3 mL) basil*

In a large soup pot, sauté onion in oil until soft, stirring with a wooden spoon. Add remaining ingredients. Cover and cook gently for about 45 minutes, stirring occasionally.

**Calories per cup: 211, Fat: 7 g (1 g saturated), Protein: 9 g,
Cholesterol: 0 mg, Carbohydrates: 30 g, Sodium: 41 mg**

◆ Senate Bean Soup ◆

Save one cup mashed potatoes for this soup unless you like it thinner. And don't forget to soak the beans the night before.

1	*pound (450 g) dry beans, such as great northern, pea, or marrow beans*
41/2	*quarts (4.3 L) water*
2	*teaspoons (10 mL) liquid hickory smoke*
2	*bay leaves*
1/4	*teaspoon (1 mL) white pepper*
2	*medium onions, finely chopped*
2	*carrots, finely chopped*
2	*stalks celery, finely chopped*

2   *cloves garlic, minced*
1   *cup (250 mL) mashed potatoes*

Cover beans with cold water and soak overnight. The next day, drain off the soaking water. In a soup pot, combine the soaked beans, water, liquid smoke, bay leaves, and white pepper. Bring to a boil, turn down heat, and simmer until beans are tender, about 2 to $2^{1/2}$ hours. Stir in the chopped vegetables, and mashed potatoes. Cook for an additional 30 minutes. Remove the bay leaf. The soup can be served as is, or puréed in a food mill, blender, or food processor.

Calories per cup: 159, Fat: 2 g (0 g saturated), Protein: 9 g, Cholesterol: 0 mg, Carbohydrates: 28 g, Sodium: 19 mg

◆ Corn Chowder ◆

MAKES 2³/₄ CUPS

It's the long cooking and browning of the onion that adds the flavor. Double the recipe if you want more than three servings. A great recipe to serve people who don't drink milk and need calcium!

2   *tablespoons (30 mL) unsalted margarine*
1   *medium onion, finely chopped*
2   *medium potatoes, peeled and cut into cubes*
2   *cups (500 mL) skim milk*
10 *ounces (300 g) frozen corn**
1/8 *teaspoon (¹/2 mL) fresh pepper*

In a skillet melt the margarine over medium heat. Cook the onion until the pieces are browned. Mix onion, potato cubes, and milk in a saucepan. Simmer over medium low heat for 20 minutes, but do not let it boil. Add the corn and pepper. Simmer for another 5 minutes.

* If you like thicker corn chowder, subtitute a can of no-salt-added cream-style corn.

Calories per cup: 296, Fat: 10 g (2 g saturated), Protein: 11 g, Cholesterol: 4 mg, Carbohydrates: 46 g, Sodium: 104 mg

◆ Potato Leek Soup ◆

Make this delicious soup whenever your supermarket has leeks.

> 2 *tablespoons (30 mL) unsalted margarine*
> 4 *medium leeks*
> 2 *pounds (900 g) potatoes (about 6 medium)*
> 2 *cups (500 mL) water*
> 3/4 *cup (180 mL) skim milk*

Melt the margarine in a soup pot. Thinly slice the white part of the leeks. Cook leeks gently in the melted margarine for 10 minutes or so until they are soft. Meanwhile, peel and dice the potatoes and add to the soup pot with the leeks. Add the water, cover the pot, and simmer until the potatoes are tender, about 30 minutes. Remove some of the potato pieces to a bowl, depending on how "chunky" you like your soup. Put the remainder of the soup through a sieve or mash it with a potato masher. Add the milk and reserved potatoes. Heat over low heat, but be careful not to let it boil.

**Calories per cup: 240, Fat: 5 g (1 g saturated), Protein: 6 g,
Cholesterol: 1 mg, Carbohydrates: 45 g, Sodium: 44 mg**

◆ Cream of Broccoli Soup ◆

> 10 *ounces (300 g) frozen chopped broccoli**
> 3/4 *cup (180 mL) water*
> 2 *tablespoons (30 mL) unsalted margarine*
> 1 *small onion, diced*
> 5 *tablespoons (75 mL) flour*
> 2 *cups (500 mL) skim milk*
> 1/8 *teaspoon (1/2 mL) white pepper*
>   *dash allspice or*
> 2 *tablespoons (30 mL) sherry (not cooking sherry)*

Cook the broccoli in the water, covered, for 4 or 5 minutes. Meanwhile, melt the margarine in a soup pot, add the onion, and sauté for 5 minutes. Sprinkle flour over the onions, stir, and cook over low heat for a minute or so. Add the broccoli and its cooking water; stir. Add the milk and white pepper. Simmer but do not boil. Stir in the sherry or allspice. Cook gently a few minutes more. Serve warm or cold.

You can substitute 2 cups of fresh broccoli. We have also used a package of frozen broccoli and cauliflower with red peppers—a colorful variation.

Calories per cup: 163, Fat: 6 g (1 g saturated), Protein: 8 g, Cholesterol: 3 mg, Carbohydrates: 19 g, Sodium: 84 mg

◆ Gazpacho ◆

MAKES 4 CUPS

This cold vegetable soup is luscious when tomatoes are in season—juicy and low in cost.

Gazpacho is usually served with side dishes of chopped onion, tomato, green pepper, and cucumber for guests to sprinkle, the toppings they like best.

- 1 *medium cucumber, peeled and coarsely chopped*
- 2 *large fresh tomatoes, chopped*
- 1 *medium onion, chopped*
- 1/2 *green pepper, seeded and chopped*
- 1 *clove garlic, chopped*
- 4 *slices low-sodium bread, trimmed of crusts and crumbled (if you want a thick gazpacho)*
- 1 *cup (250 mL) water*
- 2 *tablespoons (30 mL) red wine vinegar*
- 1 *tablespoon (15 mL) olive oil*
- 1/4 *cup (60 mL) no-salt-added tomato paste*

Mix all the ingredients in a large bowl. Blend small amounts at a time in a blender until you have a smooth purée. Chill several hours before serving.

Calories per cup: 146, Fat: 5 g (1 g saturated), Protein: 4 g, Cholesterol: 0 mg, Carbohydrates: 24 g, Sodium: 29 mg

◆ Cold Cantaloupe Soup ◆

MAKES 6 CUPS

An elegant first course and less work than fresh fruit cocktail.

1   *ripe cantaloupe, seeded*
1/2   *teaspoon (2 mL) cinnamon*
1   *tablespoon (15 mL) lemon juice*
2   *cups (500 mL) orange juice*

Scoop out the cantaloupe and beat in a blender or food processor. Add the cinnamon and lemon juice. Blend until the mixture is smooth. In a serving bowl, stir the cantaloupe and orange juice. Chill at least 2 hours before serving.

**Calories per cup: 68, Fat: 0 g (0 g saturated), Protein: 1 g,
Cholesterol: 0 mg, Carbohydrates: 16 g, Sodium: 10 mg**

SALADS

◆◆◆◆◆

All your life you've probably heard that raw fruits and vegetables are good for you. They are! But surveys at popular salad bars have an interesting twist. People interviewed were asked why they chose the salad bar over other foods. Most replied that they were trying to lose weight. With generous salads smothered in salad dressing, these "low-calorie" lunches averaged 1,000 calories! Many salad dressings pack 100 calories per level tablespoon (15 mL). A person who spoons or pours on a generous layer of salad dressing may be inadvertently adding one to two thousand calories.

Whether you're making a salad at home or choosing items from a restaurant salad bar, you need to avoid the items that are high in sodium. Avoid these: canned chickpeas (garbanzo beans), croutons, olives, three-bean salad, cottage cheese, cheese, pickled beets, pickles, bacon-flavored bits, canned items such as onion rings, and bottled or dry prepared salad dressings.

Moderately high in sodium, these vegetables should be eaten only in moderate amounts: spinach, celery, carrots.

There are many low-sodium salad ingredients. Eat all you like of these: lettuce, tomatoes, green pepper slices, cucumber slices, onion slices, radishes, mushroom slices, canned or fresh fruit, oil, vinegar, lemon juice, and salad dressings from this book (pages 52 to 56).

◆ Tomato and Cucumber Salad ◆

MAKES 4 SERVINGS

2 *medium garden-ripe tomatoes*
1 *medium cucumber*
1 *cup (250 mL) Good and Good for You Dressing (page 52)*

Cut out the stem ends of the tomatoes and slice into chunks. Peel the cucumber and cut into chunks; mix the vegetables in a bowl, preferably glass. Pour the salad dressing over the vegetables. Cover and refrigerate an hour or two. Serve chilled.

Calories: 105, Fat: 3 g (0 g saturated), Protein: 2 g, Cholesterol: 0 mg, Carbohydrates: 21 g, Sodium: 13 mg

◆ Macaroni Salad ◆

Best made well in advance.

> 4   *ounces (120 g) dry macaroni*
> 2   *tablespoons (30 mL) water*
> 1/3 *cup (80 mL) Mayonnaise (page 43)*
> 1   *small onion or scallion (optional)*
> 3   *tablespoons (45 mL) cider vinegar*
> 2   *teaspoons (10 mL) celery seed*
> 2   *teaspoons (10 mL) dry mustard (less for milder flavor)*
> 1   *tablespoon (15 mL) sugar*
> 6   *tablespoons (90 mL) green or red pepper, finely diced*
>   *dash white pepper*
> 1/4 *teaspoon (1 mL) onion powder*

Cook macaroni as directed on the box without the salt; drain, rinse with water, and drain again. Mix macaroni in a bowl with all remaining ingredients. Chill. Serve on lettuce leaves, if desired.

**Calories: 252, Fat: 13 g (1 g saturated), Protein: 5 g,
Cholesterol: 11 mg, Carbohydrates: 30 g, Sodium: 8 mg**

◆ Classic Cucumbers in Vinegar ◆

A traditional summertime favorite. Good at a cookout. Make it ahead to blend the flavors.

> 1   *medium cucumber, peeled and sliced thin*
> 1   *cup (250 mL) vinegar*
> 1 1/2 *tablespoons sugar (22 mL)*

Combine the ingredients in a nonmetal bowl; cover and refrigerate. The vinegar mixture may be reused several times.

**Calories: 33, Fat: 0 g (0 g saturated), Protein: 0 g, Cholesterol: 0 mg,
Carbohydrates: 10 g, Sodium: 2 mg**

◆ Macaroni Salad, Italian Style ◆

A curly macaroni such as rotelle or fusilli makes an attractive salad.

    1/2 pound (240 g) macaroni
      3 tablespoons (45 mL) olive oil
    1/2 green pepper, diced
    1/2 medium onion, diced
      2 tablespoons (30 mL) vinegar
      3 tablespoons (45 mL) pimientos, chopped
    1/2 teaspoon (2 mL) garlic powder
      1 teaspoon (5 mL) onion powder
    1/4 teaspoon (1 mL) white pepper

Cook macaroni in boiling water according to package directions except leave out the salt; drain. Heat the olive oil in a frying pan and sauté the green pepper and onion until soft. Toss the macaroni with the green pepper and onion. Add the seasonings and toss again. Cover and refrigerate. Let sit at least an hour to blend the flavors.

Calories: 158, Fat: 6 g (1 g saturated), Protein: 4 g, Cholesterol: 0 mg, Carbohydrates: 23 g, Sodium: 3 mg

◆ Quick Potato Salad ◆

If this unsalted version seems a little bland to you, sprinkle on a seasoning your family likes such as garlic powder, dill, or the Unsalt Shaker (page 39). Nice served on lettuce leaves.*

      4 medium potatoes, peeled and quartered
      1 bay leaf
    1/2 teaspoon (2 mL) onion powder
      2 tablespoons (30 mL) vinegar
    1/4 cup (60 mL) boiling water
      1 tablespoon (15 mL) safflower oil
    1/4 cup (60 mL) Mayonnaise (page 43)
    3/4 teaspoon (4 mL) dry mustard
         chopped parsley, chopped onion, celery seed (optional)
         paprika (optional)

Pour enough water to cover potatoes in a large pan; add bay leaf and onion powder. Cook until potatoes are tender, about 20 minutes or longer; drain. When cool enough to handle, peel and dice or slice into a bowl. Combine the vinegar, the boiling water, and oil. Pour over potatoes and toss well. (Potatoes that are coated in this way will be moist without too much mayonnaise.) Cool. Combine mayonnaise and desired seasonings and add to potatoes. Sprinkle top with paprika, if desired.

* You can also add strips of cold leftover meat or drained low-sodium tuna for a main course salad. Also, you can cook potatoes in their jackets a day in advance; peel when ready to make the salad.

Calories: 192, Fat: 13 g (1 g saturated), Protein: 2 g, Cholesterol: 9 mg, Carbohydrates: 18 g, Sodium: 8 mg

◆ Marinated Bean Salad ◆

MAKES 3 CUPS

Make this salad year round.* Canned unsalted vegetables would work well here. If these are not available, you can use frozen green beans. If you're not familiar with cooking dry beans, see Beans (page 192).

> 2 *cups (500 mL) fresh, frozen, or canned unsalted green beans or part green and part wax beans*
> 1 *cup (250 mL) dry kidney beans, cooked without salt*
> 1 *small onion, chopped*
> 1/2 *cup (125 mL) cider vinegar*
> 1/4 *cup (60 mL) safflower oil*
> 1/4 *cup (60 mL) sugar*

Mix all ingredients; refrigerate several hours or overnight to blend the flavors.

* Or try with only kidney beans and some diced celery and green pepper. Sodium and calorie contents will be slightly higher, however.

Calories per 1/2 cup: 233, Fat: 9 g (1 g saturated), Protein: 8 g, Cholesterol: 0 mg, Carbohydrates: 32 g, Sodium: 9 mg

◆ Coleslaw ◆

This coleslaw is good as a side dish or as a sandwich ingredient. You can double the recipe and use an average-size cabbage.

> 1   *pound (450 g) small head cabbage, shredded, about 3¹/₂*
> *cups (875 mL)*
> 1   *carrot*
> 1   *small onion*
> ¹/₂   *cup (125 mL) Mayonnaise (page 43)*
> 1   *tablespoon (15 mL) sugar*
> 1   *tablespoon (15 mL) cider vinegar*
> *freshly ground pepper*
> ¹/₄   *to ¹/₂ teaspoon (1 to 2 mL) celery seed (optional)*

Shred the cabbage and carrot using a food processor, a blender, or a hand grater. Dice the onion. Mix the cabbage, carrot, and onion in a large bowl. In a small bowl combine the mayonnaise, sugar, vinegar, and pepper, and celery seed, if desired. Toss with shredded vegetables. Refrigerate until you are ready to serve. It tastes better if you make it a few hours before serving.

Calories per ¹/₂ cup: 74, Fat: 6 g (0 g saturated), Protein: 1 g,
Cholesterol: 5 mg, Carbohydrates: 6 g, Sodium: 12 mg

◆ Pineapple Coleslaw ◆

You can make this ahead and allow the flavors to blend for a delicious variation. Omit the carrot, onion, and sugar in coleslaw (above). Add 8 ounces (225 g) crushed pineapple.

Calories per ¹/₂ cup: 102, Fat: 9 g (1 g saturated), Protein: 1 g,
Cholesterol: 9 mg, Carbohydrates: 5 g, Sodium: 9 mg

FRUIT SALADS

You really don't need formal recipes for making fruit salads—just combine fresh available fruits with different colors and textures. Frozen or canned fruits, all naturally low in sodium, can also be used. A fruit salad looks special when served on a few leaves of lettuce or other green. Chopped walnuts on top are also nice.

Try these salad ideas: banana slices, orange sections, seedless green grapes, unsalted nuts; orange slices, pineapple chunks, banana slices; pears or peach slices sprinkled with lightly toasted unsalted almond slivers; sweet grapes and pear slices; pineapple chunks with fresh berries (blueberries, raspberries, strawberries); apples and grapes with melon balls; or melon balls with cherries and grapes.

Slice apples, pears, and peaches with a stainless steel knife to keep them from turning brown. Also, toss the fruit with a sprinkling of lemon, grapefruit, or pineapple juice to prevent browning on the cut surfaces.

◆ Waldorf Salad ◆

MAKES 4 SERVINGS

This pretty salad can be served on lettuce leaves.

    2 large firm ripe apples
    2 teaspoons (10 mL) lemon juice
    2 tablespoons (30 mL) Mayonnaise (page 43)
    2 tablespoons (30 mL) walnuts, coarsely chopped

Wash, quarter and core the apples. Dice with peel on. Toss in bowl with lemon juice. Add mayonnaise, toss to coat the apples; mix in the walnuts. Store in covered container in refrigerator until serving time.

Calories: 104, Fat: 7 g (1 g saturated), Protein: 1 g, Cholesterol: 4 mg, Carbohydrates: 11 g, Sodium: 1 mg

GELATIN SALADS

If your family likes gelatin salads, you can use either plain unflavored gelatin (such as Knox, which has only a trace of sodium) or flavored gelatin (such as Jell-O, which has about 270 mg of sodium in a 3-ounce [90-g] package). If you use flavored gelatin, you must count the milligrams of sodium in the person's daily total. You can figure about 55 mg in each 1/2 cup (125 mL). Dietetic gelatin (D-Zerta brand) has only 6 mg in a small serving. This does have the brightly colored dye already in it—good if your family expects gelatins to be bright-colored. But D-Zerta contains saccharin, a disadvantage for people who do not want to ingest artificial dyes or sweeteners.

Or make gelatins from scratch, just as easy as using a mix. Of course there are more ingredients to get together, but the steps are just about the same—hot water, cold water, and so on. The moulded gelatin salad recipes that follow include vegetable and fruit versions to start you off. When you begin to use unflavored gelatin you will certainly create your own combinations. All fresh, frozen, or canned fruits work well except fresh pineapple.

◆ Seasonal Fruit Gelatin Salad ◆

MAKES 4 SERVINGS

- 2 envelopes unflavored gelatin
- 1/4 cup (60 mL) cold water
- 1/2 cup (125 mL) boiling water
- 1/3 cup (80 mL) sugar
- 1 cup (250 mL) apple, orange, or cranberry juice
- 2 drops food coloring if desired (optional)
- 2 tablespoons (30 mL) lemon juice
- 2 cups (500 mL) small pieces of fruit such as fresh or frozen cantaloupe balls, seedless grapes, apple pieces, canned pineapple chunks

Stir the gelatin into cold water to soften. Add the boiling water and stir until the gelatin dissolves. Add the sugar, juice, and food coloring, if desired; stir. To be sure that the pieces of fruit will be evenly distributed, chill the mixture until it is as thick as unbeaten egg white, about 30 to 45 minutes. Fold in the fruit and put into a lightly oiled or sprayed mould. To unmould, see Vegetable-Pineapple Gelatin Salad (below).

Calories: 138, Fat: 0 g (0 g saturated), Protein: 4 g, Cholesterol: 0 mg, Carbohydrates: 32 g, Sodium: 17 mg

◆ Vegetable-Pineapple Gelatin Salad ◆

2   carrots, grated
1   cup (250 mL) cabbage, grated
20 ounces (600 g) crushed pineapple and juice from can
    small amount water
2   envelopes unflavored gelatin
1/4 cup (60 mL) sugar
1   cup (250 mL) ice water
2   tablespoons (30 mL) lemon juice
2   drops yellow food coloring (optional)

Combine the grated carrots and cabbage in a bowl. Drain and reserve the juice from a can of pineapple and add the drained pineapple to the carrots and cabbage. Combine the reserved pineapple juice with enough water to make 2 cups (500 mL). Pour this liquid into a saucepan; bring to a boil. Add the gelatin and sugar and stir until dissolved. Stir in 1 cup of ice water, the lemon juice, and optional food coloring. To be sure the pieces do not sink to the bottom, chill this mixture until it is slightly thicker than an unbeaten egg white, about 45 minutes. Fold in the pineapple and grated vegetables and pour into a prepared mould. (To be sure gelatin will unmould without sticking, you can spray the mould with a vegetable coating spray such as Pam.)

To unmould a gelatin salad, fill a large bowl with hot water. Hold the mould in the water for about 20 seconds so that it is immersed to the rim. Remove the mould from the water and hold the serving plate upside down over the mould. With the mould and plate held firmly together, flip the whole thing over so that the serving plate is on the bottom. Still holding the mould and the plate together, give the mould a little shake. When you feel the gelatin dropping onto the plate, lift off the mould.

Calories: 125, Fat: 0 g (0 g saturated), Protein: 4 g, Cholesterol: 0 mg, Carbohydrates: 29 g, Sodium: 22 mg

VEGETABLES

◆◆◆◆◆

Low-sodium dieters who have been advised to limit their meat portion to 3 ounces (90 g) of cooked meat begin to enjoy vegetables that fill their dinner plate. Leafy vegetables, potatoes, and squashes can round out a meal and prevent the low-sodium dieter from feeling deprived. Fortunately, these foods are all naturally low in sodium.

Another reason to eat more vegetables in addition to filling up the dinner plate? Vegetables (and fruits, too) are good sources of vitamins and potassium, which are important, as doctors and researchers have pointed out.

This chapter offers you low-sodium recipes for old favorites as well as some new ideas—all using fresh vegetables. When substituting frozen vegetables, never add salt to cooking water.

CHOOSING VEGETABLES
◆◆

All regular canned vegetables are very high in sodium. Repeated rinsings in fresh water can remove quite a lot of the salt that was added in the canning process. But after all the effort in rinsing them, you won't end up with a very tasty food.

Canned unsalted vegetables, increasingly made by large food companies, are just as convenient as the regular ones, but unfortunately are also rather tasteless. The special dietetic low-sodium canned vegetables are available but quite expensive. Some brands have added potassium chloride (leaves an unpleasant aftertaste) while others do not; the label will advise you. Try just one can to see if you like the taste. But our taste testers rated them as tasteless.

The good news is that fresh and frozen vegetables retain vegetables' natural taste and most are unsalted. The canning process destroys some of the vegetable vitamins and minerals. Frozen vegetables retain more freshness, flavor, and nutrients than canned ones do. Frozen peas and lima beans are higher in sodium than fresh ones since they are soaked in a salty solution before freezing to keep them plump. Vegetables frozen with added salt, butter, or fancy sauces are also high in sodium—too high for anyone on a restricted diet. Be sure to read the labels before you buy.

Reading Sodium Numbers on Convenience Foods

When you are trying to decide which foods are low enough in sodium to buy, be very careful. Manufacturers' nutrition information is often figured on the basis of very small servings. For example, a 3-ounce (90-g) serving of a vegetable, such as peas or green beans, is only 6 tablespoons (90 mL)— slightly more than half of the smallest jar of baby food peas. An average serving for an adult is closer to 1 cup (250 mL). A 1-cup (250-mL) serving of Green Giant small onions in a creamy cheese-flavored sauce has 725 mg of sodium.

So if you read on a package of Birds Eye small onions with cream sauce that a 3-ounce (90-g) serving has only 355 mg, do not be falsely reassured that the product is moderately low in sodium. The entire package contains 1,065 mg of sodium.

Vegetables That Are Good Sources of Calcium

If you need to keep your sodium intake low, you may not be eating large amounts of dairy products with necessary calcium. One logical solution is to eat more of the vegetables that are good sources of calcium. These include: broccoli, spinach, kale, turnip greens, beet greens, and collards.

Choose Wisely: Fresh Vegetables Are Worth the Effort

To help you choose vegetables wisely to cut down on sodium, we gave you the sodium content of common vegetables for 1 cup (250 mL) of each. We arranged vegetables in alphabetical order, rather than an arrangement based on the sodium content, because it will be much easier for the cook to find the desired vegetable.

If the cook wants to cook turnips, for example, she or he can find it quickly in an alphabetical list. But in a list by sodium content, she or he would have to look at white turnip in the high group and yellow turnip in the low group.

Also, the differences in sodium are minor when vegetables are compared with other foods. Certainly carrots and celery are higher in sodium, but this does not mean that people ought to give them up and miss out on the fiber and vitamins. When vegetables are considered in the context of foods in general, we find that there really is no such thing as a fresh vegetable that is high in sodium.

ASPARAGUS

——◆◆——

Wash the asparagus and cut or snap off the pale part of the bottom. Cut the stalks in small pieces (2 inch or 5 cm) and cook in a vegetable steamer or a saucepan until tender, about 10 minutes. Or bunch the whole stalks and bind them together using a wide rubber band. Set the asparagus in a tall pot with the cut ends down. Add water to a level of 3 inches (8 cm), cover, and cook until the asparagus is tender, about 15 minutes. (This is a good method because the tender top end of the stalk is cooked less than the tough woody end.) Serve asparagus with lemon wedges to add a refreshing flavor.

Sodium, 1 cup (250 mL): • Fresh, 3 mg • Frozen, 2 mg • Canned, 740 mg

GREEN AND WAX BEANS

——◆◆——

Cook plain frozen green or wax beans according to the directions on the package, except leave out the salt in the cooking water.

To cook fresh green beans, wash beans and cut or snap off the ends; cut lengthwise into strips, or snap them into pieces or on the diagonal for a fancy look; or leave the beans whole. Steam beans or cook them in a small amount of boiling water for 15 to 20 minutes. Never add baking soda to the water since baking soda is very high in sodium.

**Sodium, 1 cup (250 mL): Fresh, 8 mg • Canned wax beans, 690 mg
• Canned green beans, 710 mg • Frozen cut green beans, 6 mg
• Frozen French green beans with toasted almonds, 670 mg**

Green Beans with Mushrooms
◆ and Almonds ◆

More like the fancy frozen green beans.

 1 *pound (450 g) fresh green beans or frozen green beans*
 2 *tablespoons (30 mL) unsalted margarine*
 1 *small onion, diced*
10 *small mushrooms, sliced*
    dash white pepper
 3 *tablespoons (45 mL) sliced almonds*

In a saucepan with a small amount of water, add the fresh or frozen green beans; cook until tender; drain. Meanwhile, melt the margarine and add the onion, mushroom, and white pepper. Cook gently 5 minutes or so. Add the almonds and cook for another 2 or 3 minutes. Toss with the hot cooked beans just before serving.

Calories: 147, Fat: 10 g (1 g saturated), Protein: 5 g, Cholesterol: 0 mg, Carbohydrates: 14 g, Sodium: 12 mg

LIMA BEANS
————◆◆————

Fresh limas are low in sodium. To cook fresh limas, just remove them from their pods and then cook in a small amount of unsalted water for a half hour or so.

BEETS
————◆◆————

Fresh beets are higher in sodium than most vegetables, with 22 mg in a medium-size beet. Canned beets are even higher with 545 mg in a 1-cup (250-mL) serving.

BROCCOLI

To cook frozen broccoli, just follow the package directions, except leave out the salt.

To prepare fresh broccoli, cut a slice off the bottom of each stem. Leave the broccoli whole or slice the stalk into "coins" and divide the top into florets. Steam broccoli or cook it in a small amount of unsalted water for 15 minutes or so.

Sodium, 1 cup (250 mL): • Fresh, 16 mg • Frozen deluxe florets, 30 mg • Frozen broccoli spears in butter sauce, 875 mg

Lemon and "Butter" Sauce ◆ for Broccoli ◆

MAKES 4 SERVINGS

Make your broccoli more like the packaged kind with butter sauce by using the following recipe.

2 **tablespoons (30 mL) unsalted margarine**
1 **tablespoon (15 mL) lemon juice**
    dash pepper

Melt the margarine. Stir in the lemon juice and pepper. Toss over cooked, drained broccoli.

Calories: 52, Fat: 6 g (1 g saturated), Protein: 0 g, Cholesterol: 0 mg, Carbohydrates: 0 g, Sodium: 0 mg

BRUSSELS SPROUTS

———◆◆———

Cook plain frozen brussels sprouts according to package directions but leave out the salt in the water.

To prepare fresh brussels sprouts, trim the bottoms, discarding any discolored leaves; with a sharp knife score an "X" on the flat bottom. Steam brussels sprouts or cook them in a small amount of unsalted water for about 15 or 20 minutes until tender.

Brussels sprouts are traditionally served with brown butter. The following recipe can be made for fresh or frozen brussels sprouts.

Sodium, 1 cup (250 mL): • Fresh, 16 mg • Frozen, 15 mg • Frozen baby brussels sprouts in butter sauce, 865 mg

◆ Brown "Butter" for Brussels Sprouts ◆

MAKES 4 SERVINGS

2   *tablespoons (30 mL) unsalted margarine*
1   *tablespoon (15 mL) lemon juice*
     ground black pepper

Melt the margarine and cook over low heat until brown. Stir in the lemon juice and pepper. Toss with cooked brussels sprouts.

Calories: 52, Fat: 6 g (1 g saturated), Protein: 0 g, Cholesterol: 0 mg, Carbohydrates: 0 g, Sodium: 0 mg

CABBAGE

———◆◆———

A medium-sized cabbage has 218 mg of sodium, but when cabbage is bought as coleslaw or sauerkraut, both versions are high in sodium. For example, canned sauerkraut (shredded cabbage in brine) has 1,554 mg in 1 cup (250 mL). Prepared "deli" coleslaw varies but may have as much as 322 mg in 1 cup (250 mL). There are two delicious low-sodium coleslaw recipes in the salad chapter (page 111). Unfortunately, there is no way to make sauerkraut without salt since it's essential to the process.

❖ Cabbage with Apples ❖

1 medium head of red or white cabbage
2 medium apples, peeled and sliced
1 medium onion, chopped
2 tablespoons (30 mL) unsalted margarine
1/4 cup (60 mL) vinegar
2 tablespoons (30 mL) sugar
1 teaspoon (5 mL) crushed caraway seeds
2 tablespoons (30 mL) water

Shred the cabbage using a food processor, hand grater, or a knife. Mix the apples and onion with the cabbage. Melt the margarine in a large saucepan. Add the vegetables and cook and stir for about 5 minutes. Add the remaining ingredients; cover the pot and cook gently for 35 minutes; add more water, if needed. Remove the cover and cook for 10 minutes more to boil down any excess liquid.

Calories: 75, Fat: 3 g (1 g saturated), Protein: 1 g, Cholesterol: 0 mg, Carbohydrates: 12 g, Sodium: 8 mg

CARROTS

If you are on a sodium-restricted diet, you may be advised to eat fresh carrots in measured amounts. This may seem strange at first, since most of us think of carrots as a food to munch freely when trying to lose weight.

Peel or just scrub carrots before cooking; slice into rings or into sticks. Then steam or cook in a small amount of water until crisp, about 6 minutes, longer if you like them tender.

Sodium, 1 cup (250 mL): • Fresh, grated, 52 mg • Canned, 510 mg • Frozen carrots with brown sugar glaze, 1,000 mg

◆ Queen Cauliflower ◆

If you want to "dress up" plain caulifower, try this recipe.

- 1 *cauliflower*
- 1 *tablespoon (15 mL) unsalted margarine*
- 1 *tablespoon (15 mL) oil*
- 1 *tablespoon (15 mL) wheat germ*
- 1 *tablespoon (15 mL) unsalted bread crumbs or crushed low-sodium cornflakes*

Trim leaves and stem of the cauliflower, but leave it whole and put it into a cooking pot with a tight-fitting lid. Add 2 cups (500 mL) water and cover tightly. Cook over high heat until the water begins to boil; turn down the heat and allow cauliflower to cook in the steam until fork tender, about 15 to 20 minutes, depending on the size of the cauliflower. In a saucepan melt the margarine. Stir in the oil, wheat germ, and bread crumbs. Press the mixture onto the top of the cauliflower, like a crown. (This can be done ahead of time.) Just before serving, set the cauliflower in a pie plate and bake in a 350°F (175°C) oven 5 to 10 minutes until warm.

Calories: 45, Fat: 3 g (0 g saturated), Protein: 1 g, Cholesterol: 0 mg, Carbohydrates: 3 g, Sodium: 15 mg

CELERY

Celery is higher in sodium than most vegetables—25 mg in a single stalk. For that reason, celery is usually used only in small amounts to flavor a sodium-restricted diet.

CORN

—◆◆—

Fresh or frozen ears of corn can be served plain or with unsalted margarine. Add onion or garlic powder (or both) to melted margarine or keep the Unsalt Shaker (page 39) on the table.

You can use fresh or frozen cut corn to make the delicious Corn Relish (page 50).

Sodium, 1 cup (250 mL) except where noted: • Fresh, 1 ear, 1 mg • Frozen, 1 small ear, 4 mg • Frozen kernels, 2 mg • Frozen cream-style corn, 480 mg • Frozen corn in butter sauce, 765 mg • Canned whole kernel corn, 420 mg • Canned cream-style corn, 530 mg

◆ Barbecued Corn on the Cob ◆

MAKES 4 SERVINGS

This is the oven method. Or cook outdoors on a grill. Follow the same instructions except roast corn over glowing coals, turning occasionally.

    2   tablespoons (30 mL) unsalted margarine
    1   cup (250 mL) low-sodium ketchup
    2   tablespoons (30 mL) vinegar
    2   teaspoons (10 mL) dry mustard
    1/4 teaspoon (1 mL) ginger
    1/4 teaspoon (1 mL) onion powder
    1/4 teaspoon (1 mL) liquid hickory smoke (optional)
    4   ears of corn, fresh or frozen

To make the barbecue sauce, combine all of the ingredients except the corn in a small saucepan; heat gently and stir until the margarine melts. Cut 4 pieces of aluminum foil into approximately 12-inch (30-cm) squares. Lay an ear of corn on each square. Brush the sauce on each ear, spreading the sauce over the surface of the corn. Seal the foil but don't wrap it tightly around the corn, allowing room for steam. Arrange the ears on a cookie sheet, seam side up. Roast in 400°F (205°C) oven for 45 minutes.

Calories: 201, Fat: 8 g (1 g saturated), Protein: 4 g, Cholesterol: 0 mg, Carbohydrates: 35 g, Sodium: 26 mg

◆ Corn and Zucchini Casserole ◆

MAKES 6 SERVINGS

Cut corn is a good addition to vegetable casseroles. The following recipe is a hearty autumn favorite.

    4   medium zucchini, about 1 pound (450 g)
    2   teaspoons (10 mL) unsalted margarine
    1   medium onion, diced
   10   ounces (300 g) frozen corn
    4   ounces (120 g) no-salt Swiss cheese, grated
    2   eggs or equivalent egg substitute

Wash zucchini, slice into pieces, and put in a saucepan with enough water to cover the zucchini. Cover the pan. Bring to a boil and cook for about 15 minutes. While the zucchini cooks, melt the margarine in a saucepan; add the onion and cook gently until tender. In another saucepan, bring 1/2 cup (125 mL) water to a boil. Add the corn, cover, and boil 2 to 3 minutes. Drain and set aside. Mash the cooked zucchini with a fork, combine with all of the ingredients in a casserole. Bake in 350°F (175°C) oven for 35 to 40 minutes, until top is golden brown.

**Calories: 174, Fat: 10 g (5 g saturated), Protein: 10 g,
Cholesterol: 90 mg, Carbohydrates: 15 g, Sodium: 32 mg**

CUCUMBERS

Cucumbers are very low in sodium—only 10 mg in a medium-sized one; they are also low in calories with 25 calories in a medium cucumber. There is a recipe for Classic Cucumbers in Vinegar (page 108). You can use cucumbers in salads, with tomatoes (page 107), and in sandwiches for a crunchy addition. Cucumbers are crisper when chilled.

EGGPLANT

Eggplant is low in sodium with only 5 mg in a whole medium eggplant. Don't use the traditional eggplant procedure of salting eggplant to draw the bitterness out. And avoid Parmesan cheese which also increases the sodium content.

Eggplant can be delicious if you try the recipe for Moussaka (page 190).

MUSHROOMS

Fresh mushrooms are low in sodium (17 mg) and calories (32 calories) per 1/4 pound (110 g). Mushrooms can be a flavorful addition to hot and cold dishes.

But canned mushrooms are very high in sodium with 242 mg in 2 ounces (60 g). Canned with buttery flavoring, mushrooms are even higher and cannot be part of a low-sodium diet.

To prepare fresh mushrooms, wash them carefully but don't use too much water or soak them because they will get spongy; just wipe them off gently with a damp paper towel. If the mushrooms are large, cut the stem into "coins" before cutting the crown. If the mushrooms are small or medium, cut the whole mushroom lengthwise through the stem.

Try the Marinated Mushrooms (page 78) and the Mushroom Barley Soup (page 97).

OKRA

Okra, a flavorful vegetable, is low in sodium and adds body to the liquid in which it's cooked. To cook fresh okra, cut off the stems and tips and steam or cover with water and cook gently for 10 minutes or so.

Sodium, 1 cup (250 mL): • Fresh, 3 mg • Frozen, 4 mg • Frozen Southern okra gumbo, 210 mg

◆ Okra and Tomatoes ◆

MAKES 4 SERVINGS

1   *tablespoon (15 mL) unsalted margarine*
1   *medium onion, diced*
1/2   *pound (225 g) fresh or frozen (defrosted) okra, sliced*
3   *medium tomatoes, cut into chunks*
    pinch sugar
    ground black pepper

Melt the margarine in a large skillet. Sauté the onion; slice the okra and add. Fry gently for 5 minutes or so. Add the remaining ingredients. Cook gently, partially covered, for 15 to 20 minutes. Serve in small bowls.

Calories: 75, Fat: 3 g (1 g saturated), Protein: 2 g, Cholesterol: 0 mg, Carbohydrates: 11 g, Sodium: 14 mg

ONIONS

———◆◆———

Onions add flavor to many hot and cold dishes. Don't miss the recipes for delicious Onion Soup (page 98) and Vegetable Tempura or Onion Rings (page 82).

◆ Boiled Onions ◆

Serve onions boiled the traditional way. Choose the tiny pearl onions or small white onions; remove the skins and root ends but leave the onions whole. Cover with water and boil until the onions are fork tender; drain. Serve boiled onions with a little unsalted margarine and black pepper.

Sodium, 1 cup (250 mL) except where noted: • 1 medium fresh onion, 10 mg • Fresh diced onion, 17 mg • 6 fresh green onions or scallions, 6 mg • Small onions in a creamy cheese-flavored sauce, 1 cup, 725 mg

PARSNIPS

———◆◆———

Parsnips look like pale carrots. A medium parsnip has 19 mg of sodium. Many soup recipes in this book call for soup vegetables. These packages (from your market) contain one or two parsnips and for good reason—they add a lot of flavor.

◆ Roasted Parsnips ◆

MAKES 6 SERVINGS

Parsnips make a delightful accompaniment to meat dishes.

   2 *pounds (900 g) parsnips*
   1 *tablespoon (15 mL) safflower oil*
 1/4 *teaspoon (1 mL) ground black pepper*
   1 *teaspoon (5 mL) dried parsley*

Peel and cut up the parsnips into 1-inch (2.5 cm) pieces. Add oil, pepper, and parsley. Mix until coated. Roast in a 425°F (220°C) oven for 25 minutes. Turn parsnips; continue to roast, turning every 5 minutes until tender and brown, about 20 more minutes. Serve hot.

Calories: 134, Fat: 3 g (0 g saturated), Protein: 2 g, Cholesterol: 0 mg, Carbohydrates: 27 g, Sodium: 16 mg

PEAS

——◆◆——

Fresh peas can be removed from their pod just before cooking. Steam or cook peas in a small amount of unsalted water, from 10 to 20 minutes until tender.

Frozen peas, like lima beans, are soaked in brine before freezing to keep them plump, making them fairly high in sodium. A person on a strict low-sodium diet is best advised to avoid frozen peas, except in measured amounts.

Sodium, 1 cup (250 mL): • Fresh, 3 mg •Frozen, 187 mg • Frozen peas and onions, 612 mg • Canned early peas, 700 mg

POTATOES

——◆◆——

For those who believe a meal is not a meal unless there are potatoes, here are 8 recipes! Potatoes are readily available, easy to prepare, and low in sodium.

Sodium, 1 cup (250 mL) except where noted: • 1 medium fresh potato, 5 mg • Frozen french fries (unsalted), 6 mg • Frozen hashed brown potatoes, 460 mg • Packaged au gratin potatoes, 710 mg • Packaged potato pancakes, per 3 pancakes, 490 mg • Packaged mashed potatoes, 660 mg

◆ Baked Potatoes ◆

Just put scrubbed potatoes in the oven and bake them at a temperature between 350°F and 400°F (175°C to 205°C). At the lower temperature, potatoes take longer to cook—tender when pricked with a fork.

For topping your potato, use unsalted margarine. If you are watching your calorie intake and also limiting cholesterol, sour cream and other combinations made from cream are taboo. Chopped chives or diced parsley are great on any kind of potato dish.

◆ Baked New Potatoes ◆

12   *small new potatoes*
1¹/2 *tablespoons (22 mL) safflower oil*
    dash paprika

Wash, peel, and pat dry the potatoes. Line a baking dish with aluminum foil to make cleanup easier. Brush the safflower oil on the baking dish. Add the potatoes and turn each one well to coat with oil. Sprinkle with paprika, turning the potatoes again. Bake in 400°F (205°C) oven for about 1 hour, or until the potatoes are brown and soft.

Calories: 223, Fat: 5 g (0 g saturated), Protein: 4 g, Cholesterol: 0 mg, Carbohydrates: 41 g, Sodium: 8 mg

◆ Boiled Potatoes ◆

These boiled potatoes have seasonings added to the cooking water to increase the flavor. You can also add other seasonings that appeal to you— chopped chives, chopped parsley, a clove of garlic (remove before serving), a peeled onion, thyme, rosemary, curry, dry mustard, or a dash from the Unsalt Shaker (page 39).

5   *medium potatoes*
1   *bay leaf*
¹/4 *teaspoon (1 mL) onion powder*
    dash white pepper

Wash and peel potatoes but leave whole, if small; quarter if large. Drop in saucepan, add cold water to cover, with a seasoning or two that appeal to you. Bring to a boil and boil gently for about 20 minutes or until tender to the touch of a fork. Drain and serve.

Calories: 146, Fat: 0 g (0 g saturated), Protein: 4 g, Cholesterol: 0 mg, Carbohydrates: 33 g, Sodium: 11 mg

♦ Mashed Potatoes ♦

This trick—adding a bay leaf, onion powder, and a hearty dash of white pepper—also helps to take away the bland taste from other cooked potato recipes.

  5 *medium potatoes*
1/4 *teaspoon (1 mL) onion powder*
  1 *bay leaf*
     dash white pepper
1/3 *cup (80 mL) skim milk*
  3 *tablespoons (45 mL) unsalted margarine*

Wash, peel, and quarter the potatoes; put potatoes in a saucepan with cold water to just cover. Add onion powder, bay leaf, and white pepper. Boil for about 20 minutes or until fork tender. Drain off the water by putting potatoes in colander (you can save the potato cooking water to add to homemade soups). Remove the bay leaf. While the potatoes are in the colander, combine milk and margarine in the saucepan; heat briefly. In a bowl, add the cooked potatoes. Mash with a potato masher or an electric mixer. Serve immediately or keep hot in a double boiler.

Calories: 193, Fat: 9 g (2 g saturated), Protein: 4 g, Cholesterol: 0 mg, Carbohydrates: 26 g, Sodium: 19 mg

♦ Scandinavian Mashed Potatoes ♦

To add flavor to plain mashed potatoes, borrow a trick from Scandinavians and add a turnip to the potatoes. You can substitute a turnip for one potato and cook in the same pan. Since turnip is tougher than potato, dice the turnip into smaller pieces. Mash as for Mashed Potatoes (above).

◆ Oven Fries ◆

This is a tastier version of the fries you get in restaurants.

    4   good quality baking potatoes
    2   tablespoons (30 mL) safflower oil
    1   teaspoon (5 mL) paprika
  1/2   teaspoon (2 mL) onion powder

Wash the potatoes and peel, if you like. Cut the potatoes lengthwise and then cut each half into 3 long strips. Place on foil-lined cookie sheet. Combine the oil, paprika, and onion powder in a small bowl. Brush on potato sticks with basting brush or clean fingers. Roast in oven 350° to 475°F (175° to 260°C) until fork tender, about 20 to 30 minutes.

Calories: 283, Fat: 7 g (1 g saturated), Protein: 5 g, Cholesterol: 0 mg, Carbohydrates: 52 g, Sodium: 17 mg

◆ Parsley Potatoes ◆

Small new potatoes, about 3 per person, are also excellent choices.

    4   medium potatoes
    4   tablespoons (60 mL) unsalted margarine
    1   clove garlic, crushed
        dash dry mustard
    2   tablespoons (30 mL) chopped fresh parsley
  1/2   teaspoon (2 mL) lemon juice
        ground black pepper

Peel the potatoes or leave unpeeled, if you prefer; halve or quarter them. Place them in a saucepan with cold water to cover and cook over high heat until they start to boil. Lower heat and cook gently until fork tender, 15 to 20 minutes. Melt the margarine in a saucepan and remove from heat. Stir in the garlic, mustard, parsley, lemon juice, and pepper. Let stand until potatoes are done (this will increase the flavor). Before serving, gently reheat margarine mixture and pour over the potatoes; or you can strain the mixture by pouring through a sieve.

Calories: 214, Fat: 12 g (2 g saturated), Protein: 3 g, Cholesterol: 0 mg, Carbohydrates: 26 g, Sodium: 10 mg

◆ Potato Pancakes ◆

MAKES 8 SERVINGS

A delicious addition to any meal, but especially good with plain meats such as pork chops. Applesauce is often served with potato pancakes. Make just before serving.

3 *medium potatoes*
1 *small onion (optional)*
1 *tablespoon (15 mL) flour*
1 *egg or equivalent egg substitute*
2 *tablespoons (30 mL) skim milk*
1 *tablespoon (15 mL) unsalted margarine, melted*

Preheat a griddle or frying pan over medium heat. Peel the potatoes and onion, if using, and cut them into small pieces. Put them into a blender or food processor. Sprinkle with flour, add the egg and milk, and blend just enough to mix (if you blend too much you'll liquefy the potatoes). Add the margarine. Spoon the batter onto the hot frying pan, about 1/4 cup (60 mL) for each pancake. When the pancakes are brown around the edges, turn them over and cook on the other side.

Calories per pancake: 68, Fat: 2 g (1 g saturated), Protein: 2 g, Cholesterol: 27 mg, Carbohydrates: 11 g, Sodium: 13 mg

SWEET POTATOES AND YAMS

Sweet potatoes and yams are flavorful and almost as versatile as white potatoes. A medium sweet potato has only 14 mg of sodium. But canned sweet potatoes are high in sodium, 122 mg in 1 cup (250 mL).

Don't overlook the easiest way to cook sweet potatoes—bake them as you would white potatoes. Depending on the oven temperature and the size of the potato, it will take 45 to 70 minutes to cook a sweet potato until it's fork tender.

Cook sweet potatoes or yams in their jackets in unsalted water; drain and peel.

◆ Candied Sweet Potatoes ◆

This is the way many people expect sweet potatoes on special occasions.

> *4 medium sweet potatoes*
> *1 tablespoon (15 mL) unsalted margarine*
> *1/2 cup (125 mL) brown sugar*
> *1/4 cup (60 mL) water*

In a large saucepan, cover potatoes with water and boil for 30 minutes or so until they are fork tender. Drain and cool slightly; remove their skins and cut them in half. Melt the margarine in a large frying pan. Mix in the brown sugar and water. Add the potatoes and cook very gently over low heat; turn the potatoes every now and then, and cook for about 15 minutes to "candy" the potatoes.

Calories: 248, Fat: 3 g (1 g saturated), Protein: 2 g, Cholesterol: 0 mg, Carbohydrates: 54 g, Sodium: 19 mg

SPINACH AND OTHER LEAFY GREENS

Spinach is rather high in sodium—94 mg in 1 cup (250 mL), cooked without salt. Plain frozen spinach is about the same as fresh. A strict low-sodium dieter is advised to eat fresh or frozen spinach in measured amounts. And canned spinach has more than 900 mg of sodium in a cup (250 mL). Frozen spinach in cream or butter sauce is as high in sodium as canned spinach.

Kale, collards, beet greens, curly-leafed endive, escarole, and turnip greens can be cooked the same as spinach. Pick over greens carefully, remove any tough or split stems, and wash thoroughly. Cut the leaves before cooking, if you like, using a sharp scissors. Steam the leaves or cook them in very little water until tender, not mushy, from 5 to 15 minutes.

WINTER SQUASHES

All winter squashes or marrows are low in sodium—1 cup (250 mL) has only 2 mg of sodium. Peel and cut up butternut and hubbard squash before cooking. Partially cover with water and boil until fork tender, a half hour or so. You may like to mash the squash before serving.

Frozen butternut and hubbard squash, easier to prepare, are also low in sodium.

◆ Baked Acorn Squash ◆

MAKES 4 SERVINGS

Acorn squash, the easiest of all squashes to prepare, is a good choice when your oven is on for other dishes.

2 *large acorn squashes (more if they're small)*
4 *tablespoons (60 mL) maple syrup*
4 *teaspoons (20 mL) unsalted margarine*

Cut the squash in half, remove the seeds and stringy part to make a "well" in the center; put the halves on a cookie sheet, cut side up. Add a fourth of the maple syrup and a fourth of the unsalted margarine in each "well." (Some cooks like to substitute another syrup or brown sugar.) Bake in 400°F (205°C) oven until soft when pierced with a fork.

Calories: 176, Fat: 12 g (2 g saturated), Protein: 1 g, Cholesterol: 0 mg, Carbohydrates: 19 g, Sodium: 4 mg

TOMATOES

Enjoy the tomato sauce recipes (pages 61–62).

Sodium, 1 cup (250 mL) except where noted: • 1 fresh tomato, 4 mg • Canned whole peeled tomatoes, 1 cup, 440 mg • Canned stewed tomatoes, 1 cup, 710 mg • Canned Libby's stewed tomatoes, 1 cup, 585 mg • Canned low-sodium tomatoes, 1 cup, 30 mg

◆ Fried Tomatoes ◆

Have you ever fried fresh tomatoes? They are an old-fashioned favorite that can really round out a meal.

- 4 *medium tomatoes (ripe or green as you prefer or have available)*
- 1/4 *cup (60 mL) cornmeal*
- 1/4 *teaspoon (1 mL) pepper*
- 1/2 *teaspoon (2 mL) sugar*
- 1 *teaspoon (5 mL) paprika*
- 1 *tablespoon (15 mL) safflower oil*

Slice the tomatoes into 1/4-inch (6-mm) slices. Combine cornmeal, pepper, sugar, and paprika in a shallow bowl. Dip the tomato slices into the cornmeal mixture and turn to coat well on both sides. Heat the oil in a skillet over medium-high heat. Fry the tomato slices until brown on both sides, turning with a pancake turner; drain on paper towels and serve hot.

Calories: 91, Fat: 4 g (0 g saturated), Protein: 2 g, Cholesterol: 0 mg, Carbohydrates: 13 g, Sodium: 12 mg

TURNIPS

Cooked white turnips have 78 mg of sodium in a 1-cup (250-mL) serving; yellow turnips are not so high, with only 10 mg in the same amount. Turnips are often tucked into "soup greens" because they contribute so much taste to the soup. Scandinavian Mashed Potatoes (page 129) are flavored with turnips.

To cook fresh turnips, wash, peel, dice, and cook until tender in boiling, unsalted water. Drain and mash with a potato masher. Season with unsalted margarine, pepper, or grated nutmeg.

ZUCCHINI AND SUMMER SQUASH

◆◆

Fresh summer squash and zucchini cook in the same time and so easily. Scrub vegetables and cut large ones into slices or wedges and leave very small ones whole. Cook in a small amount of water about 10 to 15 minutes or until tender. You can also steam them; the exact time depends on the size of the slices. Serve hot or cold.

Sodium, 1 cup (250 mL): • Fresh, 2 mg of sodium • Frozen baby zucchini, 4 mg • Canned zucchini in tomato sauce, 832 mg

◆ Five-Minute Zucchini ◆

MAKES 4 SERVINGS

Faster than a frozen vegetable and delicious, this recipe can be made just before serving. It also works with summer squash. Good with freshly ground pepper and a sprinkling of garlic powder.

2   *medium zucchini or summer squash*
1   *tablespoon (15 mL) unsalted margarine*
1   *tablespoon (15 mL) olive oil*

Wash the zucchini and shred using a food processor or hand grater. Heat the margarine and oil over medium heat. Add the shredded squash. Cook for a few minutes, stirring frequently. Serve warm.

Calories: 69, Fat: 6 g (1 g saturated), Protein: 1 g, Cholesterol: 0 mg, Carbohydrates: 3 g, Sodium: 3 mg

PASTA AND PIZZA

◆◆◆◆◆

Spaghetti and other shapes of pasta are logical parts of a low-sodium diet because they have only a very small amount of sodium, plus no fat or cholesterol!

Pasta has protein, but it's an incomplete protein. For this reason, it's traditionally served with a small amount of a complete protein food, such as cheese or meat. If you are able to find a supplier of tasty low-sodium cheese, you can grate a small amount to add to plain pasta. Otherwise, leave it out or measure the small amounts of regular salted cheese that you use very carefully.

A serving of pasta is supposed to be two ounces (60 g), which is a small serving.

The traditional ingredients in commercial spaghetti sauces are so high in sodium that they must be avoided: canned plum tomatoes, canned tomato sauce or purée, and most prepared spaghetti sauces.

Fresh tomatoes would be a nutritious addition to a sauce when and if they are available where you live.

◆ Spaghetti and White Clam Sauce ◆

MAKES 4 SERVINGS

Canned clams and clam juice may be convenient, but they are outrageously high in sodium. If you and your family love clam sauce, wait to buy fresh clams. Hard-shelled clams (also called quahogs, cherry stones, little necks) are quite high in sodium—465 mg in 1 cup (250 mL). Soft-shelled clams are much lower—82 mg in 1 cup (250 mL)—but very perishable. If you live where soft-shelled clams are available, substitute them.

1/4 cup raw (60 mL) clams,* diced
1/3 cup (80 mL) olive oil
  3 cloves garlic, finely minced
  2 tablespoons (30 mL) parsley, finely chopped (optional)
  2 teaspoons (10 mL) cornstarch
1/2 cup (125 mL) water

1/2 cup (125 mL) vermouth
     dash white pepper
1/2 teaspoon (2 mL) oregano (optional)
     garlic powder to taste (optional)
  8 ounces (225 g) linguini or spaghetti cooked
     without salt

Prepare the clams: use a knife or steam them open. To steam: Pour 1 cup (250 mL) water into a large saucepan; cover and bring to a boil. Scrub the outsides of the clams with a vegetable brush; add the clams to the boiling water. Cover and steam over high heat, approximately 5 minutes. Check after 2 minutes to see if the shells are open. When they are open, turn off the heat. Remove the clams from the shells and dice. Some cooks prefer to use only the parts with a firm texture and discard the soft "bellies."

To make the clam sauce: Heat the olive oil in a frying pan and cook the garlic, parsley, and clams over low heat for 3 to 5 minutes. While this is cooking, in a small bowl stir the cornstarch in the water and vermouth until smooth; add to the olive oil and clams. Sprinkle with pepper and oregano, if desired. Cook over low heat for a minute or so until sauce thickens slightly. Cook linguini according to package directions, except leave out the salt. Drain linguini and turn into a serving dish. Pour the sauce over the linguini and toss. Some cooks like to sprinkle garlic powder on their serving.

* Since clams are fairly high in sodium, the amount used must be small. To get the 1/4 cup (60 mL) of diced clams, you can buy approximately 12 very small hard-shell clams (2 inches or 5 cm across at the widest), or 5 medium-size clams (3 inches or 8 cm across at the widest), or 3 large clams.

**Calories: 411, Fat: 19 g (3 g saturated), Protein: 9 g,
Cholesterol: 5 mg, Carbohydrates: 46 g, Sodium: 16 mg**

◆ Spaghetti with Tuna ◆

Substitute one small can of low-sodium tuna for the clams in Spaghetti and White Clam Sauce (opposite page).

◆ Macaroni and Cheese ◆

  2 tablespoons (30 mL) unsalted margarine
  2 tablespoons (30 mL) flour
1/8 teaspoon (.5 mL) white pepper, less for a milder taste
1/2 teaspoon (2 mL) dry mustard
1/4 teaspoon (1 mL) onion powder
  1 cup (250 mL) skim milk
1/4 cup (60 mL) dry vermouth
1/8 teaspoon (.5 mL) turmeric, to make the casserole
    yellow (optional)
1 1/2 cups (375 mL) low-sodium cheese, such as no-salt
    Swiss-type, grated
  8 ounces (225 g) macaroni, elbow macaroni, tubetti, or
    other shapes

To make the sauce, melt the margarine over low heat in a large saucepan. Stir in the flour, pepper, mustard, and onion powder and cook over low heat for a couple of minutes. Add the milk and vermouth and stir over medium heat until the sauce thickens. Add the turmeric and cheese; stir until the cheese is melted. Cook the macaroni according to package directions, except leave out the salt; drain the macaroni; add to the cheese sauce; stir to combine. Serve hot.

**Calories: 319, Fat: 14 g (7 g saturated), Protein: 14 g,
Cholesterol: 29 mg, Carbohydrates: 33 g, Sodium: 31 mg**

◆ Lasagne ◆

MAKES 6 SERVINGS

  1 pound (450 g) very lean ground beef
 12 ounces (340 g) no-salt-added tomato paste
  2 cups (500 mL) water
  1 teaspoon (5 mL) basil
1/8 teaspoon (.5 mL) pepper
  1 teaspoon (5 mL) onion powder
1/2 teaspoon (2 mL) garlic powder
  2 tablespoons (30 mL) sugar
  2 tablespoons (30 mL) cider vinegar

3   tablespoons (45 mL) unsalted margarine
1/4 cup (60 mL) flour
1   cup (250 mL) skim milk
1/2 pound (225 g) low-sodium cheese (such as no-salt-added
    Swiss), grated
1/2 lb. (225 g) lasagne noodles

Make the sauce: In a large skillet, brown the meat; drain off any fat. Add the tomato paste, water, seasonings, sugar, and vinegar; simmer 25 minutes.

While the sauce is simmering, make the cheese sauce: Melt the margarine over low heat and add the flour; stir with a wire whisk for a couple of minutes; add the milk and stir with the wire whisk; cook over low heat for about 5 to 10 minutes; remove from the heat and stir in the grated cheese. Cook the lasagne noodles as directed on the box, except do not add salt to the cooking water; drain.

In a shallow baking dish assemble the lasagne: Spoon a little of the ground beef sauce, spread a layer of a third of the cooked noodles, add a layer of cheese sauce. Repeat until all are used up, ending with a cheese layer. Bake in 350°F (175°C) oven for about 30 minutes; let stand for about 10 minutes before cutting. You can also assemble the lasagne ahead of time, refrigerate, and heat later. Allow more time to heat through, if it has been refrigerated.

Calories: 617, Fat: 32 g (14 g saturated), Protein: 32 g,
Cholesterol: 91 mg, Carbohydrates: 51 g, Sodium: 132 mg

◆ Vegetarian Lasagne ◆

MAKES 6 SERVINGS

You can have this lasagne ready to pop in the oven in the time it takes to boil the noodles, if your sauce is all ready.

4   tablespoons (60 mL) unsalted margarine
2   small zucchini, sliced thin
1/2 pound (225 g) mushrooms, thin sliced
2   tablespoons (30 mL) cornstarch
2   tablespoons (30 mL) cold water
1/2 cup (125 mL) skim milk
8   ounces (225 g) lasagne noodles
3   cups (750 mL) Tomato Sauce (page 61)
1/2 pound (225 g) unsalted cheese, such as unsalted
    Swiss, grated

To make the vegetable-cream sauce: Melt the margarine over low heat in a skillet; add the sliced zucchini and mushrooms and cook until they are lightly browned. In a small bowl, dissolve the cornstarch in the water. Add the milk and stir together. Add this mixture to the zucchini and mushrooms. Cook over medium heat for about 10 minutes, or until the sauce is smooth and thick.

Meanwhile, cook the lasagne noodles as directed on the box, except leave out the salt.

To assemble, start with a thin layer of the tomato sauce. Add a layer of cooked drained noodles. Cover with approximately a third of the mushroom-zucchini mixture. Add a third of the grated cheese. Repeat with layers of tomato sauce, noodles, and mushroom-zucchini and end with cheese. Bake in 350°F (175°C) oven for about 20 minutes; let stand for a few minutes before slicing.

Calories: 490, Fat: 21 g (10 g saturated), Protein: 19 g,
Cholesterol: 38 mg, Carbohydrates: 56 g, Sodium: 78 mg

◆ Stuffed Shells ◆

MAKES 6 SERVINGS

This vegetarian meal can be made ahead and baked just before dinner. It calls for tofu, which is becoming relatively popular. It is made from soy and has virtually no sodium, fat, or cholesterol. You will find it in the produce section of the grocery store. If you don't see it, ask! You may want to double the filling recipe so that you will not have ricotta cheese and tofu left over. If so, freeze the filling for a future convenient meal.

  8 *ounces (225 g) jumbo shells*
  1 *tablespoon (15 mL) olive or safflower oil*
  1 *medium onion, finely chopped*
  1 *clove garlic, finely minced*
1/4 *cup (60 mL) water*
  2 *tablespoons (30 mL) lemon juice*
  1 *cup (250 mL) tofu*
  2 *tablespoons (30 mL) flour*
  1 *egg or equivalent egg substitute*
  1 *cup (250 mL) ricotta cheese*
  3 *tablespoons (45 mL) parsley, finely chopped*

1/4   *teaspoon (1 mL) onion powder*

1/4   *teaspoon (1 mL) garlic powder*

1/2   *teaspoon (2 mL) oregano*

1/8   *teaspoon (.5 mL) white pepper*

  1   *cup (250 mL) grated low-sodium cheese (such as no-salt-added Swiss)*

  2   *cups (500 mL) Tomato Sauce (page 61)*

Cook the shells in boiling water as directed on the box, except do not add salt to the cooking water; drain. Meanwhile, heat the oil in a large skillet. Pan-fry the onion and garlic. Put the water, lemon juice, tofu, and flour into a blender or food processor. Purée until the mixture is very smooth. Add this mixture to the onion and garlic. In a bowl, beat the egg or egg substitute lightly. Add the ricotta cheese, parsley, seasonings and grated cheese. Stir to combine. Spoon a thin layer of the tomato sauce in a large baking dish. Using a spoon, fill each cooked and drained shell with the cheese mixture. Place the stuffed shells in a single layer in the dish. Cover with tomato sauce. You may wish to reserve part of the tomato sauce to serve heated with the shells. Bake in 350°F (175°C) oven for approximately 30 minutes.

Calories: 457, Fat: 16 g (7 g saturated), Protein: 22 g, Cholesterol: 67 mg, Carbohydrates: 57 g, Sodium: 127 mg

◆ Pasta Primavera ◆

MAKES 4 SERVINGS

An easy side dish that combines vegetables with pasta (carbohydrate). Yet it's fancy enough for any company meal. If you want to make it the main dish, you may want to add small amounts of a protein food, such as small pieces of cooked chicken or other meat, low-sodium canned tuna, or low-sodium cheese.

  2   *tablespoons (30 mL) olive oil*

  2   *tablespoons (30 mL) unsalted margarine*

  2   *cloves garlic, finely minced*

  2   *cups (500 mL) broccoli,* fresh or frozen, cut into fairly small pieces*

  1   *cup (250 mL) sweet red or green peppers,* cut into thin strips*

  1   *cup (250 mL) carrots,* cut into thin strips, approximately 1 to 1¹/2 inches (2.5 to 4 cm) long*

8 ounces (225 g) linguini or another pasta
ground black pepper
garlic powder (optional)

Heat the oil and margarine in a frying pan; add the garlic and vegetables and cook for approximately 10 minutes. The vegetables should still have some crispness. Cook the linguini as directed on the box, but leave out the salt. Drain the linguini and toss in a large bowl with the vegetables using two large spoons. Grind the pepper on top and toss again. Garlic lovers will want garlic powder sprinkled on top. It helps to make up for the missing Parmesan cheese.

*You can also add or substitute other fresh vegetables that are available, such as mushroom slices, cherry tomatoes, sliced zucchini, or yellow summer squash. As long as the total is approximately 4 cups (1 L) of small vegetable pieces, the choice is up to you. It's most appealing when there are vegetables in more than one color.

Calories: 355, Fat: 14 g (2 g saturated), Protein: 9 g, Cholesterol: 0 mg, Carbohydrates: 50 g, Sodium: 24 mg

◆ Macaroni and Beef Casserole ◆

MAKES 4 SERVINGS

1 pound (450 g) lean ground beef
1 small onion, finely chopped
1 tablespoon (15 mL) safflower oil
1 teaspoon (5 mL) oregano
6 ounces (170 mL) no-salt-added tomato paste, diluted
with 1 cup (250 mL) water
8 ounces (225 g) macaroni
1/8 teaspoon (.5 mL) cumin (optional)

Over medium heat, cook ground beef in skillet, breaking up with a fork; cook until no pink color remains. Drain off any fat by spreading meat on a paper towel. Sauté chopped onion in oil until soft. Add oregano, tomato paste, and water and stir to combine. Add cooked meat. Cook macaroni in unsalted water for about 9 to 12 minutes; drain macaroni. Toss with the beef sauce.

Calories: 587, Fat: 28 g (10 g saturated), Protein: 29 g, Cholesterol: 85 mg, Carbohydrates: 53 g, Sodium: 121 mg

NOODLES

———◆◆———

Noodles are low in sodium—1 mg in a 2-ounce (60-g) serving. Commercially prepared noodle dishes, however, are very high. A person eating one-fourth of a box of Betty Crocker noodles romanoff takes in 705 mg of sodium. Although "egg noodles" are made with egg, the amount of egg and cholesterol is quite small. A two-ounce (60-g) serving of cooked noodles has 18 mg of cholesterol. (To put this in perspective remember that the yolk of a large egg has 250 mg of cholesterol.) Cholesterol-free egg noodles are available in many markets.

Here are some ideas for noodles cooked in unsalted water and served with unsalted margarine: Serve noodles with other dishes that have a flavorful sauce such as Beef Goulash (page 173), Chicken Marsala (page 165), Chicken Marengo (page 159), Beef Bourguignon (page 173) or Swiss Steak (page 172); use noodles in recipes that traditionally call for other types of pasta, such as Pasta Primavera (page 141); toss noodles with small amounts of left-over Tomato Sauce (page 61). Make a flavorful noodle dish such as Garlic-Flavored Noodles (page 144) or Fresh Parsley Pesto and Fettucine (below).

◆ Fresh Parsley Pesto and Fettucine ◆

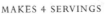

MAKES 4 SERVINGS

Green sauce for noodles? Yes. Try this when you feel adventurous and are pressed for time. This is especially good when served with a generous tossed salad. Fresh basil in place of fresh parsley is the traditional pesto. In addition to the fresh basil, traditional pesto is made with pine nuts. Use pine nuts, or substitute less expensive walnuts, as we have.

1/2 teaspoon (2 mL) basil, dried, or double amount of
  fresh basil
1/2 cup (125 mL) fresh parsley clusters
  2 large cloves garlic
1/2 cup (125 mL) walnuts
  4 teaspoons (20 mL) lemon juice
  4 ounces (120 g) no-salt Swiss cheese
  2 teaspoons (10 mL) olive oil
  8 ounces (225 g) fettucine or egg noodles

Combine the basil, parsley, garlic, walnuts, cheese, and lemon juice in the blender or food processor. Turn on the blender and slowly add the olive oil; blend until smooth. Stop the blender and scrape down the sides. Cook the fettucine without salt. Drain and turn into a warm bowl. Pour sauce over the fettucine. Serve warm.

**Calories: 437, Fat: 22 g (8 g saturated), Protein: 17 g,
Cholesterol: 82 mg, Carbohydrates: 44 g, Sodium: 23 mg**

◆ Garlic-Flavored Noodles ◆

MAKES 4 SERVINGS

3   tablespoons (45 mL) unsalted margarine
1   tablespoon (15 mL) olive oil
1   clove garlic, crushed
1   tablespoon (15 mL) fresh parsley, chopped fine
1   teaspoon (5 mL) lemon juice
8   ounces (225 g) noodles

Melt the margarine in a skillet; add the oil and garlic. Cook gently for 5 minutes; add the parsley and lemon juice; stir to combine. Cook the noodles in boiling water according to package directions—except leave out the salt in the cooking water; drain. Combine the noodles and sauce in a bowl; toss well before serving.

**Calories: 298, Fat: 12 g (2 g saturated), Protein: 8 g,
Cholesterol: 54 mg, Carbohydrates: 41 g, Sodium: 13 mg**

◆ Pizza ◆

MAKES 4 SERVINGS

You can make this family-pleasing pizza quickly, possibly in less time than it would take to have it delivered from a pizza parlor. The dough doesn't need to rise, so you can make and eat it right away. To prevent the pizza from sticking to the pan, you can use a nonstick pan, or sprinkle a fine layer of cornmeal on the pan, or coat the pan with vegetable or olive oil.

How many pizzas do you want to make? If you like to make extra, double this recipe. You can roll the extra dough into pizzas that would be the right size for your family and bake and freeze the baked dough. Or you can wrap the raw dough and freeze it for a short time.

3/4 cup (185 mL) lukewarm water (neither hot nor cold
    to the touch)

1 envelope packaged dry yeast

1 tablespoon (15 mL) sugar

2 cups (500 mL) flour, preferably bread flour or
    all-purpose flour (not self-rising flour)

1/8 teaspoon ground black pepper

2 tablespoons (30 mL) olive oil
    cornmeal to sprinkle on the pans

1/2 recipe Tomato Sauce (page 61)
    1/2 recipe Pizza Toppings (recipe follows)
    no-salt Swiss or low-sodium cheese

Pour 1/4 cup (60 mL) of the lukewarm water into a small bowl; stir in the yeast
and sugar; let stand for 5 minutes. In a large mixing bowl, combine the yeast
mixture, the remaining 1/2 cup (125 mL) of lukewarm water, about 1 1/2 cups
(375 mL) of flour, the pepper, and the olive oil. Stir with a large spoon.

Dust a little of the remaining flour on your work area or bread board; make
a pile of the rest of the flour off to one side of the work area. Put the dough
on the floured surface; knead for about 3 to 5 minutes until the dough is
shiny and elastic; use the reserved flour while you knead to keep the dough
from sticking to the work surface. Divide the dough into parts according to
the number and size of pizzas you want to make. One 12-inch (30-cm)
pizza and one 8-inch (20-cm) pizza is a popular choice. Use a rolling pin to
roll out the dough into "pizza" shapes and the thickness you like. Sprinkle a
light coating of cornmeal on your pie pans, cookie sheets, or pizza pans.
Shape the dough on the pans. Spread with sauce and top with your favorite
topping and cheese. Bake in 450°F (230°C) oven for about 15 to 20 minutes; using a pancake turner, you can carefully lift an edge of the pizza to
see if the bottom is lightly browned. Serve warm. You might like to try a
sprinkle of garlic powder on your pizza just before serving.

It would be almost impossible to list how many mg of sodium or calories
you are getting. How thick is the crust? What are the toppings?

◆ Pizza Toppings ◆

Pan-fry thin slices of mushrooms, green or red peppers, or onion in a small amount of olive oil with a dash of basil and oregano. Or, leave the vegetables raw if you like a crunchy topping.

To make ground beef taste like sausage (which is too high in sodium): Make fennel tea by pouring 1/4 cup (60 mL) boiling water over 1 tablespoon (15 mL) fennel seeds; steep for a few minutes. Strain the fennel tea into a skillet. Add 1/4 pound (120 g) of ground beef and pan-fry. Drain the meat on paper before using it as a pizza topping.

FISH AND SEAFOOD

$$\blacklozenge\blacklozenge\blacklozenge\blacklozenge\blacklozenge$$

If you or someone in your family has been placed on any kind of diet, chances are that fish was recommended because it is low in calories and fat. Commercially frozen fish is usually immersed in brine during the freezing process. Good fresh fish does taste better. Ideally, you should try to find a local market or department with a quick fish turnover. Buy and serve fish the same day for maximum flavor and freshness.

Even though "saltwater" fish swim around in the salty ocean, the sodium content is not higher than that of freshwater fish. Although the sodium content varies in different fish, it should not be your first consideration. Select fresh fish according to availability and reasonable prices.

FREEZING FISH

If you have fresh fish and would like to freeze it for later use, here is the way an old New England fisherman recommends that you do it: Choose only the freshest fish for freezing. To prepare the fish, first clean and fillet it, then rinse well. Select sturdy freezer containers. If the container is not adequate, the fish will dry out. Place the fillets in the freezer container in the amount you will defrost for one meal. Cover the fish with fresh water. Leave an inch of head space for expansion. Seal the container.

Use your frozen fish in recipes that have a tasty sauce: Shrimp or Fish Creole (page 155); Horseradish Gravy (page 45).

If you are absolutely unable to find fresh fish, buy frozen fish and rinse it before cooking. It has been shown that rinsing canned tuna fish through a plastic strainer drastically reduces the sodium content. Rinsing the tuna under running tap water for three minutes removes nearly all of the sodium that had been added during processing. You may want to rinse defrosted fish fillets and use them in place of fresh fillets.

SHELLFISH

— ◆◆ —

Shellfish is high enough in sodium and cholesterol to be considered off-limits to most people who need to cut down: lobster has 212 mg of sodium, 72 mg of cholesterol, and 81 calories in a 3-ounce (90-g) serving; scallops have 217 mg of sodium, 30 mg of cholesterol, and 95 calories in a 3-ounce (90-g) serving; canned crab has 1,700 mg of sodium per cup (250 mL); sodium content of frozen crabmeat may vary. Unfortunately, USDA handbooks do not list fresh crab's nutritional content. Shrimp are also high in cholesterol.

You may be fortunate enough to live in an area where people go crabbing to catch fresh crabs. If so, you probably know how to cook fresh crabs. Just remember to leave out all the salty cooking aids; read the label on anything you plan to use. Crabmeat that comes in the small, expensive packages may have been "freshened" in brine.

Shrimp are high in cholesterol—45 mg in 5 large shrimp. Check with your doctor or dietitian if you are on a low-cholesterol diet. But shrimp are a fairly good source of calcium.

Aside from the cholesterol, fresh shrimp make a special treat. Be sure to buy fresh shrimp, since canned and frozen shrimp have much added sodium. If you can't buy fresh shrimp, don't buy it at all. A 3-ounce (90-g) portion of fresh shrimp has 119 mg of sodium, fairly high for a protein food; the same amount of chicken has only 56 mg of sodium. Buy 1 pound (450 g) to serve four, leaving 12 ounces (340 g) of shrimp after the shells are discarded.

◆ Fish Baked in Foil ◆

MAKES 4 SERVINGS

This method works well on an outdoor grill—easy and very little mess to clean up.

> 1 pound (450 g) fresh fish fillets
> dash paprika
> 4 onion slices
> 4 green pepper slices
> 4 fresh lemon slices
> ground black pepper

Rinse, pat dry, and cut the fish into four pieces. Cut heavy aluminum foil into 4 pieces about 12" by 12". Put a piece of fish on each square of foil;

sprinkle generously with paprika. Lay a slice of onion and green pepper on each piece; squeeze the lemon slice over the fish and lay it on the top. Fold the foil around the fish to seal. For oven baking, put the foil packages on a cookie sheet. Bake in 425°F (220°C) oven for 15 minutes or so. For an outdoor grill, put the packages on the grill. Fish will flake easily when it's done.

**Calories: 178, Fat: 8 g (1 g saturated), Protein: 24 g,
Cholesterol: 66 mg, Carbohydrates: 4 g, Sodium: 60 mg**

◆ Broiled Fish Steaks ◆

MAKES 4 SERVINGS

Good for salmon or swordfish steaks. Using a charcoal grill is another good way to cook fish steaks.

1 pound (450 g) salmon or swordfish steaks
2 tablespoons (30 mL) safflower oil
2 tablespoons (30 mL) lemon juice

Preheat the broiler with the broiler pan six inches from the heat. Combine the oil and lemon juice and brush the broiler rack lightly with some of the mixture to prevent the fish from sticking. Brush both sides of the fish lightly with more of the lemon juice and oil. Broil for five minutes. Baste the fish again; turn it over and baste again. Broil for another five minutes or until the fish flakes easily when touched with a fork.

**Calories: 194, Fat: 11 g (1 g saturated), Protein: 23 g,
Cholesterol: 59 mg, Carbohydrates: 1 g, Sodium: 76 mg**

◆ Broiled Marinated Fish or Shrimp ◆

MAKES 4 SERVINGS

2 tablespoons (30 mL) olive oil
1 tablespoon (15 mL) parsley, finely chopped
1/4 cup (60 mL) lemon juice
2 cloves garlic, chopped
1 cup (250 mL) white wine
1/8 teaspoon (.5 mL) black or white pepper
1 pound (450 g) boneless fish fillets or shrimp, cleaned

Mix oil, parsley, lemon juice, garlic, wine, and pepper in a nonmetal bowl. Put the fish fillets into marinade and refrigerate for at least two hours. Preheat the broiler and brush the hot rack with the marinade. Broil close to the heat for approximately 5 minutes until fish flakes when touched with a fork; broil shrimp about 3 minutes.

**Calories: 228, Fat: 9 g (1 g saturated), Protein: 23 g,
Cholesterol: 172 mg, Carbohydrates: 4 g, Sodium: 174 mg**

◆ Broiled Fish ◆

MAKES 4 SERVINGS

1   *pound (450 g) fresh fish fillets*
2   *tablespoons (30 mL) unsalted margarine*
2   *teaspoons (10 mL) lemon juice*
    ground black pepper

Wash and dry the fillets. Place the margarine, lemon juice, and pepper in a saucepan over low heat. Brush a broiler pan with some of the melted margarine mixture. Place the fish on the rack. Brush with remaining margarine mixture. Broil a few inches from the heat for about 10 minutes, turning once, or until the fish flakes easily with a fork.

**Calories: 219, Fat: 13 g (2 g saturated), Protein: 24 g,
Cholesterol: 66 mg, Carbohydrates: 0 g, Sodium: 59 mg**

◆ Baked Stuffed Fish ◆

MAKES 6 SERVINGS

This recipe is especially good for large fish and takes very little effort.

1   *large fish, cleaned with head and tail removed*
1   *medium onion*
1   *green pepper*
3   *tablespoons (45 mL) lemon juice*
2   *tablespoons (30 mL) chopped fresh parsley*
1/4 *teaspoon (1 mL) paprika*
    ground black pepper

Wash the fish and pat dry. Put the fish on its side in a pan large enough to accommodate the fish. Slice the onion and the green pepper. Lift up the top half of the fish and arrange the vegetables in the cavity. Sprinkle lemon juice, parsley, paprika, and pepper over the vegetables. Pull the top of the fish over the filling; cover the pan loosely with foil. Bake in 425°F (220°C) oven for about 30 minutes until the fish flakes easily with a fork.

Nutritional information may vary according to size and type of fish.

◆ Baked Breaded Fish ◆

MAKES 4 SERVINGS

This is a great way to serve fish to guests who usually don't eat fish. The fish is moist and tender when it's baked in Roll and Bake Coating Mix.

1 pound (450 g) fresh fish fillets
1 cup (250 mL) Roll and Bake Coating Mix (page 42)
1/3 cup (80 mL) lemon juice

Wash, dry, and cut fish into serving-size pieces. Put the coating mix in one bowl and the juice in another. Line a baking pan with aluminum foil to make cleanup easier. Dip each piece of fish into the juice and into the coating mix, using your hand to press the mix onto the fish. Place in a baking pan; bake in 350°F (175°C) oven for about 10 to 15 minutes, depending on the thickness of the fish; fish is done when it flakes easily with a fork.

Calories: 178, 8 g fat (1 g saturated), Protein: 24 g, Cholesterol: 66 mg, Carbohydrates: 3 g, Sodium: 59 mg

◆ Fish in Wine ◆

MAKES 4 SERVINGS

If you've never cooked fish before, this is a good first recipe. The fish and wine may vary somewhat in sodium content depending on the varieties you choose.

1 pound (450 g) fresh fish fillets
1 medium onion, thinly sliced
1 green pepper, thinly sliced
3 tablespoons (45 mL) lemon juice
3/4 cup (190 mL) dry white wine, not cooking wine
1/4 cup (60 mL) Roll and Bake Coating Mix (page 42)

Wash the fillets and leave them whole. Line a baking pan with aluminum foil to make cleanup easier and spread fillets on the foil. Cover with the vegetables and the lemon juice. Pour the wine over the top and sprinkle on the coating mix. Bake in 350°F (175°C) oven until tender, about 20 minutes.

Calories: 172, 2 g fat (0 g saturated), Protein: 24 g, Cholesterol: 59 mg, Carbohydrates: 7 g, Sodium: 103 mg

◆ Sautéed Fish ◆

This method of cooking fish on the stovetop is easy and tasty.

> 1   *pound (450 g) fresh fish fillets*
> 1/3 *cup (80 mL) lemon juice*
> 1/3 *cup (80 mL) Roll and Bake Coating Mix (page 42)*
> 1   *tablespoon (15 mL) safflower oil*
> 1   *medium onion, chopped*
> 1   *clove garlic, chopped*

Wash, dry, and cut the fish into serving-size pieces. Pour lemon juice into one bowl and coating mix into another. Dip each piece in lemon juice, then place each in coating mix and use your hand to press the coating on. Heat the oil in a skillet. Sauté the onion and garlic gently for about 5 minutes. Slip in the fish and sauté for about 5 minutes; turn the fish over with a spatula and fry gently until browned.

Calories: 171, 5 g fat (1 g saturated), Protein: 24 g, Cholesterol: 58 mg, Carbohydrates: 7 g, Sodium: 100 mg

◆ Batter-Fried Fish or Shrimp ◆

> 4   *tablespoons (60 mL) flour*
> 1   *tablespoon (15 mL) cornstarch*
> 1/2 *teaspoon (2 mL) low-sodium baking powder (shake before using)*
> 1/4 *cup (60 mL) water*
> 1   *tablespoon (15 mL) egg substitute*
> 1   *pound (450 g) boneless fish fillets or shrimp*
>   *oil for frying*

Mix 3 tablespoons (45 mL) flour with the cornstarch, baking powder, water, and egg substitute in a bowl. Beat with a wire whisk until the batter is smooth and foamy. Wash the fish, pat dry, and cut into serving-size pieces; dust lightly with the remaining flour. Turn each piece over in the batter to coat well. Pour oil in a frying pan and heat to 375°F (190°C); an electric frying pan is best. Slip each fish slice into the hot oil. Cook fish for 5 to 7 minutes on each side, until golden brown; fry shrimp for 3 minutes. Drain on a double layer of paper towels. Serve plain or with lemon juice or vinegar.

**Calories: 149, Fat: 2 g (0 g saturated), Protein: 24 g,
Cholesterol: 40 mg, Carbohydrates: 8 g, Sodium: 78 mg**

◆ Pan-Fried Fish ◆

MAKES 4 SERVINGS

This is a recipe traditionally used for fresh trout that is not filleted before cooking.

1   *pound (450 g) fresh fish fillets, or whole cleaned fish**
2   *tablespoons (30 mL) flour*
1/4 *teaspoon (1 mL) paprika*
     dash white pepper
1   *tablespoon (15 mL) unsalted margarine*
1   *tablespoon (15 mL) safflower oil*

Rinse the fish, pat dry, and cut into serving pieces. Meanwhile, mix the flour, paprika, and white pepper together on a large plate. Coat each piece of fish with the flour mixture. Melt the margarine in a frying pan. Add the oil and heat so it's good and hot. Slide the fish into the hot frying pan and cook for 3 or 4 minutes on each side. The fish should be golden brown and flake easily. Whole fish will need to cook longer.

* You may want to pan-fry your fish Southern style: Dip the fish into the flour mixture and then into egg substitute and coat with cornmeal.

**Calories: 246, Fat: 14 g (2 g saturated), Protein: 25 g,
Cholesterol: 69 mg, Carbohydrates: 3 g, Sodium: 62 mg**

SERVING FISH AND SEAFOOD

◆◆

Just about any fish tastes better with lemon juice, and lemon wedges add a nice touch. Some people prefer to sprinkle vinegar on their fish when served. Specialty fish restaurants often keep malt vinegar on the tables. Tartar Sauce (page 48) is low in sodium, but higher in fat and calories.

◆ Shrimp Scampi ◆

MAKES 4 SERVINGS

Scampi is traditionally served with spaghetti or linguini tossed with olive oil. Two ounces of pasta add 210 calories, but only a trace of sodium.

1   pound (450 g) fresh shrimp in shells
3   tablespoons (45 mL) unsalted margarine
1   tablespoon (15 mL) olive or safflower oil
1   clove garlic, halved
1   tablespoon (15 mL) parsley, chopped
1   teaspoon (5 mL) lemon juice

Remove the shrimp shells and black "vein." Wash the shrimp. Melt the margarine in a frying pan. Add the oil and garlic; sauté for a few minutes. Add the shrimp, parsley, and lemon juice. Cook slowly over low heat, turning, until shrimp turns pink, about 5 minutes. Remove the garlic Serve immediately.

**Calories: 228, Fat: 14 g (2 g saturated), Protein: 23 g,
Cholesterol: 172 mg, Carbohydrates: 2 g, Sodium: 169 mg**

◆ Shrimp or Fish Creole ◆

Don't think that only convenience foods are convenient. This dish is very fast and easy.

1   tablespoon *(15 mL) olive oil*
1   *medium onion, finely chopped*
1/2   *green pepper, finely chopped*
6   *ounces (170 mL) no-salt-added tomato paste*
    ground black pepper
1/2   *teaspoon (2 mL) onion powder*
2   *teaspoons (10 mL) sugar*
2   *teaspoons (10 mL) lemon juice*
3   *dashes Tabasco sauce (more if you like it hotter)*
1 1/2   *cup (375 mL) water*
1   *pound (450 g) fresh shrimp, shelled, or fish fillets, washed*

Heat the oil in a large frying pan. Add the onion and green pepper and sauté over medium heat for approximately five minutes. Add the tomato paste, seasonings, sugar, lemon juice, and water and simmer over low heat. Add the shrimp or fish to the sauce and simmer for approximately 5 to 8 minutes, depending on the size of the shrimp or fish.

**Calories: 105, Fat: 3 g (0 g saturated), Protein: 13 g,
Cholesterol: 86 mg, Carbohydrates: 8 g, Sodium: 105 mg**

POULTRY

◆◆◆◆◆

Chicken is economical, low in fat and cholesterol, and fairly low in sodium. No wonder anyone on a special diet is usually advised to eat the white meat, which comes from the chicken breast—lower in sodium and calories. Therefore, the recipes in this book call for chicken breasts. Whole chickens, however, are less expensive and you may prefer to use them cut in serving pieces. If you do substitute the whole chicken, serve the breast portion to the person who needs to be especially careful about his or her diet.

If you are trying to cut down on fat or calories, it makes sense to remove the chicken skin before you cook it. A person who is on a strict diet is usually told to limit the serving to 3 ounces (90 g) of cooked chicken or about one breast. A kitchen scale is the most accurate way to know how large a serving is.

With the recipes that follow you can substitute other cuts of chicken. Allow less time for boneless chicken cutlets to cook.

◆ Barbecued Chicken ◆

MAKES 4 SERVINGS

If you like barbecue chicken the way restaurants serve it, use Barbecue Sauce.

4 chicken breasts (2 pounds / 1 kg), trimmed
Barbecue Sauce (page 46) or a marinade (pages 57–60)

Several hours or the day before planning to serve, wash chicken and discard the skin. Mix together the barbecue sauce or marinade in a nonmetal bowl. Put chicken pieces in the sauce or marinade; cover and refrigerate for several hours or overnight.

To barbecue, oven method: Preheat the oven to 400°F (205°C). Arrange the chicken in a baking pan and spoon about a third of the sauce or marinade over the chicken. Cover with aluminum foil. Bake for about 20 minutes. Uncover, turn the chicken over, and baste. Cover again and continue baking 20 minutes. Remove aluminum foil, and cook uncovered for 5 to 10 minutes to brown. Serve warm with extra sauce or marinade and with cooked rice.

Indoor or outdoor charcoal broiling method: Arrange the chicken on the broiler pan; brush with sauce or marinade. Broil, checking every 2 to 3 minutes to avoid overcooking. After 5 to 6 minutes, turn the chicken. Brush again with the marinade and broil until the chicken is tender.

Nutritional information varies.

◆ Chicken Fricassee ◆

MAKES 4 SERVINGS

A classic recipe that is so easy to fix. It almost cooks by itself. Excellent with Quick Biscuits (page 69).

> 4 *chicken breasts(2 pounds / 1 kg), trimmed*
> 1/4 *cup (60 mL) flour*
> 1/2 *teaspoon (2 mL) white pepper*
> 2 *tablespoons (30 mL) safflower oil*
> 1 *medium onion, diced fine*
> 1 *clove garlic, minced*
> 2 *cups (500 mL) water*
> 2 *tablespoons (30 mL) cornstarch*
> 1/3 *cup (80 mL) fresh parsley, chopped*

Wash and skin the chicken. Remove any visible fat. Mix the flour and pepper together on a plate. Coat each piece of chicken by rolling it in the flour mixture. Heat the oil in a large saucepan or Dutch oven. Add the onion and garlic; cook gently for 2 to 3 minutes; add the chicken and cook for a few minutes on each side until golden brown. Add the water; cover the pot tightly and gently simmer for about 45 minutes, or until tender; remove the chicken to a plate.

Measure the cornstarch into a bowl. Gradually stir in a cup of the cooking liquid and pour back into the cooking pot. Heat and stir until sauce thickens. Stir in the parsley. Slip the chicken back in and reheat.

Calories: 368, Fat: 10 g (1 g saturated), Protein: 54 g, Cholesterol: 132 mg, Carbohydrates: 13 g, Sodium: 152 mg

◆ Quick Lemon Chicken ◆

You can also use thin slices of turkey cutlets or veal cutlets and garnish with freshly chopped parsley.

1/3   *(90 mL) cup flour*
    dash white or black pepper
1 1/4 *pounds (600 g) boneless chicken breasts or cutlets*
1   *tablespoon (15 mL) unsalted margarine*
1   *tablespoon (15 mL) safflower oil*
6   *tablespoons (90 mL) lemon juice*
2   *tablespoons (30 mL) sugar*

Mix the flour and pepper together in a bowl. Coat the cutlets with the flour mixture. Heat the margarine with the oil in a large frying pan. Add the chicken and cook over medium high heat until golden brown on both sides. Remove the chicken to a platter to keep warm. Sprinkle lemon juice and sugar into the frying pan and stir over low heat, scraping the bottom of the pan frequently, about 2 to 3 minutes; pour it over the cooked chicken. Serve warm.

**Calories: 279, Fat: 8 g (1 g saturated), Protein: 34 g,
Cholesterol: 82 mg, Carbohydrates: 16 g, Sodium: 93 mg**

◆ Honey Chicken ◆

Easy enough for everyday and special enough for company!

4   *chicken breasts (2 pounds / 1 kg), trimmed*
4   *tablespoons (60 mL) unsalted margarine*
1/2 *cup (125 mL) honey*
1   *(5 mL) teaspoon curry powder*
1/2 *teaspoon (2 mL) dry mustard*

Wash, dry, and remove skin and fat from chicken. In a saucepan, melt the margarine, stir in the honey, curry powder, and dry mustard; remove from heat. Pour about half the sauce mixture into a baking dish. Roll each piece of chicken and arrange in a baking dish with the round side up. Pour any remaining sauce over the chicken. Bake in 375°F (190°C) oven for about 1 hour.

Calories: 482, Fat: 14 g (3 g saturated), Protein: 53 g,
Cholesterol: 132 mg, Carbohydrates: 35 g, Sodium: 150 mg

◆ Baked Chicken in Wine ◆

MAKES 4 SERVINGS

Wonderful for company.*

4 chicken breasts (2 pound / 1 kg), trimmed
1 cup (250 mL) white wine (not cooking wine)
1 teaspoon (5 mL) garlic powder
1 teaspoon (5 mL) onion powder
1 teaspoon (5 mL) paprika
2 tablespoons (30 mL) fresh parsley, minced

Wash the chicken; remove and discard skin. If you like, line a baking pan with aluminum foil to make cleanup easier. Place chicken pieces on the foil. Mix remaining ingredients in a small bowl. Pour over chicken and cover with aluminum foil. Bake for about 40 minutes or until fork tender.

*To roast whole chicken, see note under Roast Turkey (page 167).

Calories: 295, Fat: 3g (1 g saturated), Protein: 53 g,
Cholesterol: 132 mg, Carbohydrates: 2 g, Sodium: 154 mg

◆ Chicken Marengo ◆

MAKES 4 SERVINGS

Since this recipe makes a tasty sauce, serve rice or noodles at the same meal.

4 chicken breasts (2 pounds / 1 kg), trimmed
2 tablespoons (30 mL) olive oil
1 onion, minced
1 clove garlic, mashed
2 large tomatoes, peeled
1/2 teaspoon (2 mL) paprika
1/2 cup (125 mL) vermouth
1 cup (250 mL) mushrooms, sliced

Wash the chicken and discard the skin. Heat the oil in a large casserole. Add the chicken breasts and sauté briefly until golden brown on both sides. Remove the chicken. Add the onion and garlic to the casserole and cook gently for about 5 minutes. Add the tomatoes to the onion and garlic and cook until mushy. Tuck the chicken into the sauce. Add the paprika, vermouth, and mushrooms. Simmer for about 40 minutes, or until done.

**Calories: 359, Fat: 10 g (2 g saturated), Protein: 54 g,
Cholesterol: 132 mg, Carbohydrates: 7 g, Sodium: 157 mg**

◆ Chicken Cacciatore ◆

MAKES 4 SERVINGS

If you are using a whole fryer, serve the breast to the person who needs to cut down on sodium.

    4   *chicken breasts (2 pounds/1 kg), trimmed*
    3   *tablespoons (45 mL) flour*
    2   *tablespoons (30 mL) safflower oil*
    1   *medium onion, chopped*
    1   *clove garlic, finely chopped*
    1   *fresh tomato, cut up*
  1/2   *green pepper, chopped*
    1   *cup (250 mL) fresh mushrooms, chopped*
    6   *ounces (170 mL) no-salt-added tomato paste*
 11/3   *cups (320 mL) water*
  1/2   *teaspoon (2 mL) basil*
    1   *bay leaf*
        ground black pepper

In a paper bag, shake the chicken pieces with the flour. Heat the oil in a large frying pan. Brown the chicken pieces lightly on all sides. Add all the vegetables; cook gently over low heat. Dilute the tomato paste with the water. Add the basil, bay leaf, and pepper to the sauce and pour over the chicken and vegetables. Cover and continue simmering over low heat until the chicken is tender, about 45 minutes, or longer if you like it very tender. Remove the bay leaf. Serve the chicken cacciatore over spaghetti or other pasta, cooked without salt, of course.

**Calories: 393, Fat: 10 g (1 g saturated), Protein: 56 g,
Cholesterol: 132 mg, Carbohydrates: 19 g, Sodium: 190 mg**

◆ Creamed Chicken ◆

Serve over toast, or for a fancier touch, use as filling for Crêpes (page 237) or in Popovers (page 213). If you like, you can add sliced mushrooms, diced green pepper or pimentos as you melt the margarine to make the cream sauce. Creamed chicken can be seasoned at the table with a sprinkling from the Unsalt Shaker (page 39).

    3 cups (750 mL) water
    1 medium onion, peeled and quartered
1 1/2 pounds (680 g) chicken breasts
    4 tablespoons (60 mL) unsalted margarine
  1/4 cup (60 mL) flour
    2 tablespoons (30 mL) sherry (not cooking sherry)
       dash white pepper
  1/2 teaspoon (2 mL) onion powder

Combine water and onion in a large saucepan. Remove the skin from the chicken. Cut each breast in half down the back. Add to the saucepan; you may need to cut the chicken into smaller pieces so that it is covered by the water. Bring to a boil, reduce the heat, and simmer until tender, approximately 45 minutes. Remove the chicken from the broth and place on a plate to cool. Using a slotted spoon, discard onion; save the broth.

While the chicken is cooling, make a white sauce in a separate saucepan: Melt the margarine over low heat, add the flour, and cook over low heat for a few minutes, stirring with a wire whisk. Measure 2 cups (500 mL) of the broth and add to the saucepan; add the sherry and seasonings and stir the mixture over low heat until the sauce is thickened. Cut up the chicken into small chunks, discarding the bones, and add chicken to the sauce and stir. If this is more than you need at the meal, refrigerate or freeze the extra for a convenient meal at another time.

**Calories: 222, Fat: 9 g (2 g saturated), Protein: 27 g,
Cholesterol: 66 mg, Carbohydrates: 6 g, Sodium: 75 mg**

◆ Baked "Fried" Chicken ◆

Quick and easy to pop in the oven for a tasty family favorite. Especially good for people who don't want the fat and calories in traditional fried chicken.

- 4 chicken breasts (2 pounds / 1 kg), trimmed
- 1/2 cup (125 mL) lemon juice or orange juice
- 1/3 cup (90 mL) Roll and Bake Coating Mix (page 42)

Remove and discard skin from chicken. Pour juice into a bowl or flat pan, and the coating mix in another. If you like, line a baking pan with aluminum foil to make cleanup easier. Dip each piece of chicken into the juice to moisten, then into the coating mix; use your fingers to press the mix onto the chicken. Arrange in a baking pan and bake in 350°F (175°C) oven until tender, about 45 to 50 minutes.

**Calories: 270, Fat: 3 g (1 g saturated), Protein: 53 g,
Cholesterol: 132 mg, Carbohydrates: 5 g, Sodium: 148 mg**

◆ Southern Fried Chicken ◆

- 4 chicken breasts (2 pounds / 1 kg), trimmed
- 1/2 cup (125 mL) flour
- 1/2 teaspoon (2 mL) white or black pepper
- 1/2 teaspoon (2 mL) paprika
-      safflower or other oil for frying

Wash the chicken. Remove and discard the skin. Mix together the flour, pepper, and paprika. Dredge the chicken pieces in the spice mixture. (To dredge, you can put the mixture and chicken into a bag and shake to coat.) Let the chicken stand.

Meanwhile, pour oil 1/2 inch (1 cm) deep into the skillet. Heat over moderate heat until hot. Add the chicken and cover tightly; brown on one side and turn over. Turn the heat down so that the chicken will brown more slowly; do not replace cover. Continue cooking until done, about 30 additional minutes.

**Calories: 494, Fat: 18 g (5 g saturated), Protein: 64 g,
Cholesterol: 174 mg, Carbohydrates: 16 g, Sodium: 149 mg**

◆ Stir-Fried Chicken ◆

It's fun to cook this in a wok, but a large saucepan or Dutch oven can be used. Traditionally, Chinese foods have smaller amounts of high-protein food, and lots of vegetables. Prepare chicken and vegetables in advance and have them ready. Cooking takes a few minutes.

   2   *tablespoons (30 mL) oil, preferably peanut oil*
 1/4   *teaspoon (1 mL) thyme*
       pinch rosemary
       pinch oregano
 1/4   *teaspoon (1 mL) onion powder*
   1   *clove garlic, crushed*
   1   *medium onion, chopped*
   1   *carrot, sliced*
 1/2   *green pepper, diced*
 1/4   *head of cabbage, shredded fine*
  10   *ounces (300 g) chicken breast*, cut into 1/2-inch wide strips*
   1   *tablespoon (15 mL) sherry wine (optional)*

Heat the oil, thyme, rosemary, oregano, onion powder, and garlic in the wok until the oil is very hot and you can smell the seasonings. Add the onion and stir-fry in the hot oil for about 10 seconds. Add the green pepper and carrot and stir-fry for about 10 seconds. Toss in the cabbage and stir-fry until limp and golden. Move vegetables to one side, drop the chicken into the wok, and stir-fry until color changes from pink to white and the pieces are cooked through, about 4 minutes. Drizzle in the sherry, if using. Mix chicken with the vegetables. Delicious with rice, cooked without salt, of course.

* If you buy chicken breasts with the bone in, buy about 1 1/4 pounds (600 g) and bone before cooking. Also, you may want to make some chicken stock by cooking the bones with herbs in water. See Chicken Stock (page 96).

Calories: 168, Fat: 8 g (1 g saturated), Protein: 17 g,
Cholesterol: 41 mg, Carbohydrates: 6 g, Sodium: 56 mg

◆ Maryland Fried Chicken ◆

4   *chicken breasts (2 pounds/1 kg), trimmed*
1/3 *cup (90 mL) flour*
1   *egg* or equivalent egg substitute*
1   *tablespoon (15 mL) water*
1/2 *cup (125 mL) Roll and Bake Coating Mix (page 42)*
    safflower or other oil for frying

Wash the chicken. Remove and discard skin. Sprinkle the flour into a large paper bag, add the chicken, and shake. Mix egg with water in a pan; spread Roll and Bake Mix in another pan. Dip each piece in the egg and then in the coating mix; repeat with each piece of chicken. (If you use one hand for the egg and the other hand for crumbs, the process is much less messy.) Let the chicken stand.

Meanwhile, pour enough oil into the skillet to make a layer 1/2-inch (1 cm) deep. Brown chicken on one side and turn over. Turn the heat down so that the chicken will brown more slowly. Do not replace cover. Continue cooking until done, about 30 additional minutes.

* Actually, very little of the egg and flour cling to the chicken.

**Calories: 356, Fat: 9 g (1 g saturated), Protein: 55 g,
Cholesterol: 185 mg, Carbohydrates: 10 g, Sodium: 164 mg**

◆ Chicken or Veal Scaloppine ◆

A delicious special treat. Or use sliced turkey breast, an economical "veal substitute." Good with pasta, garlic bread, and a green salad.

1 1/4 *pounds (600 g) boneless chicken breasts, sliced, or*
     lean veal, cut for "scaloppine"
  3   *tablespoons (45 mL) flour*
     dash white pepper
  1   *tablespoon (15 mL) unsalted margarine*
  1   *tablespoon (15 mL) safflower oil*
 2/3 *cup (160 mL) dry vermouth*
 1/2 *teaspoon (2 mL) basil*
  1   *tablespoon (15 mL) lemon juice*

1   onion, finely chopped
1   clove garlic, finely minced
6   ounces (170 mL) no-salt-added tomato paste
1 1/4   cups (300 mL) water

Using a mallet or rolling pin, pound the chicken between 2 slices of waxed paper until very thin, careful not to break the flesh apart. Combine flour and white pepper on a dinner plate. Coat chicken with flour on both sides, shaking off excess flour.

Heat oil and margarine in a large skillet. Add chicken and cook on both sides, about 8 minutes. Remove chicken and add the vermouth to the skillet. Cook over fairly high heat for about 5 minutes, stirring frequently. Turn down heat and add remaining ingredients. Stir and add the cooked chicken and cook over low heat for another 5 minutes.

Calories: 308, Fat: 8 g (1 g saturated), Protein: 35 g, Cholesterol: 82 mg, Carbohydrates: 16 g, Sodium: 134 mg

◆ Chicken, Turkey, or Veal Marsala ◆

MAKES 4 SERVINGS

This recipe is traditionally made with thin slices of veal, but you can save money: substitute 6 boneless chicken cutlets, fresh turkey slices, or thinly sliced turkey "cutlets."

1/4   cup (60 mL) flour
        dash white pepper
        dash oregano
        dash basil
1 1/4   pounds (600 g) cutlets (chicken, turkey, or veal)
1   tablespoon (15 mL) safflower oil
1   tablespoon (15 mL) unsalted margarine
1/2   pound (225 g) mushrooms, sliced
1   cup (250 mL) Marsala wine or dry sherry

Mix flour, white pepper, oregano, and basil together on a plate. Wash and dry the cutlets and coat each with the flour mixture. Reserve any leftover flour. Heat oil and margarine in a frying pan. Add the cutlets and sauté gently until brown on both sides and tender, about 15 minutes. Remove the cutlets to a dish. Add the mushrooms and 1/4 cup (60 mL) of the wine; cook for about 5 minutes over low heat. Scrape the bottom of the pan to loosen any flour. Stir in any reserved flour and the remaining Marsala. Simmer until the mixture thickens, stirring constantly. Slip the cooked cutlets into the sauce. Cook gently for about 5 minutes or more.

Calories: 295, Fat: 8 g (1 g saturated), Protein: 35 g, Cholesterol: 82 mg, Carbohydrates: 9 g, Sodium: 99 mg

◆ Sweet-and-Sour Chicken ◆

MAKES 4 SERVINGS

A family pleaser, very fast, and good with rice.

1 1/4   pounds (600 g) boneless chicken breast cutlets
1   tablespoon (15 mL) safflower oil
1   medium onion, finely chopped
2   cloves garlic, finely minced
1   cup (250 mL) water
1/2   cup (125 mL) juice drained from pineapple can
1   tablespoon (15 mL) molasses
3   tablespoons (45 mL) sugar, more if you like it sweeter
1/4   teaspoon (1 mL) ginger
1/2   cup (125 mL) vinegar
3   tablespoons (45 mL)cornstarch
1   cup (250 mL) pineapple chunks, drained
1   green pepper, cut in chunks

Trim and remove any fat or skin from the chicken; leave whole or cut into chunks, as you prefer. Heat oil in skillet and cook onion and garlic for about 5 minutes; push onion and garlic to side of pan. Add chicken and brown on both sides. Add 3/4 cup (180 mL) of the water. Turn heat down to simmer and cook over low heat, about 10 minutes for small strips of chicken, 15 minutes for larger pieces of chicken.

Remove chicken to a plate. To make Sweet-and-Sour Sauce: Stir together pineapple juice, remaining 1/4 cup (60 mL) water, molasses, sugar, ginger, vinegar, and cornstarch in skillet. Add pineapple and green pepper chunks; bring to boil. Stir, turn down heat, and simmer for about 10 minutes. Add chicken and heat through. Serve warm.

Calories: 309, Fat: 5 g (1 g saturated), Protein: 34 g, Cholesterol: 82 mg, Carbohydrates: 32 g, Sodium: 97 mg

Cornish Game Hens with
◆ Rice Stuffing ◆

MAKES 8 SERVINGS

The cooked meat averages 6 ounces (180 g) per game hen. You can serve half of a game hen to a strict dieter.

- 1 tablespoon (15 mL) unsalted margarine
- 1 small onion, minced
- 1 small apple, cored, peeled, and minced
- 2 cups (500 mL) cooked rice (cooked without salt)
- 1/2 teaspoon (2 mL) sage
- 1/2 teaspoon (2 mL) thyme
- 1/3 cup (80 mL) vermouth
    dash pepper
- 4 Cornish game hens—each weighs about 1 pound (450 g) when wrapping and giblets are removed

To make the stuffing, melt the margarine in a small pan, add the onion and apple, and cook gently for 5 minutes or so, stirring occasionally. Combine with the rice, sage, thyme, vermouth, and pepper in a bowl. Wash the hens, and spoon the stuffing into the cavities without overfilling. Place the hens on a rack in a shallow pan. Add a layer of water to the bottom of the pan. Cover pan with a tent of aluminum foil. Set pan in 400°F (205°C) oven and immediately turn the heat down to 325°F (165°C). Roast about 50 to 60 minutes until tender. Serve warm.

**Calories: 423, Fat: 25 g (7 g saturated), Protein: 30 g,
Cholesterol: 170 mg, Carbohydrates: 15 g, Sodium: 104 mg**

◆ Roast Turkey ◆

Buy a turkey that is not prebasted with salted butter. A fresh turkey may be best. Clean the turkey and dry it. Brush with a small amount of unsalted margarine, if desired.

To roast, plan 20 minutes per pound for birds up to 6 pounds (2.7 kg). For larger birds allow 15 minutes per pound (450 g). If the bird is stuffed, add an extra 5 minutes per pound. Roast in 325°F (165°C) oven. If you use a tent of aluminum foil, remove it the last half hour of cooking to brown.

To roast chicken, follow the same directions.

◆ Stuffings ◆

Many people are used to the taste of stuffing, sold dry and packaged in bags. No matter how you "doctor" it up, the product is still very salty (about 4,000 mg in a small bag). Although sage and other seasonings are used, the major seasoning is still salt. If you stuff a turkey with packaged stuffing, the saltiness is bound to be in the liquid that drips out. If you baste the bird with the pan drippings, you will be, in effect, basting with a salted liquid. A person who really needs to cut down on salt should not eat turkey meat from a bird that was basted with a salted liquid. But fortunately, it is very easy to make the salty stuffing in a separate dish, for family members who do not need to cut down.

We do not think you can make flavorful stuffing from low-sodium bread and unsalted margarine. You may want to try some combinations of seasonings. Or better still, try our rice stuffing.

◆ Rice Stuffing for Turkey ◆

Double the stuffing recipe for Cornish Game Hens with Rice Stuffing (page 166) to make enough stuffing for a 12-pound (5.4-kg) turkey.

MEATS

◆◆◆◆◆

Red meats—beef, veal, lamb, pork, especially—have been criticized for their high fat and cholesterol, expense, and for requiring a disproportionally high share of the world's agricultural resources. Animals consume 90 percent of all corn, barley, oats, and soy. But the fact remains that many people love meats and choose them for dinner over other foods.

Organ meats, such as liver, have not been very popular. Although they are rich in iron, they are often not recommended for a person who needs to cut down on cholesterol. You may want to check with your doctor or dietitian to see if he or she recommends organ meats.

Red meats are relatively low in sodium and beef is the lowest; you can figure that a small serving (three ounces or 90 g) of cooked meat has, for beef, 55 mg of sodium; lamb, 58 mg of sodium; pork, 59 mg of sodium; and veal, 69 mg of sodium.

If the doctor has told you, or someone you cook for, to limit the number of times per week that red meat is eaten, then you certainly want the meat to taste as good as possible.

Many of the most popular ways of cooking meat don't require any special low-sodium recipes. Just roast, broil, pan-fry, or cook it over a charcoal grill. As the author and former *New York Times* food editor Craig Claiborne says, charcoal broiling is an excellent way of adding flavor to unsalted meats. Just be sure to leave out all of the high-sodium cooking aids (soy sauce, tenderizer, MSG, etc.).

Veal is often recommended as being a better choice than beef or pork for people who need to cut down on fat. Major drawbacks to veal are the price and higher sodium and calorie contents than chicken. If veal fits into your economic and sodium budget, you can use some of the recipes in the chapter on chicken, such as Chicken, Turkey or Veal Marsala (page 165) or Chicken or Veal Scaloppine (page 164).

Lean cuts of red meat are the best choice because they have less saturated fat. The lean cuts, such as round, can be tenderized: braise or cook in a liquid over low heat for several hours; marinate the meat for several hours; pound with a meat mallet; and use unsalted meat tenderizer—1 teaspoon (5 mL) per pound (450 g) of meat—a very generous coating. The tenderizer not only works very well on tough meat cuts but is also made without the potassium chloride, a chemical that leaves an unpleasant aftertaste in many commercial low-sodium products.

BEEF

◆ Broiled Steak ◆

MAKES 4 SERVINGS

1   pound (450 g) boneless beef steak (buy more if there
    is bone)
1   teaspoon (5 mL) unsalted meat tenderizer (optional)

Prepare the cooking surface: preheat the broiler or prepare a charcoal fire.
If you are using a less than perfectly tender cut of meat, sprinkle it generously with unsalted meat tenderizer. (Do not use regular meat tenderizer,
which is very high in sodium.) Place the meat on a broiler pan (or on the
charcoal grill) and broil a few inches from the heat. Turn over after 2 to 3
minutes; broil on the second side. A rare steak may take approximately 3
minutes; a well-done steak may take 6 minutes. Cut into the steak as soon
as you think it may be done to see if the steak has cooked long enough. You
can always cook it a minute or two longer.

**Calories: 293, Fat: 18 g (7 g saturated), Protein: 32 g,
Cholesterol: 102 mg, Carbohydrates: 0 g, Sodium: 71 mg**

◆ Steak au Poivre ◆

MAKES 4 SERVINGS

Steak with pepper has so much flavor, you won't miss the salt!

2   tablespoons (30 mL) freshly ground black pepper
1   pound (450 g) boneless, tender beef steak (buy more if
    there is bone)

Sprinkle one-half the pepper onto one side of the meat and pound it in with
a meat mallet; repeat on the other side. Broil the meat over a charcoal grill
or on the broiler rack; or pan-fry the meat in an oiled skillet.

**Calories: 301, Fat: 18 g (7 g saturated), Protein: 32 g,
Cholesterol: 102 mg, Carbohydrates: 2 g, Sodium: 73 mg**

London Broil

To marinate 2 to 3 pounds (900–1,400 g) of a less tender cut of beef: Select a marinade (page 57–60) and double the amounts.

Marinate meat for several hours or overnight. Broil until done as described in Broiled Steak (page opposite). Slice the meat on the diagonal.

Nutritional information varies with cut of beef

Beef Teriyaki

Served with rice and a crisp salad.

> 1 *pound (450 g) lean boneless beef, such as sirloin or round*
> 1/4 *cup (60 mL) Soy Sauce Substitute (page 49)*
> 1/4 *teaspoon (1 mL) dry mustard*
> 3 *tablespoons (45 mL) sherry, not cooking sherry*
> 1/4 *cup (60 mL) water*

Place the meat in the freezer to partially freeze it so that it will be easier to slice. Meanwhile, make the marinade: combine Soy Sauce Substitute, mustard, sherry, and water in a nonmetal bowl. Remove meat from freezer and slice across the grain into thin slices. Place the pieces of meat in the marinade; cover. Refrigerate it if you will be marinating it for more than 15 minutes.*

When ready to cook, preheat the broiler. Broil the meat a few inches from the heat for 5 minutes. Turn over and broil for an additional 3 to 8 minutes, depending on how rare or well-done you like it. You can also cube the beef and skewer before broiling, as for shish kebab. If you want to serve the marinade as a sauce, heat it in a saucepan just to the boiling point, reduce heat, and simmer.

* If you use a tough cut of meat such as round, let it sit in the marinade for at least several hours or overnight. If you use a tender cut of meat such as sirloin or tenderloin, you can marinate it for just 15 minutes and make the process much quicker.

**Calories: 162, Fat: 4 g (2 g saturated), Protein: 24 g,
Cholesterol: 69 mg, Carbohydrates: 3 g, Sodium: 68 mg**

◆ Swiss Steak ◆

Slow cooking can really tenderize bottom round cut 1-inch (2.5 cm) thick or so.

- 2 tablespoons (30 mL) flour
- 1/4 teaspoon (1 mL) dry mustard
  ground black pepper
- 1/4 teaspoon (1 mL) paprika
- 1 pound round (450 g) beef steak
- 1 tablespoon (15 mL) safflower oil
- 1 large onion, sliced into thin rings
- 1 clove garlic, minced
- 1 fresh tomato, peeled and chopped
- 6 ounces (170 mL) no-salt-added tomato paste
- 2 cups (500 mL) water
- 1 teaspoon (5 mL) unsalted meat tenderizer, sprinkled on right before cooking (optional)

Combine the flour, mustard, pepper, and paprika and spread half of this mixture onto one side of the meat. Pound it in with a meat mallet (or the side of a heavy saucer). Sprinkle the remaining flour mixture on the other side of the meat and pound it in.

Heat the oil in a skillet over medium heat; brown the meat on both sides. Remove the meat, temporarily, to a plate. To the skillet add the onion, garlic, tomato, tomato paste, and water; stir to combine. Add the meat to the sauce. Cover the pan and simmer over low heat for approximately 1 1/2 hours or until tender.

Calories: 371, Fat: 19 g (6 g saturated), Protein: 34 g,
Cholesterol: 91 mg, Carbohydrates: 15 g, Sodium: 110 mg

◆ Beef Goulash ◆

Serve with noodles or boiled potatoes.

- 2 tablespoons (30 mL) safflower oil
- 1 large onion, chopped
- 1–2 cloves garlic, finely minced
- 1 pound (450 g) lean beef, cubed
  ground fresh pepper
- 1 teaspoon (5 mL) marjoram
- 2 cups (475 mL) water
- 1/4 cup (60 mL) low-sodium ketchup or Ketchup (page 42)
- 2 tablespoons (30 mL) paprika
- 1/4 cup (60 mL) yogurt (optional)

Heat the oil in a Dutch oven or casserole. Add the onion and garlic and stir over low heat for a few minutes. Add the cubes of meat and brown on all sides over medium heat. Add the pepper, marjoram, and 1 1/2 cups (355 mL) of the water. Bring to a boil, reduce heat, and simmer for about 1 hour. Mix the ketchup, paprika, and remaining water and add to the goulash. Simmer for about 10 minutes more. If you like, add the yogurt and stir over low heat without boiling.

Calories: 296, Fat: 17 g (4 g saturated), Protein: 26 g,
Cholesterol: 71 mg, Carbohydrates: 10 g, Sodium: 77 mg

◆ Beef Bourguignon ◆

Good with noodles.

- 1 1/2 tablespoons (22 mL) safflower oil
- 1 medium onion, finely chopped
- 1 clove garlic, finely minced
- 1 pound (450 g) lean beef, trimmed of fat and cubed
- 12 small onions, peeled
  ground fresh pepper
- 1/4 teaspoon (1 mL) thyme
- 1 tablespoon (15 mL) lemon juice
- 1/2 teaspoon (2 mL) marjoram

1   bay leaf
1   cup (250 mL) water
1   cup (250 mL) Burgundy
1   cup (250 mL) fresh mushrooms, sliced

Heat the oil in a Dutch oven or casserole. Add onion and garlic and sauté for a few minutes. Add the cubes of meat and brown on all sides. Add the onions, seasonings, lemon juice, water, and Burgundy; simmer for about 1 1/2 to 2 hours. Add mushrooms and simmer for another 30 minutes.

Calories: 402, Fat: 14 g (3 g saturated), Protein: 28 g, Cholesterol: 70 mg, Carbohydrates: 33 g, Sodium: 78 mg

◆ Old-Fashioned Beef Stew ◆

MAKES 4 SERVINGS

2   tablespoons (30 mL) flour
     ground black pepper
1   pound (450 g) lean beef, cut into cubes
2   tablespoons (30 mL) safflower oil
1   tablespoon (15 mL) wine vinegar
2   bay leaves
1/2 teaspoon (2 mL) onion powder
1/2 teaspoon (2 mL) garlic powder
1   teaspoon (5 mL) no-salt-added tomato paste
1/2 teaspoon (2 mL) basil
3   cups (750 mL) hot water
1/2 cup (125 mL) vermouth
4   medium potatoes, peeled and cut into chunks
2   carrots, peeled and cut into chunks
4   medium onions, peeled and quartered

In a paper bag, shake the cubes of meat with flour and pepper to coat lightly. Heat the oil in a Dutch oven or casserole dish. Brown the meat in the oil, turning frequently. Add all the seasonings, vinegar, tomato paste, water and vermouth; stir to mix. Heat just to the boiling point. Turn down heat, cover, and simmer for 1 1/4 hours, or until almost done. Add the potatoes, carrots, and onions and stir; cover and simmer for 40 minutes until potatoes are cooked.

Calories: 523, Fat: 22 g (6 g saturated), Protein: 42 g, Cholesterol: 115 mg, Carbohydrates: 34 g, Sodium: 98 mg

◆ Beef Roast ◆

For many families, Sunday just isn't Sunday without a roast. Roasts are fairly expensive and certainly need attention. Set the roast on a rack in a shallow roasting pan. Use a meat thermometer.

A good rule of thumb: Roast at 325°F (165°C) for 20 minutes a pound for all meat except pork. Pork should be roasted at 350°F (175°C). Remember that meat continues to cook for 15 minutes or so after you've removed it from the oven; take the roast out when the thermometer indicates that it is not quite done for your personal preference.

◆ Pot Roast ◆

MAKES 8 SERVINGS

When serving a pot roast,* you'll surely have more meat than four moderate servings. Leftover cooked meat can be ground or thinly sliced to make sandwich filling.

    1   *4-pound (1.8 kg) lean trimmed beef suitable for*
        pot roast
    1   *clove garlic, peeled*
    2   *tablespoons (30 mL) flour*
        ground black pepper
    2   *tablespoons (30 mL) safflower oil*
    2   *cups (500 mL) water*
  1/2   *cup (125 mL) vermouth*
  1/8   *teaspoon (.5 mL) Tabasco sauce*
    2   *teaspoons (10 mL) leaf thyme*
    3   *medium onions, quartered*
    1   *potato, pared and quartered, per person (optional)*
  1/2   *carrot, pared (optional)*

Trim off any visible fat. Rub the garlic around the meat. Combine the flour and pepper and coat the meat.

Heat the oil in a Dutch oven or casserole. Brown the meat over medium-high heat on all sides. Add the water, vermouth, seasonings, and onions. Reduce the heat to a gentle simmer. Cover and simmer for approximately three hours. Turn the meat over during the cooking process, if convenient, but cook very slowly. Add carrots and potatoes during the last hour of cooking. (You can figure that each potato adds 6 mg of sodium. Each half of a carrot adds 17 mg of sodium.)

If you want to eliminate more fat, make pot roast a day early, chill the cooked roast, discard the layer of fat and reheat the meat in the degreased sauce over low heat.

Calories: 370, Fat: 14 g (4 g saturated), Protein: 49 g, Cholesterol: 136 mg, Carbohydrates: 8 g, Sodium: 157 mg

◆ Gravy ◆

To make the gravy: After removing fat, there should be about 2 cups (500 mL). Pour half the liquid into a saucepan and the other half in a dish. Add 3 tablespoons (45 mL) of flour to the dish and mix with a fork until there are no lumps and the mixture is smooth. Stir the flour mixture into the saucepan, blending with a wire whisk. Cook over medium heat, stirring constantly until the gravy thickens.

◆ Hash ◆

MAKES 4 SERVINGS

Still a favorite way to serve leftover beef.

2   *tablespoons (30 mL) unsalted margarine*
1   *medium onion, diced*
12 *ounces (360 g) leftover beef, such as pot roast, trimmed of all visible fat and minced or ground*
4   *medium potatoes, boiled and diced*
    ground black pepper

Melt margarine in a skillet. Add the onion and cook gently until soft. Add potatoes, stir, and cook until the potatoes are browned. Add the meat and heat thoroughly. Sprinkle with pepper. Serve hot.

Calories: 333, Fat: 20 g (7 g saturated), Protein: 18 g, Cholesterol: 59 mg, Carbohydrates: 19 g, Sodium: 63 mg

◆ Spicy Meat Loaf ◆

1 pound (450 g) lean ground beef from the round
2 tablespoons (30 mL) chopped parsley
1/2 teaspoon (2 mL) basil
1 teaspoon (5 mL) dry mustard
1 small onion, grated or finely chopped
1/4 cup (60 mL) crumbs from low-sodium bread*
2 teaspoons (10 mL) lemon juice
   ground pepper

Knead all the ingredients together. Spray a meat loaf pan or small individual baking cups or sections of a muffin pan with a vegetable coating spray. Mound the meat loaf in the pan or baking dishes. Bake the loaf in 375°F (190°C) oven for approximately one hour, individual baking dishes for approximately 15 to 25 minutes. When you remove the meat loaf from the oven, drain off the grease by holding the pan at an angle.

* You can substitute 1/4 cup (60 mL) dry oatmeal (not instant) for the bread crumbs.

Calories: 323, Fat: 24 g (10 g saturated), Protein: 21 g, Cholesterol: 85 mg, Carbohydrates: 5 g, Sodium: 81 mg

◆ Family Meat Loaf ◆

1 1/2 pounds (675 g) lean ground beef
1/2 cup (125 mL) oatmeal, not instant
1/4 cup (60 mL) wheat germ
1 egg or equivalent egg substitute
1/4 teaspoon (1 mL) onion powder
1/2 teaspoon (2 mL) basil
   ground fresh pepper
1/2 teaspoon (2 mL) oregano
1/4 cup (60 mL) no-salt-added tomato paste
1/2 cup (125 mL) water

Mix together all ingredients in a large bowl, kneading with your hands. Bake in a loaf pan in 375°F (190°C) oven for about 1 hour. Individual meat loaves in ovenproof custard cups or muffin pan bake much faster, in about 20 minutes.

Calories: 364, Fat: 25 g (10 g saturated), Protein: 24 g, Cholesterol: 121 mg, Carbohydrates: 9 g, Sodium: 166 mg

◆ Swedish Meatballs ◆

MAKES 32 MEATBALLS

These cook without being watched.

1   *pound (450 g) very lean ground beef*
1   *egg or equivalent egg substitute*
1   *small onion, grated or minced*
3   *pieces of low-sodium bread, made into about 1 cup (250 mL) of crumbs*
3/4   *teaspoon (4 mL) allspice*
1   *teaspoon (5 mL) sugar*
    dash white pepper
1/4   *teaspoon (1 mL) nutmeg*

Mix all ingredients lightly and form into small meatballs, using one tablespoon (15 mL) per meatball. Put them on a broiler pan (so that the fat will drip down and away from the meat). Bake in 375°F (190°C) oven for approximately 12 to 15 minutes. Good when served with parsley potatoes.

Calories: 41, Fat: 3 g (1 g saturated), Protein: 3 g, Cholesterol: 16 mg, Carbohydrates: 1 g, Sodium: 12 mg

◆ Swedish Meatballs with Gravy ◆

MAKES 32 MEATBALLS

Swedish meatballs are traditionally served with a sauce or gravy made in the same pan. But making a gravy from beef drippings (saturated fat) cannot be recommended. The easiest way out is to serve the meatballs without a gravy, as the recipe above suggests. If you really want a sauce, make Beef Stock (page 99).

1 pound (450 g) very lean ground beef
1 egg or equivalent egg substitute
1 small onion, grated or minced
3 pieces of low-sodium bread, made into crumbs
3/4 teaspoon (4 mL) sugar
   dash white pepper
1/4 teaspoon (1 mL) nutmeg
3 tablespoons (45 mL) flour
1/2 cup (125 mL) skim milk
1/2 cup (125 mL) homemade Beef Stock (page 99)

Mix together the meat, egg, onion, bread crumbs, sugar, and dry seasonings. Form the meat mixture into small meatballs, using one tablespoon (15 mL) per meatball.

Spray your frying pan with a vegetable coating spray and fry the meatballs; turn them to brown evenly. Shake the pan from time to time so that the meatballs do not stick to the pan. After the meatballs are cooked, about 15 minutes, remove them and put them in a bowl. Drain the fat from the pan. Add the flour and stir around in the pan for a few minutes over medium heat. Add the milk and beef stock and stir with a wire whisk. Slip the meatballs back into the pan and simmer 5 to 10 minutes. Good served over noodles or boiled potatoes.

Calories: 49, Fat: 3 g (1 g saturated), Protein: 3 g, Cholesterol: 17 mg, Carbohydrates: 2 g, Sodium: 15 mg

◆ Italian Meatballs ◆

MAKES 4 SERVINGS

By cooking the meatballs in the oven you avoid time and fuss. Using a broiler pan allows the grease to drain off. If you don't have a broiler pan with a rack, you can line a pan that has sides with aluminum foil and support a cookie-cooling rack on the top.

1 egg or equivalent egg substitute
1 teaspoon (5 mL) onion powder
1 small onion, finely grated
2 tablespoons (30 mL) no-salt-added tomato paste
2 tablespoons (30 mL) water
1 teaspoon (5 mL) sugar

1   teaspoon (5 mL) basil
1   teaspoon (5 mL) parsley, finely minced
3   cups (750 mL) low-sodium cornflakes, crushed
1   pound (450 g) lean ground beef

Mix together all the ingredients except the meat. Let stand for 10 minutes. Mix in the meat. Form meat into balls. Place the meatballs on a broiler pan. Bake in 350°F (175°C) for about 20 to 25 minutes, depending on the size of the meatballs. Serve in Tomato Sauce or Tomato Sauce with Peppers and Mushrooms (pages 61–62).

Calories: 382, Fat: 21 g (8g saturated), Protein: 25 g,
Cholesterol: 131 mg, Carbohydrates: 22 g, Sodium: 101 mg

◆ Sweet-and-Sour Meatballs ◆

MAKES 32 MEATBALLS

1   pound (450 g) very lean ground beef such as round
1   egg or equivalent egg substitute
3   pieces low-sodium bread made into about 1 cup
     (250 mL) of crumbs
1/4 teaspoon (1 mL) dry mustard
1/4 teaspoon (1 mL) ginger
     Sweet-and-Sour Pineapple Sauce (page 48)

Knead the meat, egg or egg substitute, bread crumbs, mustard, and ginger. Shape into 32 meatballs. Place the meatballs on a broiler pan. Bake in 375°F (190°C) oven for about 20 minutes.

Meanwhile, make the Sweet-and-Sour Pineapple Sauce. When the meatballs are done, lift each meatball with a slotted spoon and place in the sauce.

Calories per meatball: 54, Fat: 3 g (1 g saturated), Protein: 3 g,
Cholesterol: 16 mg, Carbohydrates: 4 g, Sodium: 12 mg

LAMB

Lamb, although fairly low in sodium, is high in fat and price. Roast leg or shoulder of lamb in a 350°F (175°C) oven for approximately 20 to 30 minutes per pound. Before roasting, some cooks like to rub the outside surface with a little oil, pepper, rosemary, or a cut clove of garlic. Others like to use a knife to make little cuts in the meat into which pieces of garlic are inserted. Set lamb on a rack in your pan.

Lamb is medium rare when the oven thermometer reads 145°F (62°C), well done when the thermometer climbs to 165°F (74°C). Leftover lamb, cut up, can be layered in Moussaka (page 190). Lamb cubes can be transformed into a curry (page 196). Lamb chops, trimmed of excess fat, are broiled a few inches from the heat.

◆ Shish Kebab ◆

MAKES 4 SERVINGS

A great way to make a small serving of meat look generous. Marinate overnight. You can also substitute lean cubes of beef.

- *1 pound (450 g) lean lamb*
- *2 green peppers, cubed*
- *12 small onions, peeled*
- *12 fresh mushroom caps*
- *12 cherry tomatoes*
- *Herb Marinade (page 60)*

Trim off any visible fat and cut the meat into 1- to 1¹/2-inch (2.5–4 cm) cubes. Combine all the marinade ingredients in a bowl. Add the meat, cover and refrigerate for several hours or overnight. When ready to cook, steam the green pepper cubes and onions for 5 minutes. Preheat the broiler, if necessary. (Charcoal broiling is great, if convenient.) Arrange the meat and vegetables on skewers: mushrooms, cherry tomatoes, meat, onion, peppers, and repeat. Brush the skewered food with the marinade. Broil until done, about 10 to 15 minutes, turning and brushing with the marinade.

Calories: 432, Fat: 14 g (3 g saturated), Protein: 34 g, Cholesterol: 74 mg, Carbohydrates: 47 g, Sodium: 99 mg

PORK

◆◆

Although pork is fairly low in sodium—59 mg in a three-ounce (90-g) serving—it is fairly high in fat. If pork is allowed on your diet, be sure to trim off all visible fat.

Pork should always be cooked thoroughly, or until the meat is white or gray on the inside—never pink. Another test is to see if the juices run clear when the meat is pricked with a fork.

◆ Pork Chops ◆

To serve four persons three ounces (90 g) of cooked meat, buy approximately 2¹/4 pounds (1 kg) of pork chops to compensate for fat and bone waste, or one chop for each person. If you are feeling more generous, you can plan to serve two thin chops. If you are buying thicker or medium pork chops, each person eats approximately 3 ounces (90 g) of cooked pork containing 59 mg of sodium. Broil, pan-fry, or bake your pork chops. Just leave out high-sodium seasonings such as Shake 'n Bake; use Roll and Bake Coating Mix (page 42).

◆ Pork Chops and Apple Rings ◆

MAKES 4 SERVINGS

A complete stovetop meal with mashed potatoes and a green or yellow steamed vegetable.

2   *tablespoons (30 mL) flour*
    dash white pepper
4   *medium pork chops*
2   *tablespoons (30 mL) safflower oil*
3   *medium apples, unpeeled*

Mix flour and white pepper on a dinner plate. Coat both sides of the chops with the flour mixture. Heat the oil in a skillet. Brown the chops on both sides. Turn the heat down slightly and continue cooking until the chops are done, about 35 minutes, depending on the thickness; there should be no pink color left inside the chops. While the chops are cooking, cut the unpeeled apples across the core into slices about 1/2 inch (1 cm) thick; remove the inside core of each apple slice. When the chops are done, remove them from the skillet and keep warm. Fry the apple slices in the same skillet, on both sides, shaking the skillet from time to time to prevent sticking. Serve the apple slices and chops together.

Calories: 359, Fat: 21 g (5 g saturated), Protein: 23 g,
Cholesterol: 75 mg, Carbohydrates: 19 g, Sodium: 67 mg

◆ Pork Chops and Scalloped Potatoes ◆

MAKES 4 SERVINGS

 1 *tablespoon (15 mL) safflower oil*
 4 *medium pork chops, fat trimmed*
 2 *tablespoons (30 mL) unsalted margarine*
 3 *tablespoons (45 mL) flour*
1/4 *teaspoon (1 mL) ground black pepper*
 2 *cups (500 mL) Chicken Stock (page 96)**
 4 *medium potatoes, peeled and thinly sliced*
 1 *medium onion, peeled and thinly sliced*

Heat oil in a large skillet over medium heat; brown the chops on both sides. Melt the margarine in a saucepan. Add the flour and pepper and stir with whisk for a couple of minutes. Add the chicken stock and cook over medium heat, stirring constantly, until the mixture boils. Layer the potato slices in a 9-inch (23-cm) square or rectangular baking pan which has been sprayed with a vegetable coating spray. Spread onion over the potatoes. Add the chicken stock and pork chops; cover with aluminum foil. Bake in 350°F (175°C) oven for approximately 45 minutes; remove the aluminum foil and bake for an additional 30 minutes.

* You can substitute milk for the broth and get more calcium, but also more sodium.

Calories: 447, Fat: 24 g (6 g saturated), Protein: 28 g,
Cholesterol: 75 mg, Carbohydrates: 28 g, Sodium: 87 mg

◆ Pan-Fried Pork Chops ◆

This is a good way to cook thin chops. Pork needs to be cooked thoroughly, but not overcooked.

1   *tablespoon (15 mL) safflower oil*
4   *thin pork chops, fat trimmed*
1   *medium onion, diced (optional)*

Heat oil in a skillet over medium-high heat. Add the chops and onions. Cook over medium heat for approximately 20 minutes; thicker chops will take longer. Pork should not be pink inside.

**Calories: 265, Fat: 18 g (5 g saturated), Protein: 23 g,
Cholesterol: 75 mg, Carbohydrates: 2 g, Sodium: 68 mg**

◆ Pork Chops with Stuffing ◆

You can use all apple juice instead of mixing it with vermouth.

4   *medium pork chops, with a "pocket" for stuffing (or just
     put the stuffing on top)*
1   *tablespoon (15 mL) unsalted margarine*
1   *medium apple, peeled and chopped*
1   *small onion, peeled and chopped*
3   *slices low-sodium bread, toasted
     ground pepper*
1/4 *teaspoon (1 mL) sage or savory*
2   *tablespoons (30 mL) apple juice*
2   *tablespoons (30 mL) vermouth*

Heat margarine in a saucepan or skillet; add the diced onion and apple and cook over low heat for a few minutes. While that mixture is cooking, crumble the toast into a bowl. Add the seasonings, apple juice, and vermouth and the cooked apple and onion.

Place the chops on a broiler pan that has a rack. Spoon the stuffing in the pocket or on top of each chop. Cover with aluminum foil. Bake in a 350°F (175°C) oven for approximately one hour.

**Calories: 340, Fat: 18 g (6 g saturated), Protein: 25 g,
Cholesterol: 75 mg, Carbohydrates: 18 g, Sodium: 74 mg**

◆ Barbecued Pork Chops ◆

Barbecue Sauce (page 46)*
4 *medium pork chops, fat trimmed*

Prepare Barbecue Sauce. Line a baking dish with aluminum foil if you want to make cleanup easier. Arrange chops in pan, cover with sauce, and close the aluminum foil. Bake in 350°F (175°C) oven for 30 to 40 minutes, depending on the thickness of the chops.

* There is quite a lot of sauce in this recipe; approximately one tablespoon of sauce clings to each chop. If you put extra sauce on your noodles, potatoes, or rice, you can figure that each additional tablespoon (15 mL) adds 3 mg of sodium.

**Calories: 236, Fat: 12 g (4 g saturated), Protein: 15 g,
Cholesterol: 50 mg, Carbohydrates: 18 g, Sodium: 55 mg**

◆ Sweet-and-Sour Pork Chops ◆

Sweet-and-Sour Chicken (page 166) can also be adapted for pork. Be sure to cook pork longer—at least 30 minutes, longer for thick chops—until the meat pinkness is gone.

◆ Barbecued Spareribs ◆

MAKES 4 SERVINGS

A person told to limit sodium or red meat intake can really get a lot of chewing satisfaction from eating spareribs! This sauce is so delicious—as good as any restaurant sauce.

21/2 *pounds (1.2 kg) meaty spareribs, country style*
2 *tablespoons (30 mL) unsalted margarine*
1 *medium onion, chopped*
2 *tablespoons (30 mL) vinegar*
2 *tablespoons (30 mL) honey*
1/4 *cup (60 mL) lemon juice*
1 *cup (250 mL) low-sodium ketchup*
1 *teaspoon (5 mL) dry mustard*
1/2 *cup (125 mL) fresh parsley, chopped*
1/2 *cup (125 mL) water*

Trim the fat that you can see from the spareribs. To remove excess fat, parboil for 5 minutes: Place the meat in a large pot and cover with cold water; leave the pot uncovered and bring the water to a boil. Turn down the heat and simmer for about 5 minutes; drain ribs in a colander. Refill the pot with cold water; plunge ribs in cold water to firm; drain. Place the ribs on the rack of a broiler pan. Bake in 450°F (230°C) oven for 25 minutes. Meanwhile, make the sauce: Melt the margarine in a saucepan; cook the onion gently until soft; add the remaining ingredients and stir; remove from heat. Baste the ribs with the sauce and reduce the heat to 300°F (150°C). Bake 45 minutes, basting frequently with sauce.

Nutritional information: difficult to calculate exactly; when spareribs are parboiled, much of the fat is lost in the water

◆ Pork Roast ◆

Roasts offer more than four moderate servings, and leftover pork is delicious served cold. Or pork can be reheated in Barbecue Sauce (page 46); or make Sweet-and-Sour Pork Chops (page 185).

Place the roast, fat side up, on a rack in a shallow pan. If you like a mild garlic taste, rub the outside surface with a cut garlic clove. Insert a meat thermometer into a meaty part. Roast in 350°F (175°C) oven for approximately 30 minutes per pound (450 g). The internal temperature on a meat thermometer should be 160°F (70°C) when you remove the roast from the oven. Let the meat rest for 10 minutes before carving.

◆ Leftover Pork in Fried Rice ◆

Chinese restaurants often serve fried rice with small pieces of cooked pork. Make Fried Rice (page 194) and add the pork after cooking the onions.

SPECIALTIES *of* *the* HOUSE

❖❖◆❖❖

Many popular meals for supper or lunch do not fall into the meat and pota-toes pattern. Casseroles and hot sandwiches are foods that people often eat, perhaps because they are easy on the food budget or perhaps because they do not require a lot of work, especially at the last minute.

Many ethnic meals that have now become popular because of their good taste first became commonly used recipes because they could stretch a small amount of the expensive protein food with less expensive foods. Asian meals with small amounts of pork or seafood are one example. Italian foods with small amounts of cheese and generous amounts of pasta are another example (see Pasta chapter, page 136).

Some ethnic foods are more easily adapted to low-sodium cooking than others. Japanese foods that depend on high-sodium ingredients such as soy sauce (1,319 mg in 1 tablespoon [15 mL]) are not adaptable to low-sodium cooking. German recipes that call for sausages or "wurst" are not adaptable. Rich French dishes made from heavy cream and butter are probably not what your doctor ordered for you.

Tex-Mex foods, Chinese foods, and curry dishes are logical additions to a low-sodium diet. The natural spices, such as chilies and combinations that make a curry, are already low in sodium.

❖ Stuffed Cabbage ❖

MAKES 4 SERVINGS

You may prefer to substitute crushed low-sodium cornflakes for the rice in this recipe. The low-sodium cornflakes would add slightly more sodium.

> 12 *large cabbage leaves, more if they are small*
> 1 *pound (450 g) lean ground beef, such as round*
> 1 *medium onion, finely chopped*
> 1/4 *cup (60 mL) green pepper, finely chopped*
> *ground black pepper*
> 1 1/2 *cups (375 mL) rice, cooked without salt*

1/2   *teaspoon (2 mL) paprika*
1/4   *teaspoon (1 mL) dry mustard*
  4   *cups Tomato Sauce (page 61), heated*

Heat some water in the bottom of a vegetable steamer in preparation for steaming the cabbage leaves. Use a knife to cut the stem off a cabbage and separate 12 large leaves. (You may need more than 12 leaves if they are small.) Wash the leaves and place them in the steamer, cover tightly, and cook for 5 minutes or so until leaves are limp. Combine the meat, chopped onion, and green pepper in a frying pan. Cook gently to brown the meat, breaking it up with a fork as it cooks. Add the black pepper, cooked rice, paprika, dry mustard, and 1/4 cup (60 mL) of the warm tomato sauce; stir to combine. Select a baking dish that is shallow and just big enough to hold the 12 cabbage rolls close together; a lasagne pan—9" by 13" (23 by 34 cm) works well. Rub with vegetable oil to prevent sticking, or line the pan with aluminum foil for easy cleanup.

Lay out the limp cabbage leaves on a counter or other work surface; divide the meat mixture among the leaves by placing a scoop of meat on each one; roll the leaves around the meat, tucking the ends inside. Place each cabbage roll, seam side down, in the baking pan. Pour remaining tomato sauce over rolls. Cover the pan tightly with aluminum foil. Bake in 350°F (175°C) oven for about 50 minutes. Serve hot.

**Calories: 609, Fat: 25 g (10 g saturated), Protein: 29 g,
Cholesterol: 85 mg, Carbohydrates: 65 g, Sodium: 195 mg**

◆ Stuffed Zucchini ◆

MAKES 4 SERVINGS

A good way to use those zucchini that grew too big! Fennel seeds make the beef taste like sweet Italian sausage. Or use a fennel "tea" (see Pizza Toppings, page 146).

1   *pound (450 g) very lean ground beef*
4   *medium zucchini, cut in half lengthwise*
2   *teaspoons (10 mL) fennel seeds*
1   *medium onion, finely diced*
1   *clove garlic, minced*
1   *slice low-sodium bread, toasted*

Half fill a large skillet with water; bring to a boil. Add the zucchini, cut side down; boil for 10 minutes; drain. Scoop out seeds and soft center; reserve. Arrange the zucchini shells in a baking pan; line the pan with foil for easy cleanup. Wrap the fennel seeds in a small piece of cheese cloth and secure the ends of the cloth with a rubber band, wrapped around and around. Put the little package of fennel seeds into skillet with the ground beef. Fry the meat with the fennel in the pan. Stir in the onion and garlic; cook gently until the meat is no longer red. Remove and discard the bag of fennel seeds. Drain the fat off from the cooked meat.

Chop the zucchini flesh and mix with the meat; fill the zucchini shells. Crumble the toast in the blender, to make approximately 1/3 cup (80 mL) of bread crumbs; sprinkle on the stuffed zucchini. Bake in 350° F (175° C) oven for about 20 minutes.

**Calories: 323, Fat: 20 g (8 g saturated), Protein: 25 g,
Cholesterol: 78 mg, Carbohydrates: 12 g, Sodium: 84 mg**

◆ Stuffed Green Peppers ◆

MAKES 4 SERVINGS

Make this delicious meal ahead and keep it in the refrigerator until dinner time. If cold, bake for an additional 10 minutes or until hot. Good with Gentle Italian seasoning in the Unsalt Shaker (page 39). Peppers may also be stuffed with other fillings—Macaroni and Beef Casserole (page 142) or Macaroni and Cheese (page 138).

   8 *green or sweet red peppers*
   1 *tablespoon (15 mL) safflower oil*
   1 *medium onion, finely chopped*
   1 *pound (450 g) lean ground beef*
   2 *tablespoons (30 mL) fresh parsley, finely chopped*
   1 *teaspoon (5 mL) basil*
 1/4 *cup (60 mL) no-salt-added tomato paste diluted with
       1/4 cup (60 mL) water*
   2 *cups (500 mL) cooked rice, cooked without salt*
   1 *cup (250 mL) Tomato Sauce (page 61, optional) or water*

Cut tops off peppers and save; discard seeds and white membranes. Put peppers and tops in a steamer and steam for about 10 minutes. Meanwhile make the filling: Heat oil in a skillet and cook the onion for a few minutes, or until soft; add meat and cook over medium heat until the meat is browned and grainy; drain off any fat; add the seasonings, tomato mixture, and the cooked rice. Lightly fill the peppers with the stuffing. Cover with pepper tops. Place in ovenproof baking pan. Add tomato sauce or water to the pan. Bake for about 20 minutes in 350°F (175°C) oven.

Calories: 571, Fat: 28 g (10 g saturated), Protein: 27 g,
Cholesterol: 85 mg, Carbohydrates: 54 g, Sodium: 127

◆ Moussaka ◆

The traditional version of moussaka is layered with lamb and eggplant in a flat pan like a lasagne pan. There are many variations of this casserole using thin slices of potatoes or zucchini, layered with or without the eggplant. When ground lamb is not available, beef is frequently substituted. And leftover meat can be diced and used, if you like.

    1   *medium eggplant*
 1¹/2   *tablespoons (22 mL) olive oil*
    1   *pound (450 g) very lean ground beef, ground lamb, or*
        finely diced cooked lamb*
    1   *medium onion, chopped*
    1   *clove garlic, minced*
    6   *tablespoons (85 mL) no-salt-added tomato paste*
  1/2   *cup (125 mL) water*
  1/4   *teaspoon (1 mL) cinnamon*
        ground pepper
    2   *tablespoons (30 mL) parsley, finely chopped*
  1/4   *cup (75 mL) + 1 tablespoon (15 mL) unsalted*
        margarine
  1/2   *cup (125 mL) flour*
    1   *cup (250 mL) skim milk*
    1   *cup (250 mL) Chicken Stock (page 96)***
        dash white pepper
  1/4   *cup (60 mL) Roll and Bake Coating Mix (page 42) or*
        use crumbs from low-sodium bread

Slice eggplant 1/2-inch (1.3 cm) thick. Brush a very thin layer of olive oil over both sides of the eggplant slices. Bake the slices until the top side is lightly browned, about 10 minutes, or broil a minute or two on each side. Make the meat mixture: Cook the meat, onion, and garlic in a large frying pan over medium heat until no pink color remains; drain off any fat and add the tomato paste, water, cinnamon, pepper, and parsley. Turn heat down and simmer until tender, about 25 minutes. While the meat mixture is simmering, make the white sauce: Melt 1/4 cup (60 mL) of the margarine over low heat; add the flour and stir with a wire whisk until well blended and cook over low heat for a couple of minutes; then add the milk, stock, and stir constantly with a whisk until thick.

To assemble the moussaka: Line a flat baking dish with aluminum foil (to make cleanup easier). Layer half the eggplant slices in bottom of baking dish with the meat mixture on top; spread evenly and cover with remaining eggplant slices. Cover with white sauce. Mix the Roll and Bake (or low-sodium bread crumbs) with the remaining tablespoon (15 mL) margarine and sprinkle the mixture on top of the casserole. Bake in 350°F (175°C) oven about 30 to 45 minutes (longer if the casserole has been made ahead of time and refrigerated). Let sit for 10 minutes to make it easier to cut into portions.

If using cooked, diced meat, add to tomato sauce during last 5 minutes while simmering.

**If you find the taste of prepackaged low-sodium chicken broth acceptable you may use it in place of the homemade stock. You may also want to try plain water as a chicken stock substitute. Using 2 cups (500 mL) of skim milk in place of the stock would increase the calcium (and sodium).*

Calories: 598, Fat: 40 g (11 g saturated), Protein: 29 g, Cholesterol: 80 mg, Carbohydrates: 32 g, Sodium: 328 mg

◆ Zucchini Moussaka ◆

MAKES 4 SERVINGS

Substitute one pound (450 g) zucchini for the eggplant for a hearty casserole. Slice zucchini into thin slices; no need to broil or bake before layering.

Calories: 584, Fat: 40 g (11 g saturated), Protein: 29 g, Cholesterol: 80 mg, Carbohydrates: 28 g, Sodium: 329 mg

BEANS

——◆◆——

Beans may have a plebeian reputation but can make scrumptious meals with imagination. Beans have so many good points that shouldn't be overlooked: They are very low in sodium, fat, and cholesterol, very nutritious, and can be combined with rice or pasta to make a complete-protein meal without the cholesterol and sodium of meat or fish; beans are inexpensive and keep very well. Many favorite ethnic bean recipes suggest beans cooked in delicious ways. Just plan ahead.

To prepare, wash the beans* and cover with water; let them soak overnight. If you haven't done this, here is an alternative method: Place the washed beans in a large cooking pot, cover with water and bring to a boil for one minute. Turn the heat off, cover, and let the beans soak for one hour. To cook: bring to a boil; turn down the heat and simmer until the beans are tender, about 2 hours. Freeze beans in one-meal portions. Beans expand in volume when cooked. For example, one pound or 2 1/2 cups (600 mL) of uncooked kidney beans, will measure 5 cups (1.2 L) after cooking. Each cup (250 mL) of cooked kidney beans contains 6 mg of sodium.

* *Beans do not cook well in hard water. If you substitute bottled water, you should have no problem in the future.*

◆ Baked Beans, an American Classic ◆

MAKES 8 SERVINGS

Dry white beans are called great northern beans or pea beans. They are still a terrific buy and provide excellent nutrition. They also are naturally low in sodium. Many people like the convenience of canned pork and beans, but the sodium content is far too high (850 mg in 1 cup or 250 mL). It's easy to make homemade baked beans as long as you plan ahead. Sweet Relish (page 50) goes well with baked beans.

Beans are a very good source of vegetable protein. But to make the protein more complete, plan to serve the beans with a product that comes from corn or rice. Many traditional recipes use these combinations—beans with corn bread or beans with rice. You may want to add a small amount of a complete protein food, such as pork. The traditional ingredient for beans is a piece of salt pork (399 mg in a small piece). A small trimmed pork chop is a logical substitute, although it can be omitted.

1   pound (450 g) dry white beans
2   medium onions, cut in half
1/4 cup (60 mL) low-sodium ketchup
1/4 cup (60 mL) white sugar
1/4 cup (60 mL) dark molasses
2   teaspoons (10 mL) dry mustard
1   small pork chop trimmed of all fat and bone* (optional)

The night before, wash the beans, place in a bowl with water to cover; soak overnight. The next morning, discard the soaking water; mix the beans with all other ingredients in a casserole.** Add water to cover. Cover the casserole. Place in 300°F (150°C) oven and bake for several hours or all day. Check beans from time to time, adding water if necessary.

* *Since you can't serve "franks and beans" to people on low-sodium diets, you may want to add additional small, thin pork chops, so that each person gets one chop with his or her beans. Each small chop adds 30 mg of sodium.*

** *A bean pot is still the best container for cooking beans.*

Calories: 292, Fat: 3 g (1 g saturated), Protein: 16 g, Cholesterol: 9 mg, Carbohydrates: 53 g, Sodium: 21 mg

RICE

Did you know that rice has traditionally been the mainstay of blood-pressure-lowering diets? Rice is a natural for anyone cutting down on salt, because there arc less than 10 mg in a cup (250 mL) of cooked rice.

The commercial flavored rices, however, are extremely high in sodium. For example, a 6-ounce (180-g) package of Uncle Ben's beef-flavored rice has almost 4,000 mg of sodium.

If plain boiled rice, cooked without salt, tastes bland, make rice more flavorful and avoid the sodium in commercial products. Serve rice with dishes that have a tasty sauce such as Baked Chicken in Wine, Chicken Marengo (page 159), Curry (page 196), Chicken Cacciatore (page 160), Swedish Meatballs with Gravy (page 178), Beef Bourguignon (page 173) and Shrimp or Fish Creole (page 155); cook the rice in chicken or beef broth and add seasonings for more flavor and color; fry the cooked rice in a little oil and add chopped vegetables; toss rice with a little low-sodium Tomato Sauce (page 61).

◆ Fried Rice ◆

Use leftover rice and heat just before eating. To increase the protein value of the dish, add a cup of chopped leftover meat when you add the rice. You can also add 1/2 cup (125 mL) of sesame seeds after the onions are cooked and before you add the rice to complement the proteins.

  2 *tablespoons (30 mL) safflower oil*
  2 *medium onions, chopped fine*
  1 *medium green pepper, chopped fine*
1/4 *teaspoon (1 mL) garlic powder*
  4 *cups (1 L) cooked rice (preferably cooked in a flavored broth)*
1/2 *cup (125 mL) water*
     ground black pepper

Heat the oil in a large skillet. Add the onions, green pepper, and garlic powder. Cook gently until the onions are soft. Add the cooked rice and water. Stir and cook gently until the rice is heated through. Add the black pepper. Stir again. Serve hot.

Calories: 197, Fat: 5 g (0 g saturated), Protein: 4 g, Cholesterol: 0 mg, Carbohydrates: 34 g, Sodium: 3 mg

◆ Rice Flavored with Chicken Stock ◆

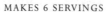

If you use a quick cooking rice, follow the directions on the box but replace the amount of water with homemade stock and add onion powder.

21/2 *cups (600 mL) Chicken Stock (page 96)*
  1 *cup (250 mL) raw converted rice*
  1 *teaspoon (5 mL) safflower oil*
1/2 *teaspoon (2 mL) onion powder*

Bring the stock to a boil in a saucepan that has a tight-fitting lid. Stir in the rice, oil, and onion powder; cover the pot tightly and cook very gently over low heat for 20 minutes. Remove from heat, uncover, and wrap in towel for 5 minutes.

Calories: 143, Fat: 2 g (0 g saturated), Protein: 4 g, Cholesterol: 0 mg, Carbohydrates: 27 g, Sodium: 52 mg

◆ Hopping John ◆

Black-eyed peas with rice, a traditional ethnic food.

   1 *cup (250 mL) black-eyed peas*
   1 *small pork chop, trimmed of all visible fat*
 1/4 *teaspoon (1 mL) liquid hickory smoke*
   4 *cups (1 L) water*
   1 *teaspoon (5 mL) chili powder (check the sodium content)*
   1 *medium onion, chopped*
2 2/3 *cups (640 mL) cooked rice, cooked without salt*

Wash and drain the beans. Combine in a casserole with pork chop, smoke flavoring, and water; cook gently for 45 minutes; add a small amount of water as needed to keep the beans from sticking. Add the chili powder and onion. Continue simmering for 30 minutes or until the beans are tender and most of the liquid is absorbed. Mix the cooked beans and the rice together. Serve warm.

**Calories: 244, Fat: 4 g (1 g saturated), Protein: 12 g,
Cholesterol: 19 mg, Carbohydrates: 41 g, Sodium: 31 mg**

◆ Louisiana Red Beans and Rice ◆

SERVES 4

   8 *ounces (225 g) dry red or kidney beans**
   2 *medium onions, chopped*
   4 *scallions, chopped*
   1 *clove garlic, finely chopped*
   1 *green or red pepper, chopped*
 1/2 *cup (125 mL) fresh parsley, finely chopped*
 1/2 *teaspoon (2 mL) cayenne pepper*
     dash ground black pepper
     dash Tabasco sauce
   3 *ounces (90 g) no-salt-added tomato paste*
 1/4 *teaspoon (1 mL) oregano*
 1/4 *teaspoon (1 mL) thyme*
 1/2 *teaspoon (2 mL) liquid hickory smoke*
2 2/3 *cups (640 mL) cooked rice, cooked without salt*

Wash red or kidney beans and soak overnight or for several hours in cold water (see page 192 for alternate method). Drain off the soaking water; put the beans into a large cooking pot and add enough water to cover. Simmer over medium heat for 15 minutes and add all other ingredients, except the rice. Cook about 2 hours, or until beans are tender. Serve beans over cooked rice.

You can double the recipe and cook all the beans, and freeze for a later low-sodium meal.

Calories: 384, Fat: 1 g (0 g saturated), Protein: 18 g, Cholesterol: 0 mg, Carbohydrates: 77 g, Sodium: 36 mg

CURRY

◆ Anything Curry ◆

MAKES 4 SERVINGS

With leftovers, you can make this glamorous dish quickly—an exotic way to use leftover meat. Chunks of cooked chicken, lamb, pork, or beef, canned low-sodium tuna, or cooked fresh shrimp can be used. The curry looks beautiful surrounded by little side dishes.*This recipe does not make a "hot" curry.

If you want to make this dish but don't have any leftover meat, simmer 4 chicken breasts in water to cover for approximately 40 minutes. Then, you will have chicken and stock.

3 tablespoons (45 mL) unsalted margarine
1 small onion, finely diced or sliced
1 tablespoon (15 mL) curry powder, less if you like a milder curry flavor
1/4 cup (60 mL) flour
3/4 teaspoon (4 mL) sugar
1/8 teaspoon (.5 mL) ginger
2 cups (500 mL) Chicken Stock (page 96) or substitute skim milk
3 cups (750 mL) diced cooked chicken, lamb, beef, fish, shrimp, etc.
1/2 teaspoon (2 mL) lemon juice

Melt the margarine in a saucepan or Dutch oven. Add the onion and curry powder. Cook gently over low heat until the onion is soft and yellow. Stir in the flour, sugar, and ginger. Add the chicken stock. Blend well and stir until mixture begins to boil. Allow it to boil for about 1 minute.

Just before serving, add chicken and lemon juice. Heat gently. Serve over rice with accompaniments, suggested below.

* Some suggested side dishes: Five-Minute Chutney (page 51); tomato wedges, or chopped tomato; pan-fried onion rings; unsalted, slivered almonds; pineapple chunks; unsalted chopped peanuts; currant jelly; chopped avocado; flaked coconut.

**Calories: 596, Fat: 18 g (4 g saturated), Protein: 88 g,
Cholesterol: 222 mg, Carbohydrates: 16 g, Sodium: 245 mg**

TEX-MEX COOKING

◆ Easy Mexican Sauce ◆

MAKES 1²/3 CUPS

You can buy convenient sauces in jars but unfortunately they all have salt. Fresh unsalted sauces are easy to make. You may prefer a very smooth sauce, or one that has finely chopped fresh vegetables.

 6 ounces (170 mL) no-salt-added tomato paste
 1 cup (250 mL) water
 1/4 cup (60 mL) vinegar
 1 tablespoon (15 mL) olive oil
 2 teaspoons (10 mL) sugar
 1 teaspoon (5 mL) chili powder
 1/2 teaspoon (2 mL) onion powder
   dash cayenne pepper
   dash Tabasco sauce

Combine all ingredients in a saucepan and simmer for a few minutes. Add more Tabasco sauce if you like it hotter. This sauce can be frozen.

**Calories per tablespoon: 12, Fat: 1 g (0 g saturated), Protein: 0 g,
Cholesterol: 0 mg, Carbohydrates: 2 g, Sodium: 7 mg**

◆ Fresh Tomato Sauce with Chili ◆

  2   *medium ripe tomatoes, peeled*
¹/2   *medium green pepper*
  2   *hot peppers or chili peppers* for people who like it hot*
¹/2   *small onion, grated*
¹/4   *teaspoon (1 mL) oregano*
¹/4   *teaspoon (1 mL) garlic powder*

Finely dice the tomato and green pepper. Dice the hot peppers and combine all the vegetables and spices in a bowl. It's best if the flavors are allowed to blend for several hours.

* If you don't have or don't like fresh chili peppers, you can substitute Salt-Free Chili Powder (page 41) or Tabasco sauce to taste.

Calories per tablespoon: 6, Fat: 0 g (0 g saturated), Protein: 0 g, Cholesterol: 0 mg, Carbohydrates: 1 g, Sodium: 1 mg

TORTILLAS

Tortillas can be made from corn flour or regular white flour. You can make them from scratch from special corn flour called *masa harina*, a product of Quaker Oats, which is available in some large or Hispanic markets. Regular cornmeal will not work.

Canned tortillas are fairly commonly available, but they contain salt. Each Old El Paso brand tortilla in a can has approximately 118 mg of sodium. Frozen tortillas may also be available. Check the label to see if salt is an ingredient. Fresh corn tortillas are often refrigerated in markets near the eggs. Check the label; you may be able to find a no-added-salt brand. At home, you can make unsalted tortillas from all-purpose flour.

◆ Flour Tortillas ◆

These are the tortillas used in making burritos.

2¹/2   *cups (625 mL) flour*
  5   *tablespoons (75 mL) unsalted margarine*
¹/2   *cup (125 mL) warm water*

Mix 2 cups (500 mL) of the flour in a medium bowl with 4 tablespoons (60 mL) margarine (clean fingers work well). When the margarine is mixed in, gradually stir in the water to make a soft dough. Divide the dough into 12 parts, the size of large walnuts; work the dough to make a smooth ball out of each part. Rub some of the reserved margarine on your clean hands and spread on the outside of each ball; place it in the bowl. Cover the bowl with a clean cloth and set it aside for 15 minutes or so.

Heat an ungreased frying pan over medium high heat or heat an electric frying pan to 375°F (190°C). Flatten one ball between the palms of your hands. Flour it on both sides. Use a rolling pin to roll out the tortilla until it is almost paper thin, 7½- to 8-inches (20 cm) across. Use small amounts of additional flour as needed. Put the tortilla in the frying pan to cook on one side until the tortilla bubbles and the underside is lightly flecked with brown. Flip the tortilla over and press it down with a spatula. Cook until the second side is also flecked with brown spots. Some cooks like to roll out all the tortillas first and cook in two or more frying pans at once.

As you cook the tortillas, stack them and cover them with a towel. If the tortillas are to be filled later and have become too brittle to roll up without cracking, you can hold them, one at a time, over steaming water, to make them flexible again.

Calories per tortilla: 137, Fat: 5 g (1 g saturated), Protein: 3 g, Cholesterol: 0 mg, Carbohydrates: 20 g, Sodium: 1 mg

◆ Burritos ◆

MAKES 12 BURRITOS

Burritos, a lot of fun to make with a group of friends, are wheat tortillas rolled around a filling. Make the filling and sauces ahead of time and have people help cook, fill, and roll the burritos.

12   *Flour Tortillas (opposite)*
    Meat Filling for Tacos or Burritos (page 201) or Refried
    Beans (page 203) or both
    Guacamole (page 202, optional)
    Easy Mexican Sauce (page 197, optional)
    low-sodium cheese, grated (optional)

On each tortilla center, spoon 2 to 3 tablespoons (30–50 mL) of the meat or refried bean filling, or you can put on a little of each. If you like, add guacamole, sauce, and cheese to the filling. Fold each side of the tortilla over about one inch as if you were making an envelope. Start at the bottom and roll up the tortilla, keeping the sides tucked in. Serve with optional garnishes as toppings. Burritos can be eaten with a knife and fork or held in the hand like a sandwich.

◆ Enchiladas ◆

MAKES 12 ENCHILADAS

Enchiladas are another popular Mexican food, consisting of a tortilla with a filling inside and sauce on the outside. Enchiladas are often topped with cheese; they also may be baked in the oven until the cheese melts.

Although traditional enchiladas are made from corn tortillas, you can also make the less traditional Flour Tortillas (page 198). "Tortilla" restaurants serve burritos topped with a spicy sauce strewn with cheese. Serve such a Mexican casserole at home!

  12 Burritos with your choice of filling (page 199)
   2 cups (500 mL) Easy Mexican Sauce (page 197)
   4 ounces (120 g) low-sodium cheese, about 2/3 cup (180 mL), grated

Arrange the stuffed burritos in a 9" by 12" (23 cm by 30 cm) flat baking pan. Pour the sauce over them. Sprinkle the cheese on top. Cover with aluminum foil. Bake in 350°F (175°C) oven for approximately 15 minutes.

◆ Tacos ◆

Tacos—Mexican equivalents of sandwiches or snacks—are crispy corn tortillas that have been folded in the middle and filled with various fillings. Many brands of no-salt-added taco shells are aids to low-sodium cooking. If you can't find a brand without added salt, estimate that each taco adds a little sodium. For example, each Ortega taco shell has 55 mg.

To heat taco shells: turn oven on to 250°F (120°C). Pull oven rack out. Take a taco shell and place it upside down, so that it is hanging suspended over a metal rod of the oven rack. Repeat with number of shells desired. Heat for a few minutes. You can leave the extra ones hanging in the oven while eating the first ones. Reheat if necessary before serving.

To assemble tacos: Scoop about 2 tablespoons (30 mL) of refried beans or other filling of your choice into a warm taco shell. You probably want to put out small bowls of different foods that people can add to their own tacos. Popular garnishes: Refried Beans (page 203), Meat Filling for Tacos or Burritos (below), chopped fresh tomato, chopped onion, chopped cucumber, shredded lettuce, and grated low-sodium cheese, such as no-salt-added Swiss. Sprinkle a small amount of olive oil and vinegar and spices over the chopped vegetables. You can also fill small bowls with sauces and let people spoon on a little sauce if they want to.

◆ Meat Filling for Tacos or Burritos ◆

MAKES 8 SERVINGS

This seasoned ground beef is a great alternative filling to refried beans. Or use leftover Chili con Carne (page 213) or Sloppy Joe filling (page 94) as taco filling.

 1 *pound (450 g) very lean ground beef*
 1 *medium onion, finely chopped*
 1 *clove garlic, minced*
 1 *teaspoon (5 mL) chili powder*
 3 *tablespoons (45 mL) no-salt-added tomato paste*
 1 *tablespoon (15 mL) vinegar*
    dash Tabasco sauce (optional)

Sauté the hamburger, onion, and garlic over medium heat; drain off the fat. Add the chili powder, tomato paste, vinegar, and Tabasco sauce. Stir and heat thoroughly.

**Calories: 145, Fat: 10 g (4 g saturated), Protein: 11 g,
Cholesterol: 39 mg, Carbohydrates: 3 g, Sodium: 47 mg**

◆ Tex-Mex Guacamole Topping ◆

It's best served fresh. If you make it a little ahead of time, cover it well with plastic wrap and refrigerate. Guacamole may turn darker, but the flavor is still good.

   2   *small ripe avocados or 1 large avocado*
   2   *teaspoons (10 mL) lime or lemon juice*
  1/2 *teaspoon (2 mL) garlic powder*
  1/2 *teaspoon (2 mL) onion powder*
       dash Tabasco sauce
   1   *chopped ripe tomato (optional)*

Slice the avocados in half; remove the pits. Using a spoon, scoop out the avocado flesh. Put the avocado, lime or lemon juice, and seasonings into a food processor or blender. (Ideally, use the mixing blade of a food processor to mash it. If you use a blender, be careful that it does not become totally liquefied.) Or mash with a fork for chunkier consistency. Add the tomato if desired.

Calories per tablespoon: 29, Fat: 3 g (0 g saturated), Protein: 0 g, Cholesterol: 0 mg, Carbohydrates: 2 g, Sodium: 2 mg

◆ Chicken Filling for Tacos ◆

MAKES 8 SERVINGS

   2   *tablespoons (30 mL) safflower oil*
   1   *medium onion, finely chopped*
   1   *clove garlic, finely chopped*
   1   *pound (450 g) boneless chicken breasts*
  1/2 *cup (125 mL) Easy Mexican Sauce (page 197)*

Heat the oil in a large skillet. Add the onion and garlic and cook gently for a few minutes until the onion is soft. Add the chicken and cook over low heat; use two forks to tear the chicken into shreds as it cooks. Chicken is cooked when it is no longer pink. Add the sauce and stir.

Calories: 110, Fat: 5 g (1 g saturated), Protein: 14 g, Cholesterol: 33 mg, Carbohydrates: 3 g, Sodium: 44 mg

◆ Refried Beans for Tacos or Burritos ◆

MAKES 8 SERVINGS

Delicious as a side dish or for Tacos (page 200) and Burritos (page 199).

 8 *ounces (225 g) red or kidney beans*
 2 *onions, chopped*
 2 *cloves garlic, minced*
 1 *bay leaf*
 1 *teaspoon (5 mL) chili powder (check the sodium content)*
 2 *tablespoons (30 mL) safflower oil*
 3 *ounces (85 g) no-salt-added tomato paste*

Cook beans according to directions under Beans (page 192), and cook beans with one onion, one clove garlic, bay leaf, and chili powder. Cook for about 2 hours, or until the beans are tender, adding water, if necessary, to prevent the beans from going dry; little liquid should be left. Discard the bay leaf. Heat the oil in a large skillet and add the remaining onion and garlic; stir and cook gently for a few minutes; turn off heat. Add about 1/4 cup (60 mL) of cooked beans to the skillet with some of the cooking liquid. Mash with a fork or a potato masher. Continue to add beans and mash them in the skillet. Serve warm.

Calories: 147, Fat: 4 g (0 g saturated), Protein: 7 g, Cholesterol: 0 mg,
Carbohydrates: 22 g, Sodium: 17 mg

◆ Chili con Carne ◆

MAKES 6 SERVINGS

With a tossed salad, this is a complete meal. This chili mixture can also be used as a filling for taco shells. If you freeze chili con carne in small amounts (as in an ice cube tray), you can defrost a cube to make a Chili Burger (page 92) out of a plain hamburger.

 1 *pound (450 g) lean ground beef*
 1 *tablespoon (15 mL) safflower oil*
 1 *green pepper, chopped*
 1 *medium onion, chopped finely*
 2 *cloves garlic, finely chopped*
 1 *teaspoon (5 mL) oregano*
1/2 *teaspoon (2.5 mL) paprika*

1   teaspoon *(5 mL) cumin*
1   teaspoon *(5 mL) chili powder*
6   ounces *(170 mL) no-salt-added tomato paste mixed with*
    2 cans of water
3   cups *(750 mL) kidney beans (cooked without salt)*
    ground fresh pepper

Cook the ground beef in a skillet over medium heat, stirring with a fork and breaking the meat into small chunks until no pink color is left. Drain off any fat. (You can put a double layer of paper towels on a dinner plate and use a slotted spoon to put the cooked meat on the towels.) In the same skillet, heat the oil over medium heat and sauté the onion, chopped pepper, and garlic for a few minutes or until tender, stirring frequently. Remove from heat and stir in seasonings. Add the tomato paste and water, drained ground beef, and kidney beans. Bring to a boil, lower heat, and simmer for about 1 hour.

Calories: 373, Fat: 19 g (7 g saturated), Protein: 23 g,
Cholesterol: 57 mg, Carbohydrates: 30 g, Sodium: 85 mg

◆ Chili non Carne ◆

If you want to make a delicious vegetarian version, just leave out the meat. Instead, use 3 green peppers, cut into small chunks, and 2 medium onions, chopped. Chili non carne is usually served over cooked rice to provide complete proteins.

POPULAR CHINESE FOODS

——◆◆——

Packaged Chinese convenience foods are high in sodium, and Chinese restaurants are off-limits for low-sodium eaters. The obvious solution is to cook from scratch at home. But many of the traditional ingredients in Chinese cooking are high in sodium. Water chestnuts (even fresh ones), soy sauce, canned bean sprouts, dried mushrooms, and of course MSG, cannot be used in low-sodium cooking.

◆ Chinese Pepper Steak ◆

MAKES 4 SERVINGS

Good served over rice or noodles.

 1   *pound (450 g) boneless steak such as round or sirloin*
 1   *tablespoon (15 mL) safflower oil*
 1   *clove garlic, peeled*
 4   *medium green or red peppers, cut into chunks*
1/4 *teaspoon (1 mL) onion powder*
 3   *tablespoons (45 mL) sherry (not cooking sherry)*
 2   *tablespoons (30 mL) lemon juice*
 1   *tablespoon (15 mL) sugar*
2/3 *cup (180 mL) boiling water*
 3   *tablespoons (45 mL) cornstarch*
 1   *tablespoon (15 mL) Soy Sauce Substitute (page 48)*

Place the meat in the freezer to partially freeze it so that it will be easier to slice; slice the meat across the grain into thin strips. If you are using a tough cut of meat, you may want to sprinkle it with an unsalted meat tenderizer.

Heat the oil in a wok or skillet over medium high heat. Add the garlic and cook for a minute or so, or until you can smell the garlic; remove garlic. Add the pieces of pepper to the wok and stir-fry for approximately 3 minutes. If you prefer the peppers less crisp, cook longer. Using a slotted spoon, remove the peppers and reserve. Add the pieces of meat and stir-fry until the pink color is gone, about 4 minutes. Mix onion powder, 2 tablespoons (30 mL) sherry, lemon juice, sugar, and boiling water. Add the sauce to the meat with the green peppers. Turn the heat down to medium low; cover and cook for approximately 5 minutes. Meanwhile, combine the cornstarch, Soy Sauce Substitute, and remaining sherry, and pour into the wok. Stir for a minute or two, or until the sauce is thickened.

Calories: 369, Fat: 22 g (8 g saturated), Protein: 23 g, Cholesterol: 76 mg, Carbohydrates: 18 g, Sodium: 65 mg

◆ Egg Rolls ◆

MAKES 16 EGG ROLLS

Wonderful for dinner or informal get-togethers. Much better than frozen or store-bought. To make tiny Egg Roll Hors d'Oeuvres, see the instructions in the Snacks and Appetizers chapter (page 81). Buy no-added-salt egg roll wrappers. (We have found them in the vegetable section and in the dairy section of large markets and in Asian specialty stores.)*

3/4 *cup (180 mL) onions, diced*
3/4 *cup (180 mL) green peppers, chopped*
1 1/2 *cups (375 mL) mung bean sprouts or other vegetables, chopped*
1 *cup (250 mL) cooked chicken or pork*
1 1/2 *tablespoons (22 mL) sherry (not cooking sherry)*
1 1/2 *tablespoons (22 mL) lemon juice*
1 1/2 *tablespoons (22 mL) sugar*
3 *teaspoons (15 mL) cornstarch*
1 *tablespoon (15 mL) peanut oil*
1 *clove garlic*
16 *no-salt-added egg roll wrappers*
2 *cups safflower or peanut oil for frying*

Prepare all the vegetables and the chicken or pork: Using a food processor to chop the vegetables or taking the time to dice the vegetables very fine makes the filling look very professional; cut the chicken or pork into narrow strips. Set the vegetables and meat aside. Combine the sherry, lemon juice, sugar, and 2 teaspoons (10 mL) cornstarch in a small bowl. Heat 1 tablespoon (15 mL) of oil in a wok or skillet over medium high heat. Add the garlic and stir-fry for a few seconds; discard the garlic. Add the vegetables to the hot oil and stir-fry for a minute. Add the meat and stir-fry for an additional minute. Add the sherry-lemon sauce and stir to combine all the ingredients. Continue stirring for a minute or two. There should be very little liquid left. Turn off the heat and set aside. To make the sealing liquid, combine the remaining teaspoon (5 mL) cornstarch and 1/2 cup (125 mL) hot water.

To stuff egg rolls: Place the wrapper on a flat working surface with one of the corners pointing towards you. Spread approximately 1/4 cup (60 mL) of filling diagonally on the wrapper. Fold the corner nearest you over the filling. Fold the sides in so that the corners touch. Moisten the last flap with the sealing liquid. Roll the egg roll and seal it by smoothing it with your finger. (Egg roll wrappers come with illustrations that make the whole process very easy.) Keep covered to prevent drying.

Pour 2 cups (500 mL) safflower or peanut oil into a wok, skillet, or electric frying pan and heat to 400°F (205°C).

Fry 2 or 3 at a time to maintain the oil temperature. Fry on the first side for 3 minutes or until the underside is crisp and brown. Using tongs or a spatula, turn the egg rolls over and fry for an additional 2 to 3 minutes. Drain on paper towels. Serve hot.

* Egg rolls are often served with dipping sauces. Hot or Mild Mustard are good dips (pages 44 and 45); Soy Sauce Substitute (page 48) or Sweet-and-Sour Marinade (page 58) can be used.

Calories per egg roll: 405, Fat: 11 g (2 g saturated), Protein: 16 g, Cholesterol: 25 mg, Carbohydrates: 59 g, Sodium: 80 mg

◆ Chow Mein ◆

MAKES 4 SERVINGS

This popular dish can also be made with cooked leftover chicken, turkey, or pork and served over rice. The convenient canned fried noodles have approximately 200 mg of sodium in a small (1/2 cup or 125 mL) serving.

1	medium onion
1/2	green pepper
6	medium mushrooms
1	cup (250 mL) mung beans, other sprouts, or shredded cabbage
10	ounces (300 g) boneless chicken breasts
3	tablespoons (45 mL) lemon juice
1	tablespoon (15 mL) sugar
3	tablespoons (45 mL) sherry (not cooking sherry)
2/3	cup (180 mL) boiling water

1   *tablespoon (15 mL) peanut oil*
1   *clove garlic, peeled*
2   *tablespoons (30 mL) cornstarch*

Prepare the vegetables: Cut the onion and green pepper into chunks; slice the mushrooms and sprouts; arrange vegetables on a plate. Cut the chicken into thin strips and have the pieces ready on a plate. Combine 2 tablespoons (30 mL) of the lemon juice, the sugar, and 2 tablespoons (30 mL) sherry in a small bowl. Stir in the boiling water; set aside.

Heat the oil in a wok or skillet over medium heat. Add the garlic for a minute or so until you can smell the garlic. Add the onions and stir-fry for 30 seconds (push the onion pieces from side to side with a wooden spoon, wok utensil, or spatula). Add the green pepper and stir-fry for another 30 seconds. Add the chicken and stir-fry for approximately 2 minutes. (Cooked leftover pieces of meat need only be stirred in for a few seconds to heat.) Add the mushrooms and stir-fry for another minute. Add the sprouts and lemon juice mixture. Stir to combine. Turn the heat down, cover, and cook for 3 minutes.

While it is cooking, combine the cornstarch with remaining lemon juice and sherry. Add this to the wok and stir for another minute or two, until the sauce has thickened.

**Calories: 261, Fat: 5 g (1 g saturated), Protein: 24 g,
Cholesterol: 41 mg, Carbohydrates: 30 g, Sodium: 58 mg**

BREADS

◆◆◆◆◆

You probably don't know anyone who doesn't like freshly baked bread. But it's too hard and too time-consuming to make, right? Wrong! Just because you have never made bread does not mean that you can't. You'll find delicious and quick recipes in this chapter, all low in sodium.

Of course, the companies that make quick bread mixes and ready-to-cook rolls have been telling us for years that only their products are convenient. Naturally these companies want us to buy their products. But don't let the ads mislead you into thinking that you need to depend on them.

Those convenient dinner rolls are outrageously high in sodium. For example, two Pillsbury crescent rolls (not packages) contain more than 1,200 mg of sodium. This is in spite of the fact that the basic ingredients (flour, yeast, shortening) start out with negligible sodium.

For a few minutes of work you can save 1,312 sodium mg per serving. And you will make the people in your family feel pampered. Extra bread or rolls can be frozen and reheated for later meals.

Homemade bread needs to be sliced thin to make toast. You may want to buy a special "bread knife" or sharpen your old knife. Bread slices more easily after it has cooled. This chapter includes recipes for quick breads, muffins, and yeast breads.

QUICK BREADS AND MUFFINS

◆◆

The secret to low-sodium quick breads and muffins: Low-sodium baking powder, which unfortunately, is not as easy to use as regular baking powder. We have found that it really helps to do two things: first, always sift the flour before measuring it; second, always shake and stir low-sodium baking powder before measuring it. Do this shaking each time you use it, beginning the first time you open the jar.

◆ Corn Muffins ◆

Muffins are easy to make. Don't use an electric mixer or you'll overbeat them.

- 2/3 cup (180 mL) cornmeal*
- 13/4 cups (480 mL) flour
- 1/4 cup (60 mL) sugar
- 2 tablespoons (30 mL) low-sodium baking powder (shake and stir before measuring)
- 1 egg or equivalent egg substitute
- 3 tablespoons (45 mL) safflower oil
- 1/2 cup (125 mL) skim milk
- 1/2 cup (125 mL) water

Prepare an 8-inch (20-cm) square pan or 12 muffin cups by spraying them with a vegetable coating spray or brushing lightly with safflower oil. Mix the dry ingredients together in a bowl, using a whisk. In another bowl, beat the eggs; add the oil, milk, and water; mix well. Pour this wet mixture over the dry mixture and stir gently, just enough to moisten. Spoon about 1/4 cup (60 mL) of batter into each muffin cup or pan. The amount in each cup will depend on the size of the muffin cups but, as a general rule, fill the cups about 2/3 to 3/4 full. Bake in 400°F (205°C) oven about 15 to 18 minutes.

Don't use the self-rising kind! This amount of self-rising cornmeal would have over 1,000 mg of sodium.

Calories per muffin: 115, Fat: 3 g (0 g saturated), Protein: 3 g, Cholesterol: 13 mg, Carbohydrates: 19 g, Sodium: 10 mg

◆ Blueberry Muffins ◆

- 3 cups (750 mL) flour (sift before measuring)
- 1/2 cup (125 mL) sugar
- 2 tablespoons (30 mL) low-sodium baking powder (shake and stir before measuring)
- 1/2 cup (125 mL) safflower oil
- 3 eggs or equivalent egg substitute
- 1/2 cup (125 mL) skim milk
- 1/2 cup (125 mL) water

1 cup (250 mL) fresh or frozen blueberries (don't defrost blueberries before using)
confectioner's sugar (optional)

Prepare muffin pans by spraying with a vegetable coating spray. Sift together the flour, sugar, and baking powder in a large bowl. In another bowl combine the oil, eggs, milk, and water. Stir until well mixed. Pour the wet ingredients into the bowl of dry ingredients and stir only until blended, but don't overmix. Add the berries and stir lightly. Spoon the batter into the muffin tins until they are two-thirds full.

Bake in 400°F (205°C) oven for 20 minutes until lightly browned. For a fancy look, sprinkle the muffins with confectioner's sugar while still hot.

Calories per muffin: 165, Fat: 6 g (1 g saturated), Protein: 3 g, Cholesterol: 32 mg, Carbohydrates: 21 g, Sodium: 15 mg

◆ Applesauce Muffins ◆

MAKES 12 MUFFINS

Good to round out a meal any time of day!

1 1/2 cups (375 mL) flour
1/4 cup (60 mL) sugar
2 tablespoons (30 mL) low-sodium baking powder (shake and stir before measuring)
1/2 teaspoon (2 mL) cinnamon
1/4 teaspoon (1 mL) nutmeg
1 egg or equivalent egg substitute
3 tablespoons (45 mL) safflower oil
1/2 cup (125 mL) applesauce
1/4 cup (60 mL) skim milk
1/4 cup (60 mL) water

Prepare 12 muffin cups by coating with a vegetable coating spray or safflower oil. Mix together the flour, sugar, baking powder, cinnamon, and nutmeg in a bowl. In another bowl, beat the egg or egg substitute; add the safflower oil, applesauce, milk, and water; mix well. Pour this wet mixture over the dry mixture and stir gently, just enough to moisten. Spoon about 1/4 cup (60 mL) of the batter into each muffin cup about 2/3 to 3/4 full.

Bake in 400°F (205°C) oven 15 to 20 minutes.

Calories per muffin: 122, Fat: 4 g (0 g saturated), Protein: 2 g, Cholesterol: 18 mg, Carbohydrates: 20 g, Sodium: 11 mg

◆ Lemon Bread ◆

1/4 cup (60 mL) unsalted margarine
3/4 cup (180 mL) sugar
  2 eggs or equivalent egg substitute
  2 teaspoons (10 mL) grated lemon peel
  2 tablespoons (30 mL) low-sodium baking powder
  2 cups (500 mL) flour (sift before measuring)
3/4 cup (180 mL) skim milk
  2 teaspoons (10 mL) fresh lemon juice
  2 tablespoons (30 mL) sugar

Prepare a bread pan by coating with a vegetable coating or with safflower oil. Combine margarine and sugar in a mixing bowl and beat until the mixture is blended and creamy. Add the eggs or the substitute and lemon peel and mix well. Sift together the flour and baking powder. Add about a quarter of the flour mixture to the mixing bowl and blend. Add a splash of milk and blend. Continue alternating flour and milk until all of the flour and milk have been added and the mixture is well blended. Pour the batter into the prepared pan. Bake in 350°F (175°C) oven 50 to 55 minutes until a toothpick inserted in the middle of the bread will come out clean. Mix the 2 teaspoons (10 mL) of lemon juice with the 2 tablespoons (30 mL) of sugar in a small dish. Spoon this mixture over the bread right when hot from the oven. Remove the bread from the pan after it has cooled.

**Calories per slice: 160, Fat: 4 g (1 g saturated), Protein: 3 g,
Cholesterol: 31 mg, Carbohydrates: 28 g, Sodium: 18 mg**

◆ Banana Nut Bread ◆

  3 tablespoons (45 mL) unsalted margarine, melted
  2 cups (500 mL) flour (sift before measuring)
1/4 cup (60 mL) sugar
  3 tablespoons (45 mL) low-sodium baking powder (shake
    and stir before measuring)
  1 egg or equivalent egg substitute
  1 cup (250 mL) mashed banana
1/4 cup (60 mL) skim milk

1/4   cup (60 mL) water
1   teaspoon (5 mL) vanilla extract
3/4   cup (180 mL) chopped walnuts

Prepare a bread pan by coating with a vegetable coating spray or unsalted margarine. Melt the unsalted margarine in a small saucepan.

Mix the flour, sugar, and baking powder in a bowl. In another bowl, beat the egg or egg substitute. Mix in the melted margarine, banana, milk, water, and vanilla. Pour this wet mixture over the dry ingredients. Add the nuts and stir gently, just enough to moisten. Spoon the batter into the prepared pan. Bake in 350°F (175°C) oven for 50 to 60 minutes. Slice when cool.

**Calories per slice: 156, Fat: 7 g (1 g saturated), Protein: 3 g,
Cholesterol: 15 mg, Carbohydrates: 22 g, Sodium: 10 mg**

◆ Popovers ◆

MAKES 6 POPOVERS

Popovers make a special breakfast, brunch, or luncheon choice. For a lunch, you may want to serve chicken salad, chicken curry, or tuna salad and let people fill their own popovers.

2   eggs or equivalent egg substitute
1   cup (250 mL) skim milk
1   tablespoon (15 mL) unsalted margarine
1   cup (15 mL) flour

"Butter" or oil 6 custard cups (a vegetable coating spray can also be used). With an electric mixer or a wire whisk, slightly beat the eggs in a bowl. Add the remaining ingredients and beat for about 1 to 2 minutes at medium speed or until smooth; do not overbeat. Ladle the mixture into the custard cups about 2/3 full. Place the cups on a baking pan in a cold oven. Turn the oven to 400°F (205°C) and bake for 35 minutes. (It's best not to peek.) Serve immediately (popovers do not stay light and high for very long).

**Calories per popover: 132, Fat: 4 g (1 g saturated), Protein: 6 g,
Cholesterol: 72 mg, Carbohydrates: 18 g, Sodium: 43 mg**

YEAST BREADS

Basic bread ingredients—flour, water, yeast, sugar or honey, oil or unsalted margarine—are all naturally low in sodium. Choose your favorite type of flour, the major ingredient. Most markets carry all-purpose flour, unbleached white flour, rye, whole wheat, and bread flour. Be sure never to use self-rising flour; it is extremely high in sodium, approximately 1,645 mg per cup (250 mL). As for bread flour and all-purpose flour, they can be substituted for each other, but you may need slightly more when using all-purpose flour.

Recipes in this book are made with active dry yeast, usually available in packages with three envelopes attached together. In this book, 1 envelope refers to one of the envelopes in the package.

Traditional yeast bread recipes always call for some salt to add flavor and control or actually slow down the yeast action. When you leave out the salt, the dough will rise faster. This means that to prevent the dough from falling you need to be careful not to let the dough rise too high . If the dough drops after it has risen, the baked bread will be flatter and have a coarser texture. It would still be entirely edible, however.

If you are using one of your own bread recipes and you omit the salt, you need to let it rise only about half the time. Recipes in this book have been tested without salt and timings have been adjusted.

QUICK YEAST BREADS

Quick yeast breads, more like thick batter than traditional kneaded bread, are easy to make because they require no kneading. Even if you have never thought about making your own bread, you can be successful with these bread recipes. And there is nothing like the smell of your own bread baking.

◆ Quick White Bread ◆

MAKES 1 LOAF (20 SLICES)

Great for people who never thought they could make bread. Also makes very nice toast. A commercial loaf of white bread contains more than 2,300 mg of sodium.

1   envelope active dry yeast
1   cup (250 mL) warm water
2   tablespoons (30 mL) sugar
2 3/4   cups (640 mL) bread flour or all-purpose flour
2   tablespoons (30 mL) safflower oil
1   egg or equivalent egg substitute
1   teaspoon (5 mL) unsalted margarine (optional)

Stir the yeast, warm water, and sugar in a large bowl until dissolved. Add about half the flour, oil, and the egg or substitute to the yeast mixture. Beat with an electric mixer for 3 to 4 minutes; gradually add remaining flour. Mix until the flour is all blended. The dough will be very sticky. Cover the bowl with a cloth and put it in a warm place to rise until doubled, about 40 minutes.

Oil a loaf pan (nonstick spray is good). Scrape the batter into the loaf pan. Smooth it into the corners. Cover the pan with the cloth and set it in a warm place. Let rise only to the top of the pan. While the dough is rising, preheat oven to 375°F (190°C). Bake for about 50 to 55 minutes. If you want the top crust to be soft, rub the margarine over the top as soon as it comes out of the oven.

Calories per slice: 86, Fat: 2 g (0 g saturated), Protein: 2 g, Cholesterol: 11 mg, Carbohydrates: 15 g, Sodium: 4 mg

◆ Quick Oatmeal Bread ◆

MAKES 1 LOAF (20 SLICES)

Very quick! It rises once. A commercial loaf of oatmeal bread would have about 3,000 mg of sodium.

1/2   cup (125 mL) boiling water
1/4   cup (60 mL) skim milk
1/2   cup (125 mL) "old-fashioned" oatmeal, not quick or instant oats
3   tablespoons (45 mL) safflower oil
1/4   cup (60 mL) molasses
1/4   cup (60 mL) warm water
pinch sugar
1   envelope active dry yeast
1   egg or equivalent egg substitute
2 3/4   cups (640 mL) all-purpose flour

Stir together the boiling water, milk, oatmeal, oil, and molasses in a mixing bowl. Cool until lukewarm. Meanwhile, put the 1/4 cup (60 mL) warm water in a small bowl. Add the pinch of sugar and stir in the yeast. Let sit for 2 to 5 minutes. Add the yeast to the oatmeal mixture. Stir in the egg and about half the flour. Beat for 3 or 4 minutes with an electric mixer, adding the remaining flour gradually. Mix until the flour is blended in and the batter is smooth; it will still be sticky. Oil a loaf pan (you can use a vegetable coating spray). Scrape the dough into the loaf pan; smooth it into the corners. Cover the pan with a cloth and set it in a warm place. Let rise only to the top of the pan. While the dough is rising, preheat oven to 375°F (190°C). Bake for about 50 to 55 minutes.

Calories per slice: 112, Fat: 3 g (0 g saturated), Protein: 3 g, Cholesterol: 11 mg, Carbohydrates: 19 g, Sodium: 7 mg

◆ Quick Anadama Bread ◆

MAKES 1 LOAF (20 SLICES)

Anadama bread combines the flavors of corn and molasses for a delicious taste. It's even better toasted.

1/2 cup (125 mL) boiling water
1/4 cup (60 mL) milk
1/2 cup (125 mL) yellow cornmeal
  3 tablespoons (45 mL) safflower oil
1/4 cup (60 mL) molasses
  1 envelope active dry yeast
1/4 cup (60 mL) warm water
    pinch sugar
  1 egg or equivalent egg substitute
2 3/4 cups (640 mL) all-purpose flour

Combine the boiling water, milk, cornmeal, oil, and molasses in a mixing bowl; stir. Cool until lukewarm. Meanwhile, pour the warm water into a small bowl, add the sugar, stir in the yeast. Let sit for 2 to 5 minutes, until doubled. Add the swollen yeast to the cornmeal mixture. Stir in the egg and about half the flour. Beat for 3 or 4 minutes with an electric mixer, adding the remaining flour gradually. Mix until the flour is all blended in and smooth but sticky. Oil a loaf pan. Scrape the batter into the loaf pan. Smooth it into the corners. Cover the pan with a cloth and set in a warm place. Let rise only to the top of the pan. While the dough is rising, preheat oven to 375°F (190°C). Bake for about 50 to 55 minutes.

Calories per slice: 110, Fat: 3 g (0 g saturated), Protein: 3 g, Cholesterol: 11 mg, Carbohydrates: 19 g, Sodium: 7 mg

◆ Quick Whole Wheat Bread ◆

 1 *cup (250 mL) warm water*
 1 *envelope active dry yeast*
 1 *cup (250 mL) whole wheat flour*
13/4 *cups (440 mL) flour*
 1/3 *cup (80 mL) white sugar*
 1 *egg or equivalent egg substitute*
 1/4 *cup (60 mL) safflower oil*

Pour the warm water in a large mixing bowl; add the yeast and stir. Cover until doubled, about 10 minutes. In another bowl, stir together the whole wheat flour, white flour, and sugar. Add about half of the flour mixture to the swollen yeast. Stir and mix in the egg or substitute and oil. Beat for 3 or 4 minutes with an electric mixer and gradually add the rest of the flour. Mix until the flour is blended but moist and sticky. Cover the bowl with a cloth, and set it in a warm place until doubled, around 30 minutes. Spray or oil a loaf pan and scrape the dough into the loaf pan. Smooth it into the corners. Cover the pan with the cloth and set it in a warm place. Let rise only to the top of the pan, about 10 minutes. While the dough is rising, preheat oven to 375°F (190°C). Bake for about 50 to 55 minutes.

Calories per slice: 102, Fat: 3 g (0 g saturated), Protein: 2 g, Cholesterol: 11 mg, Carbohydrates: 16 g, Sodium: 4 mg

◆ Quick Bran Rolls ◆

MAKES 24 ROLLS

Wonderful warmed for breakfast, and they freeze well.

 1/3 *cup (80 mL) sugar*
 1/3 *cup (80 mL) bran*
 1/2 *cup (125 mL) safflower oil*
 1/2 *cup (125 mL) boiling water*
 1/2 *cup (125 mL) warm water*

pinch sugar
1   *envelope active dry yeast*
1   *egg or equivalent egg substitute*
3   *cups (750 mL) all-purpose flour*

Combine the sugar, bran, oil, and boiling water in a large mixing bowl; stir and cool to lukewarm. In a small bowl pour the warm water, add pinch of sugar and yeast; stir. Let stand for 2 to 5 minutes until doubled. Add the egg to the lukewarm bran mixture and stir well. Mix in the swollen yeast. Gradually stir in the flour. Mix until the flour is blended in and the batter is smooth. Cover the bowl with a cloth and set it in a warm place 2 hours or so, until doubled.

Oil 24 muffin pan cups (nonstick spray is good). Stir the batter and put the batter into the muffin cups, filling each cup about halfway. Cover the pans with the cloth and set it in a warm place. Let rise only to the top of the pan. While the dough is rising, preheat oven to 375°F (190°C). Bake for about 50 to 55 minutes.

**Calories per roll: 114, Fat: 5 g (0 g saturated), Protein: 2 g,
Cholesterol: 9 mg, Carbohydrates: 16 g, Sodium: 3 mg**

KNEADED YEAST BREADS

Bread doughs are traditionally made by kneading, although quick "batter" yeast breads, in the previous section, do not require kneading. Kneading is not difficult; a seven-year-old child helped us knead recipes for this book.

Usually the wet and dry ingredients are stirred together in a bowl, by hand, electric mixer, or food processor, then turned out onto a floured surface, such as a countertop, a kitchen table, or a bread board. Place a small amount, approximately 1/2 cup (125 mL), of extra flour off to one side of the working area. Use your clean hands to push the dough around fairly vigorously: push (with the heel of the hand); fold it in on itself and turn, a quarter turn; then again, push, fold, and turn. Don't be afraid to keep adding small amounts of flour to prevent the dough from sticking. The quantity of flour called for in any bread recipe is always approximate. You may have to use more or less.

When dissolving active dry yeast, the temperature of the water is important: It should be 100° to 115°F (38–46°C), slightly warm to the touch. Too high a heat, such as very hot water, will kill the yeast. If you have any doubts about what 100°F (38°C) water feels like, test it with a thermometer until you get used to it.

The fact that temperature affects yeast can be used to your advantage. If you want the dough to rise fairly quickly, you put the dough in a warm place. This is the most common way that it is done. People often put the dough in a turned-off oven; a gas oven with a pilot usually provides the ideal temperature. Other warm places around the home include the top of a warm (but not hot) radiator, or on top of the refrigerator or any place that is free from drafts.

If you do not find it convenient to bake it right away, slow down the rising action by putting the dough in a covered bowl in the refrigerator. This way the dough will take several hours to rise and you can bake it at your convenience.

After the bread has thoroughly cooled, it can be wrapped. Since homemade low-sodium bread does not have any preservatives, it should be stored in the refrigerator or in the freezer. It may be convenient to slice the bread before freezing it, so that you can take out just one or two slices as needed.

◆ White Bread ◆

MAKES 2 LOAVES (20 SLICES EACH)

1¹/4 cups (300 mL) warm water
 2 tablespoons (30 mL) sugar
 2 envelopes active dry yeast
 2 tablespoons (30 mL) safflower oil
 3/4 cup (180 mL) warm skim milk
5¹/2 cups (1.3 L) bread flour
 1 teaspoon (5 mL) unsalted margarine* (optional)

Pour about 1/4 cup (60 mL) warm water in a large bowl. Sprinkle the sugar and yeast over the water. Stir and put the bowl in a warm place until the yeast bubbles up, about 5 minutes. If the yeast does not foam up, start with fresh yeast.

Add the remaining cup water, the safflower oil, and milk and mix well. Add most of the flour, reserving the rest to work in gradually as needed. Mix well with a large spoon. Sprinkle working surface such as a table or countertop with a thin layer of the reserved flour. Put the rest of the flour in a pile off to the side of the work area. Transfer the dough to the floured surface and knead for about 8 minutes, or until the dough is smooth and elastic; work in small amounts of flour as needed to prevent sticking. To test if you have kneaded enough, press the dough lightly. If it springs back to fill the depression that your fingers made, it has been kneaded enough. Oil bottom of a large bowl. Add the dough and turn it over so it is coated with oil. Cover the bowl with a cloth and put in a warm place until double in bulk, about 45 minutes.

Punch down the dough and turn it onto the working surface. Knead a few minutes. Divide the dough into 2 equal parts and form 2 smooth balls. Spray 2 loaf pans with vegetable spray or brush with oil. Spread the dough into the pans. Cover pans with a clean cloth and rest them in a warm place until doubled, about 30 minutes. Near the end of this rising time, preheat the oven to 375°F (190°C). Bake loaves until golden and they sound hollow when tapped, about 50 minutes.

* *If you want the loaves to have a soft crust, brush the top surface of each with a small amount of unsalted margarine right after you take the loaves out of the oven.*

Calories per slice: 75, Fat: 1 g (0 g saturated), Protein: 2 g, Cholesterol: 0 mg, Carbohydrates: 14 g, Sodium: 3 mg

◆ Soft Rolls ◆

MAKES 10 ROLLS

Shape the dough into round hamburger rolls or into long sandwich rolls. These rolls freeze well. A commercial hamburger roll has more than 200 mg of sodium.

> 1 *envelope dry yeast*
> 1 *cup (250 mL) warm water*
> 1 *tablespoon (15 mL) sugar*
> 1 *tablespoon (15 mL) safflower oil, more to oil the bowl*
> 3 *cups (750 mL) bread flour, more if necessary*
> 1 *egg or equivalent egg substitute (only half is used)*
> 3 *tablespoons (45 mL) sesame seeds (optional)*

Combine 1/4 cup (60 mL) of the warm water and the sugar in a large bowl. Sprinkle the yeast over the water and stir. Put the bowl in a warm place until the yeast bubbles up, about 5 minutes. If the yeast does not foam up, start with fresh yeast. Add the remaining 3/4 cup water (190 mL) and, 1 tablespoon (15 mL) safflower oil and mix well. Add most of the flour, reserving the rest to work in gradually as needed. Mix well with a large spoon or with your hands. Choose a working surface, such as a table or countertop and sprinkle it with a thin layer of the reserved flour. Put the rest of the flour in a pile off to the side of the work area. Transfer the dough to the floured surface and knead for about 8 to 10 minutes or until the dough is smooth and elastic; work in small amounts of flour if needed to prevent sticking. To test if you have kneaded enough, press the dough lightly. If it springs back to fill the depression that your fingers made, it has been kneaded enough. Oil the bottom of a large bowl. Add the ball of dough and turn it over to coat with oil. Cover the bowl with a cloth and rest it in a warm place until doubled, about 45 minutes.

Punch down the dough and knead a few minutes. Divide the dough in 10 equal parts* and roll to form 10 smooth balls. Spray 2 cookie sheets with vegetable spray or brush with oil.

To make round rolls: Put the balls of dough onto the cookie sheets, leaving 3 inches (8 cm) between each ball. Fold the edges under to make an even circle. Using the palm of your hands, press each ball to flatten it to 2 to 2 1/2 inches (5 to 6 cm) across.

To make long rolls, shape each dough ball between your hands into a sausage shape, about 6 inches (15 cm) long. Place the dough onto the cookie sheets allowing 3 inches (8 cm) between each.

Cover the cookie sheets with a clean cloth and place them in a warm place until doubled in bulk, about 30 minutes. Near the end of this rising time, preheat the oven to 375° F (190°C). If you want sesame seed rolls, use a pastry brush or your fingers to lightly coat the top of each roll with the beaten egg or egg substitute.** Sprinkle the tops with sesame seeds. Bake until the rolls are golden and sound hollow when tapped, about 20 minutes.

* You can make some round and some long rolls. If you want to make larger rolls, divide the dough into fewer pieces before shaping.

** If you want the rolls to have a soft crust, do not put on any glaze before baking. Instead, brush the top surface of each roll with a small amount of safflower oil right after you take the rolls out of the oven.

Calories per roll: 178, Fat: 4 g (1 g saturated), Protein: 5 g, Cholesterol: 21 mg, Carbohydrates: 31 g, Sodium: 8 mg

◆ Bread Crumbs ◆

There are two easy ways to make low-sodium bread crumbs. You can use commercial low-sodium bread or any homemade bread recipe in this book.

To make bread crumbs in a blender: Toast low-sodium bread; drop small chunks into blender one small piece at a time through the hole in the blender cover.

Rolled bread crumbs: Toast low-sodium bread until dry and crispy. Put the toast in a plastic bag or between two sheets of wax paper, and crush with a rolling pin.

It's convenient to make a large batch to store in the freezer. You can take out the amount you need and season it as you use it.

◆ Parker House Dinner Rolls ◆

MAKES 24 ROLLS

Would you think that rolls with yeast can be ready to eat in just one hour? Here they are!

- 2 *envelopes active dry yeast*
- 1/4 *cup (60 mL) warm water*
- 3 *tablespoons (45 mL) sugar*
- 3/4 *cup (180 mL) skim milk*
- 1/2 *cup (125 mL) water*
- 2 *tablespoons (30 mL) safflower oil*
- 4 *cups (1 L) bread flour or all-purpose flour, more if necessary*
- 1 *tablespoon (15 mL) unsalted margarine*

Dissolve the yeast and sugar in the warm water. Set aside for a few minutes until doubled. Meanwhile, pour the milk, 1/2 cup water, and the oil in a saucepan. Heat until just lukewarm.

Combine the milk mixture, the activated yeast, and all but 1/2 cup (125 mL) flour in a large bowl and stir with a large spoon. Knead for 8 minutes, adding extra flour if needed. Cover with a clean cloth and set in a warm place for 15 minutes.

Turn it out onto a floured countertop. Roll with a rolling pin until it is approximately 1/2 inch (1 cm) thick. Cut with a 2-inch (5-cm) biscuit cutter or plastic top. Fold each circle of dough in half, putting a dot of margarine in the middle to make Parker House rolls. Place them on a lightly oiled cookie sheet. Cover with a towel and rest them in a warm place until doubled, approximately 15 minutes. While the rolls are rising, preheat the oven to 350°F (175°C). Bake for 10 minutes.

Calories per roll: 101, Fat: 2 g (0 g saturated), Protein: 3 g, Cholesterol: 0 mg, Carbohydrates: 18 g, Sodium: 5 mg

◆ French Bread ◆

MAKES 2 LOAVES (20 SLICES PER LOAF)

Special "French" or "Italian" bread pans, to shape the loaves, are available at hardware and culinary supply stores. If your family likes long loaves, buy a set; the metal ones are not expensive.

1 1/2 cups (375 mL) warm water
*   1 envelopes active dry yeast*
*   2 teaspoons (10 mL) sugar*
* 1/2 cup (125 mL) skim milk*
*   2 tablespoons (30 mL) safflower oil, more to oil pan*
*   6 cups (1.5 L) bread flour*
*   1 teaspoon (5 mL) cornmeal for sprinkling*

Pour 1/2 cup (125 mL) of the warm water in a bowl and add the yeast and sugar. Stir until it is dissolved; let stand for about 5 minutes, or until slightly foamy. Mix the swollen yeast, the remaining cup warm water, and 2 tablespoons (30 mL) of oil in a large bowl. Stir in most of the flour with a wooden spoon, reserving a small amount of flour. With the remaining flour, make a small pile on your work surface. Sprinkle a small amount of the flour on the work surface. Turn the dough out and knead about 8 to 10 minutes, working in extra flour to prevent sticking, until smooth and elastic. To test if the dough has been kneaded enough, poke a finger into it. If the dough fills up the hole you poked, it is ready. Brush oil in a large bowl. Put the dough into the bowl and turn it over so that all sides are coated. Cover with a clean cloth and set in a warm place until doubled, about 50 to 60 minutes; do not let the dough rise too long.

Divide the dough into parts: 3 parts for large loaves; 12 parts for hard rolls. To shape the dough, roll into sausage shapes. To prepare the cookie sheets or bread pans, oil and sprinkle with cornmeal. Place the dough on the cookie sheets. Cover with a clean cloth and let rise in a warm spot about 30 minutes. Preheat the oven to 425°F (220°C). While the dough is rising, use a sharp knife to make diagonal slashes 2 inches (5 cm) apart and 1/4 inch (.5 cm) deep. Use your hand to brush the surface lightly with water. Bake large loaves about 45 minutes, small rolls about 20 minutes.

Calories per slice: 77, Fat: 1 g (0 g saturated), Protein: 2 g, Cholesterol: 0 mg, Carbohydrates: 15 g, Sodium: 2 mg

◆ Garlic Bread ◆

MAKES 1 LOAF (20 SLICES)

Did you know you could make garlic bread in less than five minutes? Garlic bread is especially delicious when served with chili or spaghetti.

1 *French Bread (page 223)*
2 *tablespoons (30 mL) unsalted margarine*
2 *tablespoons (30 mL) water*
1 1/2 *tablespoons (22 mL) garlic powder (not garlic salt)*

Slice the bread in half lengthwise.

Melt the margarine and mix with the water in a small saucepan. Brush the cut sides of the bread with the melted margarine. Sprinkle with garlic powder. Move the broiler pan 8 inches (20 cm) or so away from the flame. Preheat the broiler.

Broil for 1 to 2 minutes until the top is golden brown. Slice and serve.

Calories per slice: 89, Fat: 2 g (0 g saturated), Protein: 2 g, Cholesterol: 0 mg, Carbohydrates: 15 g, Sodium: 3 mg

◆ Rye Bread ◆

MAKES 2 LOAVES (20 SLICES PER LOAF)

2 *envelopes active dry yeast*
1 1/2 *cups (375 mL) warm water*
1/4 *cup (60 mL) honey*
3 *tablespoons (45 mL) safflower oil, more to oil pan*
2 *tablespoons (30 mL) caraway seeds (optional)*
unsalted margarine (optional)

1³/4 cups (430 mL) rye flour
  3 cups (750 mL) bread flour or all-purpose flour

In a large bowl, combine the yeast, water, safflower oil, honey, caraway seeds, and rye flour. Beat by hand or with an electric mixer until the dough is smooth. Gradually mix in approximately 2¹/2 cups (625 mL) of flour or until the dough can be easily handled; the dough will still be somewhat sticky. Pour the remaining flour to the side of the working area. Knead the dough until it is smooth, about 10 minutes; add extra flour as needed to prevent sticking. To test when the dough has been kneaded enough, touch the top with your finger; it will spring back. Oil a large bowl. Turn the dough around in the oiled surface to coat the dough. Cover with a cloth. Let rise in a warm spot for about 35 minutes.

Punch down the dough and divide it in half. Form each half into a loaf shape.* Place in oiled loaf pans and set pans in a warm spot to rise until doubled, about 45 minutes. Bake in 375°F (190°C) oven for 45 minutes.**

* Rye bread can also be shaped into an oval, placed on a cookie sheet, and allowed to double in size. Bake on the cookie sheets the same as above.

** If you want the top crust to be soft, spread with unsalted margarine when the loaves are hot from the oven.

Calories per slice: 73, Fat: 1 g (0 g saturated), Protein: 2 g, Cholesterol: 0 mg, Carbohydrates: 13 g, Sodium: 1 mg

◆ Pita Pocket Bread ◆

MAKES 12 SMALL PITAS

You can make your own low-sodium "pocket" bread. Pita rises only once for 30 minutes. That means you can make these delicious sandwich pockets in an hour or so. They are great for lunches and hot sandwiches at home. Make extras for the freezer.

    1 envelope active dry yeast
1¹/4 cups (310 mL) warm water
    2 teaspoons (10 mL) sugar
    3 cups (750 mL) bread flour, or all-purpose flour
    1 teaspoon (5 mL) safflower oil

In a large bowl, stir the yeast, water, and sugar. Set aside in a warm place until the yeast bubbles up, about 5 minutes. Stir in about 2¹/2 cups (625 mL) of the flour and the oil. Sprinkle a working surface with a thin layer of the reserved flour. Put the rest of the flour off to the side of the work area. Transfer the dough to the floured surface and knead for 8 to 10 minutes until smooth and elastic, working in small amounts of flour to prevent sticking. Divide the dough: If you want mini-pitas, make 12 balls; if you want medium pitas, make 6 balls. Roll each ball into a round about 1/4 inch (.5 cm) thick. Prepare cookie sheets by coating with a vegetable spray. Place the rounds on the sheets. Cover with a cloth. Let the rounds rise for 30 minutes while you preheat the oven to 500°F (260°C). Bake pita bread for 12 minutes or so until lightly browned.

To serve the mini-pitas, slice a lid of about 1/2 inch (1 cm) off the top of the round. Cut the medium- and large-sized pitas in half and press the inside lightly with your fingers to make the pocket.

**Calories per pita: 131, Fat: 1 g (0 g saturated), Protein: 4 g,
Cholesterol: 0 mg, Carbohydrates: 26 g, Sodium: 1 mg**

◆ Sweet Cinnamon Rolls ◆

MAKES 18 ROLLS

These rolls are delicious and great for low-sodium coffee breaks. By comparison, a plain Danish contains 250 mg of sodium.

1/4 cup (60 mL) warm water
1 envelope active dry yeast
1/4 cup (60 mL) brown sugar
1/4 cup + 3 tablespoons (105 mL) sugar
2 teaspoons (10 mL) ground cinnamon
33/4 cups (940 mL) all-purpose flour
1 cup (250 mL) skim milk
1 egg or egg substitute
1/4 cup + 2 tablespoons (90 mL) unsalted margarine, melted
1/2 cup (125 mL) honey

Pour the warm water into a small bowl, add the yeast, and stir to dissolve; cover until doubled. In another small bowl, mix together the brown sugar, 1/4 cup (60 mL) of the sugar, and the cinnamon; set aside.

In a large mixing bowl, combine the flour and remaining sugar. Add the milk, the egg, 1/4 cup of the melted margarine, and the yeast mixture. Stir until combined and put in warm place, covered, for 50 minutes until doubled.

Punch dough down, divide in half, and turn onto a lightly floured working surface. Roll half the dough into a 9-inch (23-cm) square. Brush with 1/2 tablespoon (7 mL) of the melted margarine; sprinkle with half the sugar-cinnamon mixture. Beginning on one end, roll the dough up like a jelly roll. Set roll aside and repeat with remaining half of the dough, 1/2 tablespoon (7 mL) margarine and sugar-cinnamon mixture. Cut each roll into nine 1-inch (3-cm) slices.

In a small saucepan, combine remaining tablespoon (15 mL) margarine and honey. Pour half the honey mixture into two 9-inch (23-cm) round baking pans that have been oiled or sprayed with a vegetable spray. Arrange dough slices, cut side down, in the pans. Cover and let rise until doubled, about 35 minutes. Bake in 350°F (175°C) oven for 25 to 30 minutes. Rest rolls on wire rack for 5 minutes. To remove from pans, invert a plate over the pan, flip the pan over, and the glazed part will be on top.

Calories per roll: 187, Fat: 4 g (1 g saturated), Protein: 4 g, Cholesterol: 12 mg, Carbohydrates: 34 g, Sodium: 13 mg

FRUITS *and* OTHER DESSERTS

◆◆◆◆◆

People who have been brought up to feel entitled to something sweet after dinner feel deprived without any dessert. Unfortunately, most of the traditional desserts are not good for you; they are high in calories, and some are also high in sodium even though they do not taste salty.

If you flip through the dessert chapter in a standard cookbook, you will see recipes that call for ingredients you would never see in cookbooks that promote healthy eating. Saturated fats such as lard, butter, and cream, lots of eggs, and sugar are common ingredients in standard cookbooks. Usually the recipes have only a little added salt. But high-calorie desserts that are made from a lot of eggs, sugar, and saturated fats are not good for anyone— even if the desserts are delicious and low in sodium.

FRUIT—THE HEALTHY ALTERNATIVE

—◆◆—

Don't overlook fruit for dessert. Fruit is naturally low in sodium and high in vitamins. If a family member expects dessert after dinner, maybe he or she will accept a fruit substitute, at least some of the time.

Fruits are a very logical part of a low-sodium diet because people don't generally feel the urge to salt them. They are also a good source of vitamins and potassium. A high-potassium/low-sodium diet is thought to be even better than a low-sodium diet.

Choose fresh fruit in season. It's pretty easy to know which are in season—look at the prices. The varieties "on special" are your best choice. Some fruits such as bananas are available all year round, and the price doesn't seem to fluctuate with the season. Be sure to wash fresh fruits, such as apples, before using.

All frozen fruit is low in sodium. You can buy whole fruit frozen in easy-to-pour bags or packed in syrup. We have called for frozen fruit in several recipes. If you are able to substitute fresh when it is available, this is even better.

Canned fruit is convenient, available all year round, and there are a lot of choices of fruit, combinations, syrup, and size of the can.

There is no need to buy canned fruit in the low-sodium or diet section of your supermarket. Since canned fruit is already low in sodium, you are just paying extra when you buy no-salt-added fruit.

It's hard to know if there is added sodium in dried fruit without reading the label. Sodium bisulfate, for example, may be listed on the label in fine print, even though larger letters say "sun dried."

The USDA booklet, "The Sodium Content of Your Food," lists these averages: raisins, 17 mg per cup (250 mL); dried apricots, 12 mg per cup (250 mL); prunes, 1 mg per prune; dates, 1 mg in 10 dates.

FRUIT DESSERTS

◆ Banana, Pineapple, and Rice Dessert ◆

MAKES 6 SERVINGS

Very low in sodium. Good for people who have used up their daily sodium allowance!

1   *ripe banana*
1   *cup (250 mL) cold cooked rice (cooked without salt)*
1/3 *cup (80 mL) sugar*
1 1/2 *cups (375 mL) fresh pineapple, chopped, or canned pineapple, drained*
1   *teaspoon (5 mL) vanilla extract*

Mash the banana and mix with all ingredients. Blend well. Chill before serving.

Calories: 116, Fat: 0 g (0 g saturated), Protein: 1 g, Cholesterol: 0 mg, Carbohydrates: 28 g, Sodium: 1 mg

◆ Fruit in Wine ◆

2 tablespoons (30 mL) sugar
2 tablespoons (30 mL) sweet white wine
4 fresh peaches, peeled* and sliced
1 cup (250 mL) fresh or frozen blueberries

Heat the sugar and wine in a saucepan over low heat until the sugar dissolves. Add the peaches, cover the saucepan, and simmer for approximately 5 minutes over very low heat. Stir in the blueberries. Serve hot or chilled.

To peel ripe fresh peaches more easily, drop them in boiling water for a minute or so to loosen the skins. If fresh peaches are out of season, substitute canned peaches and omit the cooking step. Instead of peaches, try strawberries with melon, pears with blueberries, cantaloupe with raspberries, nectarines with strawberries or raspberries.

Calories: 92, Fat: 0 g (0 g saturated), Protein: 1 g, Cholesterol: 0 mg, Carbohydrates: 22 g, Sodium: 3 mg

◆ Apple Crisp ◆

MAKES 6 SERVINGS

Good warm or cold anytime.

4 cups (1 L) apples, sliced
1 tablespoon (15 mL) lemon juice
1/4 cup (60 mL) flour
3/4 cup (180 mL) regular oatmeal (not quick cooking)
2 tablespoons (30 mL) brown sugar
3 tablespoons (45 mL) white sugar
1 teaspoon (5 mL) cinnamon
6 tablespoons (90 mL) unsalted margarine
   dash cloves

Arrange the apple slices in a baking pan and sprinkle with lemon juice. In a bowl, combine remaining ingredients to make a crumbly mixture; spoon over the apples. Bake in 375°F (190°C) oven for 30 minutes.

Calories: 283, Fat: 13 g (2 g saturated), Protein: 4 g, Cholesterol: 0 mg, Carbohydrates: 39 g, Sodium: 2 mg

◆ Cherries Jubilee ◆

A spectacular flaming dessert that is traditionally served over vanilla ice cream. If you do not have a chafing dish, you can make it in any ordinary skillet or frying pan.

16 *ounces (480 mL) dark sweet pitted cherries in light syrup*
2 *tablespoons (30 mL) cornstarch*
2 *tablespoons (30 mL) sugar*
1/4 *cup (60 mL) cherry-flavored brandy or Kirsch*
3 *cups (750 mL) vanilla ice cream*

Drain the cherries in a strainer over a bowl; pour the syrup into a measuring cup, adding enough water to make 1 cup (250 mL) of liquid.

In a medium saucepan, combine the cornstarch and the syrup mixture, stirring with a wire whisk. Cook over medium heat until the mixture is thickened. Add the cherries; stir. Transfer the mixture to a chafing dish and place over heat. Sprinkle the sugar on top and add the cherry brandy. Using a long-handled wooden match, ignite the dish; allow the brandy to burn itself out. Serve Cherries Jubilee over vanilla ice cream.

Calories: 225, Fat: 7 g (5 g saturated), Protein: 3 g, Cholesterol: 29 mg, Carbohydrates: 38 g, Sodium: 56 mg

◆ Bananas Foster ◆

A spectacular yet easy dessert topping that is traditionally served over vanilla ice cream. This recipe is so delicious, you may prefer it the way we do—without the ice cream. It can also be served over lemon sherbet or waffles.

A chafing dish at the dinner table makes a spectacular dessert. But it can be made just as well, and much more conveniently, in a heavy-bottomed frying pan in the kitchen.

4 *ripe bananas*
2 *teaspoons (10 mL) lemon juice*
4 *tablespoons (60 mL) unsalted margarine*
2 *tablespoons (30 mL) brown sugar*

dash cinnamon

1 *tablespoon (15 mL) white sugar*

¹/4 *cup (60 mL) light rum*

Peel the bananas; cut lengthwise and across into 4 pieces. Sprinkle with lemon juice. In a chafing dish melt the margarine over low heat. Stir in the brown sugar and cinnamon. Add the bananas and cook for approximately 2 minutes, stirring without crushing the bananas. Sprinkle with sugar and add the rum. Use a long wooden match to ignite the rum and serve as soon as it burns itself out.

Calories: 272, Fat: 12 g (2 g saturated), Protein: 1 g, Cholesterol: 0 mg, Carbohydrates: 36 g, Sodium: 3 mg

◆ Fruit Gelatin ◆

MAKES 4 SERVINGS

For cooks who would like to make their own gelatin dessert similar to the commercial packages but lower in sodium.

6 *ounces (180 g) frozen juice such as orange, defrosted*

2 *envelopes or 1 tablespoon (15 mL) unflavored gelatin*

4 *tablespoons (60 mL) sugar*

1 *cup (250 mL) fruit, such as frozen, sliced strawberries, drained*

Add enough water to the orange juice concentrate so that you have two cups (500 mL) of liquid. Heat the orange juice in a small saucepan. In a mixing bowl combine the gelatin and sugar. Gradually pour in the heated juice, stirring constantly.

Prepare a gelatin mold or four individual serving dishes by spraying with a vegetable coating spray. Pour the gelatin into the mold or dishes. Refrigerate for 45 minutes. Spoon the drained fruit into the gelatin. Refrigerate again until firm. If you made the gelatin in a mold, unmold before serving.

To unmold: Fill a large bowl with warm water. Put the gelatin mold in the water and hold it there for about 30 seconds. Put a serving plate upside down on top of the mold and flip the whole thing over. The gelatin will come out onto the plate.

Calories: 197, Fat: 0 g (0 g saturated), Protein: 4 g, Cholesterol: 0 mg, Carbohydrates: 47 g, Sodium: 11 mg

◆ Mandarin Orange Gelatin-Sherbet ◆

11 ounces (330 g) canned mandarin oranges
1 envelope or 1 tablespoon (15 mL) plain gelatin
2 tablespoons (30 mL) sugar
1 cup (250 mL) orange sherbet

Drain the liquid from a can of oranges and reserve the oranges. Combine liquid with enough water to make 1 cup (250 mL). Bring to a boil. Dissolve the gelatin and sugar in the liquid. Stir in the sherbet and the oranges and cook over low heat until dissolved.* Spray a mold with vegetable coating spray; pour gelatin into the mold; chill. To unmold, see directions for Fruit Gelatin (page opposite).

* If you like, use 2 drops each of red and yellow food color.

Calories: 110, Fat: 1 g (0 g saturated), Protein: 2 g, Cholesterol: 2 mg, Carbohydrates: 25 g, Sodium: 24 mg

◆ Cool Strawberry Fluff ◆

10 ounces (310 mL) fresh or frozen defrosted
   strawberries, sliced
2 envelopes or 2 tablespoons (30 mL) unflavored gelatin
1 cup (250 mL) coarsely crushed ice

Drop 1/2 cup (125 mL) of the strawberries into the blender container and blend the strawberries for about 5 seconds. Turn into a small saucepan and heat over low heat until they begin to boil; pour into the blender. Sprinkle the gelatin over the hot strawberries, cover, and blend for 30 seconds. Add the crushed ice and blend on a low speed for about 20 seconds. Switch to a high speed and blend for about 30 seconds more. Drop remaining strawberries in a bowl and mix in the blended mixture. Pour into individual dishes or a serving bowl. Chill.

Calories: 80, Fat: 0 g (0 g saturated), Protein: 3 g, Cholesterol: 0 mg, Carbohydrates: 18 g, Sodium: 9 mg

◆ Spicy Fried Apples ◆

This hot dessert is good by itself. But you can fill Crêpes (page 237–238) or top waffles, lemon sherbet, or vanilla ice cream with them, if you are not on a cholesterol-restricted diet.

> 4 *medium apples*
> 2 *tablespoons (30 mL) unsalted margarine*
> 2 *tablespoons (30 mL) brown sugar*
> 1/4 *teaspoon (1 mL) cinnamon*
>   *dash nutmeg*

Peel and core the apples. Slice apples into thin slices. Melt the margarine in a large skillet over low heat. Stir in the brown sugar, cinnamon, and nutmeg. Add the apples. Cook gently for 5 minutes or until tender. Stir occasionally so that the apples don't stick but cook on both sides.

Calories: 150, Fat: 6 g (1 g saturated), Protein: 0 g, Cholesterol: 0 mg, Carbohydrates: 26 g, Sodium: 2 mg

◆ Baked Apples ◆

MAKES 4 SERVINGS

> 4 *apples*
> 4 *teaspoons (20 mL) unsalted margarine*
> 8 *teaspoons (40 mL) sugar*
> 4 *dashes cinnamon*
> 4 *dashes nutmeg*

Use a small paring knife to core the apple; remove the seeds and the hard core. Peel the top quarter of the apple. Line a baking pan with aluminum foil to make cleanup easier. Set the apples in the pan. Into each apple center hole drop 1 teaspoon (5 mL) of margarine, 2 teaspoons (10 mL) of sugar and a dash each of cinnamon and nutmeg. Bake in 350°F (175°C) oven for approximately 40 minutes.

Calories: 148, Fat: 4 g (1 g saturated), Protein: 0 g, Cholesterol: 0 mg, Carbohydrates: 30 g, Sodium: 0 mg

Elegant Almonds and Fruit

The name says it all!

20 ounces (600 g) pineapple chunks, packed in juice
16 ounces (480 g) sliced peaches, fresh or canned
 2 tablespoons (30 mL) safflower oil
 4 tablespoons (60 mL) slivered almonds (unsalted)
 1 tablespoon (15 mL) lemon juice
 5 tablespoons (75 mL) unsweetened pineapple juice from
    the can of pineapple chunks

Drain the canned fruit, save the juices. Drop the fruit in a serving bowl and refrigerate. Heat oil in a small frying pan, add almonds; cook gently and stir until almonds are lightly browned; remove from heat and cool. Add lemon juice and pineapple juice to almonds and stir; toss over fruit. Refrigerate until serving time. Best served chilled.

Calories: 178, Fat: 8 g (1 g saturated), Protein: 2 g, Cholesterol: 0 mg, Carbohydrates: 28 g, Sodium: 3 mg

Waffles with Fruit

For a special treat, serve Waffles (page 67) and fruit as a dessert. If you have extra waffles, you can freeze, defrost, and make them crispy by heating in a toaster or toaster oven. For a delicious and easy topping, slice fresh strawberries or defrost a package of frozen strawberries. Fruit in Wine (page 230) can give you more ideas for toppings.

Fruit and Champagne

This recipe is festive using champagne instead of diet soda. If you decide to substitute champagne for a special occasion, you can estimate that the sodium content will be approximately the same; there will, of course, be more calories in the champagne.

 8 ounces (250 mL) champagne or low-calorie diet soda,
    such as strawberry or lemon-lime

4   cups (1 L) fresh fruit, such as strawberries, blueberries
    or diced peaches
2   teaspoons (10 mL) lemon juice
1   tablespoon (15 mL) sugar

Chill the champagne or soda. Meanwhile, combine the pieces of fruit in a bowl and sprinkle with lemon juice to prevent darkening. Sprinkle the sugar over the fruit and stir; chill. When ready to serve, place 1/4 of the fruit in each of four pretty glass dishes. Pour the champagne or diet soda over the fruit.

Calories: 98, Fat: 1 g (0 g saturated), Protein: 1 g, Cholesterol: 0 mg, Carbohydrates: 15 g, Sodium: 5 mg

NON FRUIT DESSERTS

◆ Easy Mocha Aspic ◆

MAKES 4 SERVINGS

1/2 cup (125 mL) skim milk
 1   envelope or 1 tablespoon (15 mL) unflavored gelatin
1/2 cup (125 mL) cold coffee
 3   tablespoons (45 mL) sugar
 3   tablespoons (45 mL) non-alkaline cocoa (such as
     Hershey's)
 1   teaspoon (5 mL) vanilla extract
 1   cup (250 mL) crushed ice

Pour the milk in a small saucepan and heat gently until very hot but not boiling. Combine the milk and gelatin in a blender container; blend on high speed for about 30 seconds. Add the coffee, sugar, cocoa, and vanilla; blend for another 30 seconds. Lower speed and begin adding the ice a little at a time (that should take another 30 seconds). Blend on high speed 15 seconds. Chill in individual dishes for at least 30 minutes before serving.

Calories: 66, Fat: 1 g (0 g saturated), Protein: 3 g, Cholesterol: 1 mg, Carbohydrates: 13 g, Sodium: 21 mg

◆ Ice Cream Sundaes ◆

Ice cream is relatively low in sodium, but higher in fat and cholesterol than ice milk. Sherbet is low in both sodium and fat. To make sherbet, ice milk, or ice cream seem a little more special at home, you can add: defrosted frozen strawberries, chilled cut-up fresh fruit, chilled canned fruit (such as canned peach slices), chilled crushed pineapple, a small amount of one of the newer jams made with half the sugar, a liqueur such as green crème de menthe or crème de cacao, or Chocolate Sauce (below).

Did you ever consider a fruit sundae? Instead of ice cream or sherbet use fresh, canned, or frozen fruit. Add one of the toppings suggested above. You could make a sundae of crushed pineapple with a little crème de menthe poured on top, for example.

◆ Chocolate Sauce ◆

MAKES 2/3 CUP

This not-too-sweet recipe is ideal for your sundae. It makes plain ice milk into a special dessert.

- 1/2 cup (125 mL) non-alkaline cocoa (such as Hershey's)
- 6 tablespoons (90 mL) sugar
- 1/3 cup (80 mL) water
- 1 teaspoon (5 mL) vanilla extract

Combine all ingredients in a saucepan. Stir with a wire whisk over medium heat. Bring to a boil and boil for 2 to 3 minutes, stirring constantly. Remove from heat. Serve immediately or store in the refrigerator. Can be reheated in a double boiler.

Calories per tablespoon: 40, Fat: 1 g (0 g saturated), Protein: 1 g, Cholesterol: 0 mg, Carbohydrates: 10 g, Sodium: 1 mg

◆ Crêpes ◆

MAKES 14 CRÊPES

This recipe makes fourteen 5-inch (13-cm) crêpes. You can make them in a larger skillet and use Strawberry Filling (below) or a different fruit filling such as blueberries or jam. Try jams with only half the sugar added, to cut down on calories.

3 tablespoons (45 mL) sugar
1 cup (250 mL) skim milk
2 tablespoons (30 mL) safflower oil
2 eggs or equivalent egg substitute
1/2 cup (125 mL) flour
2 teaspoons (10 mL) low-sodium baking powder (shake and stir before measuring)
1/4 teaspoon (1 mL) vanilla extract
Strawberry Filling (below)

Combine all ingredients in a blender container and blend for a minute or so; or mix in electric mixer until batter is smooth. Heat a small oiled skillet or crepe pan until a drop of water "dances" when you splash it on the hot surface. Add 1/3 cup (80 mL) of batter and move the pan around so that the batter covers evenly. Cook over medium heat on one side until edges are browned and there are bubbles throughout the crepe. Turn and cook on the other side to brown. Spoon one tablespoon (15 mL) strawberries on each crêpe and roll crêpes up. Spoon remaining strawberries or syrup over the tops.

Calories per crêpe: 62, Fat: 3 g (0 g saturated), Protein: 2 g, Cholesterol: 31 mg, Carbohydrates: 7 g, Sodium: 19 mg

◆ Strawberry Filling ◆

MAKES 1 1/4 CUPS

10 ounces (300 g) fresh strawberries or frozen strawberries, defrosted

Slice strawberries. You may use other berries, apples, peaches, or other seasonal fruit.

◆ Vanilla Pudding ◆

MAKES 4 SERVINGS

If you're used to pudding mixes, you will be pleasantly surprised at how easy this is and much, much lower in sodium: 76 mg per half cup (125 mL); commercial, 406 mg per half cup.

> 2 cups (500 mL) skim milk
> 2 tablespoons (30 mL) unsalted margarine
> 3 tablespoons (45 mL) cornstarch
> 1/2 cup (125 mL) sugar
> 1 egg or equivalent egg substitute
> 1 tablespoon (15 mL) vanilla extract

Heat the milk and the margarine in the top of a double boiler over simmering water. In a bowl, mix together the cornstarch and sugar. Add the eggs or egg substitute and blend well. Add the vanilla and blend. Pour the cornstarch mixture into the warm milk. Mix with a wire whisk over simmering water until the mixture is thick. A good way to know if it's done is to look for wire whisk patterns; if they stay in the pudding it's done. Cool pudding before serving.

Calories: 241, Fat: 7 g (2 g saturated), Protein: 6 g, Cholesterol: 56 mg, Carbohydrates: 37 g, Sodium: 81 mg

◆ Chocolate Pudding ◆

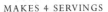

MAKES 4 SERVINGS

Enjoyment and calcium from pudding without the added sodium that commercial mixes have. Chocolate pudding from a box mix contains about 400 mg of sodium in each 1/2 cup (125 mL) serving, more than 6 times the amount in this recipe.

> 1/2 cup (125 mL) sugar
> 2 tablespoons (30 mL) non-alkaline cocoa (such as Hershey's)
> 3 tablespoons (30 mL) cornstarch
> 2 cups (30 mL) skim milk
> 1 teaspoon (5 mL) vanilla extract

Combine the sugar, cocoa, and cornstarch in a small saucepan. Add about 1/2 cup (125 mL) of the milk. Stir with a wire whisk until dissolved and the mixture is smooth. Add remaining milk and vanilla extract. Cook, stirring occasionally until thick, about 5 minutes. Cool before serving.

Calories: 172, Fat: 1 g (0 g saturated), Protein: 5 g, Cholesterol: 3 mg, Carbohydrates: 38 g, Sodium: 65 mg

◆ Rich Mocha Pudding ◆

To decrease intake of sodium and still have a rich chocolaty pudding, try this recipe.

Substitute 1 cup (250 mL) of brewed or instant coffee (decaffeinated is fine) for an equal amount of milk in the Chocolate Pudding recipe above, or 1 cup (250 mL) each of milk and coffee. Follow the directions for Chocolate Pudding above.

Calories with 1 cup coffee and 1 cup milk: 152, Fat: 1 g (0 g saturated), Protein: 3 g, Cholesterol: 1 mg, Carbohydrates: 35 g, Sodium: 35 mg

◆ Scandinavian Pudding ◆

MAKES 6 SERVINGS

A good dessert to serve to someone who has used up the day's sodium allowance. This is a variation of Klappgröt, the traditional Scandinavian dessert.

> 6 *ounces (180 g) frozen pineapple juice concentrate*
> 2¹/2 *cups (625 mL) water*
> 4 *tablespoons (60 mL) farina*
> 8 *ounces (240 g) crushed pineapple, packed in its juice, drained*

Mix the pineapple juice and water in a small saucepan. Bring to a rapid boil. Stir the mixture while gradually adding the farina. Cook gently for 5 minutes or so; remove from heat. Beat by hand or with an electric mixer until the mixture is smooth. Fold in the pineapple. Pour into individual pudding dishes and chill.

Calories: 94, Fat: 0 g (0 g saturated), Protein: 1 g, Cholesterol: 0 mg, Carbohydrates: 24 g, Sodium: 34 mg

COOKIES AND CAKES

——◆◆——

Cake mixes and homemade cakes made with regular baking powder are fairly high in sodium. So the way to cut down on the sodium in cakes is to use low-sodium baking powder. We want to warn you, however, that it is not nearly as reliable as regular baking powder. Even when you use 1 1/2 times the amount and shake the jar thoroughly, cakes sometimes turn out disappointingly flat. We also tried baking cakes from prepackaged low-sodium cake mixes and were disappointed by the results; the cakes were flat. Convenience products are high in sodium: A box of piecrust mix has 2,240 mg of sodium in a box. Try the easy piecrust recipes in this chapter.

◆ Pumpkin Cookies ◆

MAKES 100 COOKIES

Soft, moist cookies that pack well and stay fresh longer than other types of cookies.

- 1 cup (250 mL) unsalted margarine, more for cookie sheets
- 1 cup (250 mL) sugar
- 1 cup (250 mL) canned pumpkin (not pumpkin pie filling)
- 1 egg or equivalent egg substitute
- 1 teaspoon (5 mL) vanilla extract
- 2 cups (500 mL) flour
- 2 tablespoons (30 mL) low-sodium baking powder (shake and stir before measuring)
- 1 teaspoon (5 mL) cinnamon
- 1/2 cup (125 mL) raisins
- 1/2 cup (125 mL) unsalted walnuts, chopped

Prepare your cookie sheets by spraying with a vegetable spray or by rubbing lightly with unsalted margarine. Beat the margarine until soft; gradually add the sugar and beat until smooth. Add the pumpkin, egg, and vanilla. Mix well.

Sift together the flour, baking powder, and cinnamon. Add dry mixture to the pumpkin mixture; beat until smooth and rather fluffy. Stir in the raisins and chopped walnuts. Drop the batter by teaspoonfuls on cookie sheets. Bake in 375°F (190°C) oven for 10 to 15 minutes.

Calories per cookie: 40, Fat: 2 g (0 g saturated), Protein: 0 g, Cholesterol: 2 mg, Carbohydrates: 5 g, Sodium: 1 mg

◆ Holiday Walnut Cookies ◆

These rich cookies are a holiday favorite.

  1 cup (250 mL) unsalted margarine
  3 tablespoons (45 mL) sugar
  1 teaspoon (5 mL) vanilla extract
 1/2 teaspoon (2 mL) almond extract
  2 cups (500 mL) flour
  1 cup (250 mL) finely chopped unsalted walnuts
     confectioner's sugar for rolling (optional)

Beat margarine until soft and add the sugar; beat until smooth. Mix in the vanilla, almond extract, flour, and walnuts.

Roll dough into balls 1 inch (3 cm) in diameter. Place the balls on cookie sheets. Bake in 350°F (175°C) oven for 20 minutes. If desired, you can roll the cookies in confectioner's sugar while they are still hot.

Calories per cookie: 67, Fat: 5 g (1 g saturated), Protein: 1 g, Cholesterol: 0 mg, Carbohydrates: 5 g, Sodium: 0 mg

◆ Almond Sugar Cookies ◆

Perfect with a scoop of sherbet.

 1/2 cup (125 mL) unsalted margarine, softened
 1/2 cup (125 mL) sugar
 1/2 cup (125 mL) sliced almonds, finely chopped
  1 teaspoon (5 mL) vanilla extract
 1/4 teaspoon (1 mL) almond extract
  1 cup (250 mL) flour

In a mixing bowl, cream the margarine and gradually beat in the sugar. Add the almonds, vanilla, and almond extract. Mix in the flour and blend until the dough is smooth. Shape the dough into a roll about 20 inches (51 cm) long; divide the roll into two sections. Wrap each one in wax paper and refrigerate for at least 1/2 hour or longer, if you like.

Slice the dough into 1/4-inch (.5-cm) sections. Place the cookies on ungreased cookie sheets. Allow room between them since they spread out a little. Bake the cookies in 375°F (190°C) oven for 12 minutes; the edges will be lightly browned. Cool cookies on a rack. Store in an air-tight container.

Calories per cookie: 35, Fat: 2 g (0 g saturated), Protein: 1 g, Cholesterol: 0 mg, Carbohydrates: 4 g, Sodium: 0 mg

◆ Brownies ◆

MAKES 16 SQUARES

A cake-like brownie that keeps very well.

10 *tablespoons (150 mL) unsalted margarine*
6 *tablespoons (90 mL) non-alkaline cocoa*
2 *eggs or equivalent egg substitute*
1/2 *cup (125 mL) applesauce*
1/2 *cup (125 mL) sugar*
1/4 *cup (60 mL) brown sugar*
1 *teaspoon (5 mL) vanilla extract*
1 *cup (250 mL) flour*
1 1/2 *teaspoons (7 mL) low-sodium baking powder (shake and stir before measuring)*
1/2 *cup (125 mL) walnuts, chopped*

Melt margarine, stir in the cocoa, and set aside. In a large bowl beat the eggs with a fork or a wire whisk. Add the applesauce, sugars, and vanilla; mix well. Mix the flour and baking powder and add to batter; stir well to blend. Add the cocoa mixture and the walnuts. Mix until well blended. Prepare a 9-inch (23-cm) square baking pan by spreading lightly with margarine or coating with a vegetable spray. Bake in 350°F (175°C) oven for 30 minutes or so, until a toothpick comes out clean when inserted. Cool and cut into 16 squares.

Calories per square: 166, Fat: 10 g (2 g saturated), Protein: 3 g, Cholesterol: 27 mg, Carbohydrates: 18 g, Sodium: 10 mg

◆ Chocolate Chip Cookies ◆

Store-bought chocolate chip cookies have up to 60 mg of sodium in each cookie.

   1   cup (250 mL) flour
   2   teaspoons (10 mL) low-sodium baking powder (shake before measuring)
 1/2   cup (125 mL) unsalted margarine
 1/2   teaspoon (2 mL) vanilla extract
 1/4   cup (60 mL) brown sugar
 1/2   cup (125 mL) sugar
   1   egg or equivalent egg substitute
   1   cup (250 mL) chocolate chips
 1/2   cup (125 mL) chopped unsalted nuts such as walnuts (optional)

Sift the flour with baking powder twice. Beat margarine with the vanilla and sugar until fluffy and smooth. Beat in the egg. Add the flour mixture. Stir in the chips and nuts, if using. Drop by teaspoonfuls onto a cookie sheet. Bake in 375°F (190°C) oven about 10 minutes.

Calories per cookie: 60, Fat: 4 g (1 g saturated), Protein: 1 g, Cholesterol: 4 mg, Carbohydrates: 7 g, Sodium: 20 mg

◆ Peanut Butter Cookies ◆

   2   tablespoons (30 mL) unsalted margarine, more for cookie sheets
 2/3   cup (180 mL) unsalted peanut butter
 1/4   cup (60 mL) sugar
 1/4   cup (60 mL) brown sugar
   1   egg or equivalent egg substitute
 3/4   teaspoon (3 mL) vanilla extract
   1   teaspoon (5 mL) low-sodium baking powder (shake and stir before measuring)
   1   cup (250 mL) flour

Prepare cookie sheets by spraying with a vegetable spray or by rubbing lightly with unsalted margarine. Combine margarine and peanut butter in a mixer bowl and beat them using an electric mixer. Add the sugars and beat, then add the egg and vanilla; beat well. In a separate bowl, combine the baking powder and the flour; add to the peanut butter mixture and mix thoroughly. Form balls 1 inch (3 cm) in diameter and arrange them on a cookie sheet; leave about 2 inches (6 cm) between the balls. Flatten the balls with a fork. Make a second impression at right angles to the first. Bake in 350°F (175°C) oven for 10 to 12 minutes.

Calories per cookie: 80, Fat: 4 g (1 g saturated), Protein: 3 g, Cholesterol: 9 mg, Carbohydrates: 9 g, Sodium: 5 mg

◆ Fudgy Snacks with Peanuts ◆

MAKES 52 SNACKS

6	tablespoons (90 mL) unsalted margarine
1 1/2	cups (375 mL) sugar
1/2	cup (125 mL) skim milk
3	tablespoons (45 mL) non-alkaline cocoa (such as Hershey's)
1	teaspoon (5 mL) vanilla extract
1/2	cup (125 mL) unsalted peanut butter
3	cups (750 mL) quick oatmeal (not instant)*
3/4	cup (180 mL) unsalted peanuts, chopped

Slowly heat margarine in a saucepan, add the sugar, and stir until dissolved. Cooking on low heat, add the milk, cocoa, vanilla, and peanut butter; stir. Then add the oatmeal. Cook, stirring constantly, for approximately 3 minutes. Cool slightly. Drop mixture from teaspoon onto wax paper. Using your palms, shape into balls. Roll the balls in the chopped peanuts.

* Or use regular "old-fashioned" oats; put them in a blender or food processor to make the pieces smaller.

Calories per snack: 98, Fat: 4 g (1 g saturated), Protein: 3 g, Cholesterol: 0 mg, Carbohydrates: 13 g, Sodium: 2 mg

Oatmeal Cookies

3/4 cup (180 mL) unsalted margarine
3/4 cup (180 mL) brown sugar
1/2 cup (125 mL) sugar
1 egg or equivalent egg substitute
1/4 cup (60 mL) water
1 teaspoon (5 mL) vanilla extract
1 cup (250 mL) flour, sifted before measuring
2 teaspoons (10 mL) low-sodium baking powder (shake and stir before measuring)
3 cups (750 mL) oats, uncooked (not instant or quick cooking)

Prepare cookie sheets by spraying with a vegetable spray or by rubbing lightly with unsalted margarine. Combine margarine, brown sugar, sugar, egg, water, and vanilla in a mixing bowl. Beat until creamy.

Sift together the flour and baking powder and add them to the mixing bowl. Mix well; add the oats and mix again. Drop by teaspoonfuls on cookie sheets, leaving room between the cookies to spread. Bake in 350°F (175°C) oven for 12 to 15 minutes. Cool for a minute before lifting them with a spatula.

Calories per cookie: 55, Fat: 2 g (0 g saturated), Protein: 1 g, Cholesterol: 3 mg, Carbohydrates: 8 g, Sodium: 2 mg

Strawberry Layer Cake

This unusual cake is made in a way that allows low-sodium baking powder to perform well.

3 eggs or equivalent egg substitute
1/2 cup (125 mL) sugar
1 cup (250 mL) flour
2 teaspoons (10 mL) low-sodium baking powder (shake and stir before measuring)
1/2 cup (125 mL) unsalted margarine, melted

1 cup applesauce (250 mL)
10 ounces (300 g) frozen strawberries, defrosted and
drained

Lightly oil your skillet or griddle and heat it over a low flame on the top of the stove; the skillet should be approximately 6 to 8 inches (15 to 20 cm). Beat the eggs and sugar in a mixing bowl on high speed until they are thick. Sift together the flour and baking powder. Add to the egg and sugar; mix gently by hand. Add margarine and mix gently. Pour about 1/2 cup (125 mL) of batter into the heated skillet; the batter should cover the bottom of the pan and be about the thickness of a pancake. Bake in the oven 5 minutes until the cake is lightly browned. Use a spatula to remove the layer to a serving plate. Pour another 1/2 cup (125 mL) of batter into the skillet and repeat. Blend the strawberries and applesauce together. Spread a layer of fruit between each of the 3 layers and on the top. Serve within 6 hours for best results.

Calories: 294, Fat: 14 g (3 g saturated), Protein: 4 g, Cholesterol: 80 mg, Carbohydrates: 41 g, Sodium: 28 mg

◆ Pineapple Upside-Down Cake ◆

MAKES 8 SERVINGS

1/3 cup (80 mL) brown sugar
1 teaspoon (5 mL) cinnamon
5 slices (7 ounces/210 g) canned pineapple
1 cup (250 mL) flour
1 tablespoon (15 mL) low-sodium baking powder
1/2 cup (125 mL) sugar
1 egg or equivalent egg substitute
1/4 cup (60 mL) skim milk
3 tablespoons (45 mL) unsalted margarine, melted

Oil an 8-inch (20-cm) round cake pan, or spray with a vegetable spray. Combine brown sugar and cinnamon in a small bowl and sprinkle evenly on the bottom of the pan. Arrange pineapple slices on top of sugar.

To make cake batter: sift together flour and low-sodium baking powder. Add the sugar, egg, milk, and melted margarine; beat until well mixed. Pour batter on top of pineapple slices. Bake in 350°F (175°C) oven about 30 minutes or until a cake tester or toothpick inserted in the center comes out clean. Let cool about 10 to 15 minutes. Loosen sides and put a plate upside down over cake. Flip over and remove pan.

Calories: 175, Fat: 5 g (1 g saturated), Protein: 3 g, Cholesterol: 27 mg, Carbohydrates: 31 g, Sodium: 15 mg

HOMEMADE PIES

Homemade pies today are often assembled from piecrust mixes and pre-pared fillings which, unfortunately, have a lot of added sodium. If you need more information to convince you not to buy them, look at the numbers: 2 crusts from a piecrust mix, 1,968 mg; Jell-O chocolate instant pudding, 944 mg sodium (for a small pie).

Fortunately, homemade pies can be made with just a trace of sodium. This does not, however, mean that pie is nutritious. "Mom's homemade apple pie" will always have many calories and few nutrients. But when you want to bake a pie for a special occasion, at least it can be low in sodium.

◆ Piecrust for Two-Crust Pie ◆

MAKES 1 PIECRUST (TOP AND BOTTOM)

2   *cups (500 mL) flour*
1   *stick and 3 tablespoons (170 mL) unsalted margarine*
1/3   *cup (80 mL) ice water*

See directions below.

Calories per 1/8 crust: 253, Fat: 16 g (3 g saturated), Protein: 3 g, Cholesterol: 0 mg, Carbohydrates: 24 g, Sodium: 1 mg

◆ Piecrust for One-Crust Pie ◆

MAKES 1 CRUST

1 1/4   *cups (300 mL) flour*
6   *tablespoons (90 mL) unsalted margarine*
3   *tablespoons (45 mL) ice water*

Put the flour into a bowl. Using two knives or a pastry blender, cut in the margarine until the mixture resembles coarse meal. Add about two tablespoons (30 mL) of water and work it in gently with a fork. Gradually add and mix in the rest of the water using fingers or a pastry blender to work the dough into a ball. Chill dough for 30 minutes; if you are in a hurry, proceed to the next step immediately. If there is enough dough for two crusts, divide the dough in half and let half of the dough wait in the refrigerator while you roll out the first crust.

On a lightly floured surface, flatten the dough into a circle with roundish edges. Use a rolling pin to roll the dough into a circle slightly bigger around than the pie pan, rolling from the center outward. Fold the circle of dough over in half and gently lift it onto the pie pan, being careful not to stretch it. Unfold the dough and pat it gently into the pan. Using a kitchen knife, cut off any extra dough that is more than 3/4 inch (2 cm) beyond the edge of the pan. Fold the outside dough over to make a double thickness of dough around the rim of the pan. Press the dough edge down with a fork, or use your fingers to make a fluted edge. If the crust will be baked without any filling, prick the crust all over with a fork. Bake in 425°F (220°C) oven for approximately 12 to 15 minutes or until it looks as brown as you would like.

Calories per 1/8 crust: 147, Fat: 9 g (2 g saturated), Protein: 2 g, Cholesterol: 0 mg, Carbohydrates: 15 g, Sodium: 1 mg

◆ Pumpkin Pie ◆

MAKES 8 SERVINGS

> 1 *Piecrust for One-Crust Pie (opposite page)*
> 1/2 *cup (125 mL) skim milk*
> 1/2 *cup (125 mL) water*
> 1 *cup (250 mL) tofu,* cut into small chunks*
> 1 *tablespoon (15 mL) pumpkin pie spice*
> 1 *16-ounce can (450 g) no-salt-added pumpkin*
> 1 *tablespoon (15 mL) unflavored gelatin*
> 2/3 *cup (180 mL) sugar*

Prepare piecrust, bake, and cool. Put milk, 1/4 (60 mL) cup water, tofu, and pumpkin pie spice into the blender (in that order). Blend at high speed until the mixture is very smooth. Add the pumpkin to the blender and whip. In a large saucepan dissolve the gelatin in remaining 1/4 cup (60 mL) of water. Add the sugar and cook over low heat for about 5 minutes; remove the pan from the heat. Add the contents of the blender to the saucepan. Stir well to combine. Pour into the prepared pie shell. Chill for several hours.

* *If your store has more than one kind of tofu (soybean curd), choose the soft one.*

Calories: 266, Fat: 10 g (2 g saturated), Protein: 7 g, Cholesterol: 0 mg, Carbohydrates: 38 g, Sodium: 16g

◆ Cherry Pie ◆

This makes a 9-inch (23-cm) pie.

   1   *Piecrust for Two-Crust Pie (page opposite)*
   2   *pounds (900 g) canned, pitted, dark sweet cherries**
1 1/4   *cup (300 mL) sugar*
 1/3   *cup (80 mL) cornstarch*
 1/4   *teaspoon (1 mL) red food coloring (optional)*

Prepare the piecrust dough and chill in the refrigerator while you make the filling. Drain the cherries and reserve the liquid. In a saucepan, mix the sugar and the cornstarch. Stir in one cup (250 mL) of the reserved cherry liquid (discard the rest). Use a wire whisk to stir and cook over medium heat for approximately 7 minutes, or until the mixture is thick; cook for another minute. Remove from the heat and add the cherries and the optional food coloring. Stir to mix. Divide the chilled dough and roll half out to fit a 9-inch pie (23-cm) pie pan. Crimp the edges. Pour the filling into the prepared bottom crust. Roll out the second half of the dough and place it over the filling. Using a kitchen knife, make a few vent holes in the top crust (this will allow steam to escape). Crimp the edges.

Bake in 400°F (205°C) oven for approximately 50 minutes.

* *Comstock new Lite cherry pie filling is made without salt; you may want to try it instead of making homemade. If you are lucky enough to have fresh cherries, you only have to adjust the sugar to taste.*

Calories: 447, Fat: 16 g (3 g saturated), Protein: 4 g, Cholesterol: 0 mg, Carbohydrates: 73 g, Sodium: 3 mg

◆ Fruit Tart ◆

Really yummy, easy enough for a novice cook, and very impressive. Most tart pans are 9¹/2 inches (24 cm) across the bottom. If you do not have a tart pan, you can use a 9-inch (23-cm) pan. Or you could use this recipe and two 8-inch (20-cm) pie pans to make two smaller tarts.

1¹/2 cups (375 mL) flour
 1/2 cup (125 mL) unsalted margarine
   3 tablespoons (45 mL) ice water
      Vanilla Pudding (page 236)
      Fresh or canned fruit, drained*

Follow the directions for Piecrust for One-Crust Pie (page 248). Prick the crust all over with a fork and bake it at 425°F (220°C) for about 10 minutes. Let the crust cool before adding the filling. Top your tart with slices of fresh or drained canned fruit.

* Sometimes melted jelly is lightly brushed on the top of a fruit tart as a glaze. Apple jelly makes a clear glaze; strawberry jelly makes a pink glaze.

Calories (does not include fruit): 307, Fat: 15 g (3 g saturated), Protein: 5 g, Cholesterol: 28 mg, Carbohydrates: 37 g, Sodium: 41 mg

◆ Banana Cream Pie ◆

MAKES 8 SERVINGS

1 Piecrust for One-Crust Pie (page 248)
1 Vanilla Pudding (page 236)
2 large or 3 medium bananas, sliced*

Prepare piecrust for one-crust pie; bake and cool. Make vanilla pudding and stir bananas into the pudding. Put the pudding into the pie shell. If the pie will not be served right away, cover with plastic wrap and refrigerate.

* If you want the pie to look fancy, add a few slices of banana to the top just before serving.

Calories: 308, Fat: 13 g (3 g saturated), Protein: 5 g, Cholesterol: 28 mg, Carbohydrates: 44 g, Sodium: 41 mg

INDEX

◆◆◆◆◆